The Skeptic's Guide to The Adventures of Life

By Connie R. Siewert

Life is an Adventure —
Live it Richly!
Connie

For information or ordering: www.theskepticsguide.com

Editor: Lynnette McIntire

Cover Photograph: Robyn Reynolds

Cover Design: Michelle Butler

Photograph of Connie Siewert: Brian Dougherty

Photograph of Sandbox: Brian Dougherty

Photograph of Georgee: Connie Siewert

Interior Page Layout: Deborah Hill

Copy Editors: Kathryn Kienholz
                      Robyn Reynolds

Grateful acknowledgement is made to the following for permission to reprint previ-
ously published material and/or session transcript:
*Mind/Body Medicine: Exploring the power of your mind to heal your body
Part 1*, © 2002 Lisa Seelandt
The Goddess in the Office, ©1993 by Zsuzsanna E. Budapest
Session Transcript ©2001 Sylvia Browne Society of Novus Spiritus

ISBN 0-9762719-0-7

Library of Congress Cataloging-in-Publication Data is available upon request.
First Printing.
Published by Expanded Thought Press

1924 Clairmont Rd
Decatur, GA
Room 240
Rebecca

St. Michael's
Ctr

Dedicated to:

Edith's sense of strength

Reed's sense of play

Vicki's sense of right

Slava's sense of depth

Ruslan's sense of spiritual truth

And the wisdom and laughs imparted to me by my dear friends

Aric Urban, Tim Waliser, Michelle Butler and the Eclectic Ladies Network

"Each individual is gifted in some way--and challenged in others. However, always the gifts will and can be used to overcome the challenges. That is the formula for evolution of the soul and transition of the individual." *Shannon Sambells*

Let Us Be Curious
Let Us Be Courageous
Let Us Inspire The Spirit
And Evolve The Soul

Life is an Adventure-----Live it Richly!

Table of Contents

{Introduction}

I've always had a sense that something extraordinary is waiting for me right around the corner. As if something new and intriguing to delight the senses and fascinate the mind is likely to reveal itself at any given moment. With this in mind, I've always made it my mission to remain open and vigilant, ready to seize that opportunity for discovery when it decides to present itself.

It is this passion for the marvelous in life that continually stimulates me to forge onward with gusto in search of new pieces of wisdom, new ways of approaching a challenge or new solutions to a problem itself. As exciting as the new-found information often is, I find just as much pleasure in sharing my expanded awareness with others and encouraging them to travel to that same interesting space, be it a thought, a place or experience.

Over a morning Chai latte at Starbucks in May of 2004, I was having one of those sharing type conversations with the fabulously fun Whitney Greer. Whitney is an extremely quick processor who radiates a Katie Couric type energy that amplifies thoughts and always brings new insight into your world. I always find myself in a highly animated mode when we are immersed in a lively discussion and I recall telling her to "Chop, chop Whitney, we have a lot of ground to cover" as she momentarily found herself needing to take a break from our repartee. Shortly after we resumed the rhythm of our exchange, it was as if she was struck by a lightening bolt when she enthusiastically declared, "You should write a book about all these experiences you've been having…..open the door of discovery to a much broader audience." As soon as she spoke it, the thought seemed to ring true in both of us and the concept that would become *The Skeptic's Guide to The Adventures of Life* was born.

While writing this book, I've endeavored to capture my experiences in words that will help inspire self-exploration in others. I have also exorcised a number of ideas and ruminations that have been bubbling inside as I have explored who I am, how I've been affected by others and how I might have affected them. In *The Skeptic's Guide to The Adventures of Life*, I've chronicled my personal experiences and those of my healers during a three year journey to wellness through alterative sources of information and healing.

The catalyst to this healing quest happened when a breathing condition, diagnosed as asthma in the early 90's, took a turn for the worse and I was sorely feeling very middle aged. It seemed so out of balance as I have a very youthful spirit and could hardly recognize this physical body that often labored to breathe. Family members kept cautioning me that I was sinking into dangerous territory that was putting too much strain on my heart. My family doctor was encouraging me to go down that road of taking a daily pill for life to control the symptoms.

I was also caring for my long time canine companion, Zachery, a spirited tan and black Airedale who was slowly approaching the end of his time here on earth. Like me he had the spirit of one much younger than his years and on his good days, when his arthritis permitted, he would still dance around and make like a pup. But he could no longer make it up the stairs to the second floor. I would have to carry my 50lb friend at night to watch TV with me, then down and outside for his nightly business, up again for sleep and then down again early in the morning. Surely this did not help the situation, but it was what it was, and I could not bear to abandon my loyal friend in his last days as his need for comfort now surpassed mine.

My sister Vicki is an avid researcher, always seeking new information to consider, analyzing and perhaps acting on, if it can pass muster with her phenomenal sense of logic. She was probably the one most alarmed at my condition and often tried to find new ways to improve my situation. It was at her suggestion that I considered trying past life regression to see if somehow my current physical ailments were resulting from some strange misadventure of the past. She knew this would appeal to my sense of adventure and did not require the staunch physical discipline involved in some of her other recommendations. And so began the journey.

As part of this focused quest for optimum health and overall well-being, I have reveled in the most extraordinary a-ha's and breathtaking buzzes as I evidenced some truly remarkable events. I've explored past lives with an incredible hypnotherapist and spirit guide. Through Reiki, Healing Touch and Shamanic rituals, I have been introduced into the world of our energetic selves and come to understand the power that it wields over our physical bodies as well as how the suppression or abandonment of our emotional selves can be highly detrimental to our well-being. I have experienced the power of distance healing and have been given the gift of knowing momentarily what it is like to have a highly developed sixth sense. I have been cupped and had my acupoints punctured, my feet and related organs reflexed, my colon cleansed and my eyes studied as an uncanny source of information regarding my health. I have learned the vibrational affects of color, music and minerals, been counseled by the planets, angels and horses and communed with the other side.

Why is an experience with something different so frightening to some and intoxicating to others? I find myself often perplexed by some of us being pre-programmed to want our world to remain in a reliable pattern of the same day after day, while others spring out of bed hoping to come across something new and different in hopes that it will prove captivating and provide an element of fun. Still others, although curious and who would consider going there, need to preview the experience or carefully consider an idea to see how it might play out before they would feel comfortable taking that leap into that new state of doing or thinking.

While I seek opportunities to try intriguing new experiences or test drive new thoughts, I do not do so with blinders on. I may be a big picture person, but I also have an analytical side to me that makes me examine things through various lenses and from different angles, almost as if surrounded by a prism. I guess you might say I am an optimistic skeptic that is considered well grounded. I'm open to the possibilities out there, the unchartered waters waiting to be discovered, but yet not quick to jump onboard a boat riddled with holes. In fact a brilliantly funny and quick witted friend of mine, Mariette Edwards, has described this book as "Arthur Andersen meets Tinkerbell" a perfectly fitting analogy that just tickles me to my toes. She is also the one who ultimately gave me the title of this book.

Since I have such a love affair with change, I have a hard time resonating with those on the opposite side of the spectrum, those who prefer to cocoon. The idea of standing still, staying the same and being submerged in a sea of homogenized oneness is something I find positively frightening. So this book is aimed at armchair explorers, voyeurs of the experiences of others, those that might just be coaxed into exploring themselves if they can preview the experience. One who considers themselves a skeptic, yet intrigued by the idea of something new and different. Is that you? If it is, hooray we've found each other! You are exactly who I want to share my experiences with and invite you to celebrate the different paths people take and the wealth of knowledge they have to offer.

I definitely feel that I have been guided on this journey as so many fascinating people have crossed my path without me making a conscious effort to find them. They just seemed to have appeared in my life. I may have been introduced by a friend, been a neighbor, met them through business or networking with colleagues or even at local business associations. Looking back, it seems quite amazing the different avenues people have traveled towards our ultimate connection. But I am extremely thankful our lives intersected and I was able to observe first hand so many of life's deeper lessons and mysteries.

A great source of introductions has been the Eclectic Ladies Network (ELN) which is a women's social club based in Atlanta. My friend Cathy Horvath and I started the club when we found ourselves faced with having to go to premeditated networking events in an effort to expand our business network. Neither of us looked forward to the activity and we would usually entertain ourselves with a review of the more awkward moments of the evening as we drove home.

On one such evening, we started joking about the fact that if we were lucky we usually found one or two people we would enjoy having lunch with at a later date and that we should start collecting such individuals and form our own networking group. And that is exactly what we did in January 2002. Today, at any one point, our membership numbers about 100 adventuresome women. We get together for monthly parties in one of our homes for an afternoon of laughs and an always interesting potluck lunch. Typically there are only around 20 members in attendance for any given party and we spend the afternoon sharing thoughts or telling tales of some interesting life experience around the topic selected for the month. Examples of discussion fodder are "When was the last time you colored outside the lines?," "Tell us a story about new beginnings," "Who is your cherished teacher, mentor or life coach?" and "What haunts you?"

I've always believed our greatest job is to learn to think for ourselves, continually examine our beliefs and be open to stretch our imaginations so that we can move forward in time with an increased sense of who we are, why we are here and how we can best contribute while we are on Earth. My sincere hope is that by sharing my journey, I will be able to bring readers a fresh perspective on some preconceived notions, new ideas to consider and new approaches that might help along the way.

It is through "different" that we are offered the opportunity for growth, given untold wisdom and sometimes even profound enlightenment. But "different" can cause you to rethink what you have always thought to be true, stretch your boundaries of the known and in the end, create a need to redefine yourself. Are you still game? Then check quick judgment at the door, open your mind and consider something or someone different.

Sandbox Therapy
Jerry Connor MS, LPC

O ne of my fellow Eclectic Ladies, Jerry Connor, is a family psychotherapist. She is very passionate about her practice and in particular, her work with sandbox therapy. It is an experiential therapy where her clients are offered a choice of two different desk top trays, approximately 2 ft x 1 1/2 ft. One is filled with wet sand and another with dry sand, as a sort of blank canvas in which to let your subconscious mind go to work and play with an issue or challenge. The paint takes the form of miniature toy figures that represent ideas, concepts and thoughts at work deep within you. Jerry has managed to collect more than 1000 toys to choose from and she hosts them on twelve book shelves that line an entire wall of her office. She has classified the toys on these shelves into twelve categories including: people, transportation, household, nature, animals, religious/spiritual, fantasy/cartoon, housing, armies/weapons, dividers/rocks, scary/frightening, and miscellaneous.

During our monthly networking parties, Jerry always likes to tease the other ladies, "We can work on that issue in the sandbox if you like," when someone shares something particularly outrageous. She also had offered me a chance to dive in and experience this adventure to see what my subconscious might want to tell me.

Since I was a month into writing my book, I thought it was the perfect time to finally take her up on this offer and see what we could uncover. Upon my arrival I selected the dry sandbox and began mulling through what seemed like an endless array of toys to see what struck my fancy. I had no particular agenda in mind; I just started collecting toys in my hands and then would occasionally walk back to the sandbox and plop them down with a chuckle wondering if any insight would actually appear. To my surprise it did, and I thought it was so remarkable that it bore sharing with anyone about to read this book.

With tongue in cheek, I had consciously chose Catwoman to represent me. I thought that might be a fun alter ego to have. Jerry later told me that it wasn't as far fetched as it seemed because Catwoman and I share some of the same characteristics, namely being courageous, strong, strategic and assertive. I started randomly putting down other figures behind Catwoman as well as in various other places throughout the sandbox with no particular pattern or picture consciously in mind. I also ended up selecting a funky looking scientist with a full length mint green waist coat, a Bart Simpson like haircut, cool dude type funky shades and a bubbling beaker in his hand. Finally, I was about to declare that I was done, when I realized with horror that I had forgotten what had become my current life obsession, my book! I grabbed a tiny book and plopped it down in front of Catwoman.

So what did I find so awe inspiring about this whole exercise? Well when I looked behind Catwoman, I found that I had placed the following items that represented my hopes of what people would find in my writing:

Mastodon-a kind view of history
Wizard-the magic and wonder of the unknown
Buddha-kind and forgiving heart
Owl-wisdom handed down through the ages
Martian-a connection with the otherworld
East Indian Women-female mysticism
Heart-love of the experience
Brain-intellectual curiosity

If you look beside Catwoman, you will see a Guardian Angel.

My subconscious was telling me that all of these elements were in fact there supporting me in my thought process while I wrote my book.

And the cool dude scientist? Jerry explained that the method I went through to place him in the box often signifies an alter ego of the person developing the sandbox portrait. Amazingly it all seemed to personify where I was at that moment in life!

(See Pictures: Sandbox Therapy in back of book.)

Past Life Regression-Hypnotherapist
Linda Potter, Society of Novus Spiritus

I had first focused on the concept of living multiple lives when I read the book *Many Lives, Many Masters,* by Dr. Brian Weiss. Dr. Weiss is a traditional psychotherapist who accidentally led his patient to recall past-life traumas thus embarking on a discovery of how these past lives can manifest issues in our current lives. I was working at the 1996 Olympic Games at the time and the incredible pressure had caused my breathing problems, diagnosed as asthma in the early 90's, to worsen.

I was totally fascinated by Dr. Weiss' work. I thought perhaps by journeying back to previous lives I might find a reason for my current lung weakness and, with a stroke of luck, maybe even a way to make myself better. So I called his office to book an appointment, only to find there was a five year waiting list. Not easily daunted, I put myself on that list and then promptly forgot about it and moved on to the next adventure that caught my eye.

Spin ahead to six years later and a conversation I was having with my sister Vicki over the current Sylvia Browne book she had been reading. We particularly enjoyed the concept of past lives and she mentioned that representatives from Sylvia's Society of Novus Spiritus were coming to Atlanta in September. Members of the Society were now scheduling appointments with one of their hypnotherapists who would then gently guide clients back through past lives to give clues and assistance in this lifetime. Vicki is an avid personal development researcher and, like me, had learned from our mother, Edith, to be open minded about the world of possibilities. The worsening of my breathing problem had her worried and she strongly encouraged me to give past life regression a try because she had read instances where people, especially cases of asthma, had found relief from their physical conditions by releasing problems that had occurred in an earlier lifetime. I also had been experiencing stiffness in my hands and continued to be plagued by pain in my feet from time to time. So I made the call and found out the specifics. I sent my deposit in and completed the forms they sent me. One of the questions they asked was whether you had anything in particular you were hoping to address.

Along with my current health issues, I decided I would tell them about this strange image that would pop into my head from time to time. It never scared me and I didn't recall it often, but it had been with me for as long as I could remember. The scene was that my hands were raised over the top of my head, bound, and that my feet were being beaten. It was quite a strange thing to imagine I had to admit, but sometimes you just accept that life is strange and don't question it too much. I did have another piece of information that seem to fit with this weird image. When I went to a podiatrist for an assessment, he said he found it curious that my feet indicated parallel injuries in three different places on each foot. Hmmph I thought. That's pretty wild. I have no memory of ever injuring my feet. So I thought that would be a bit of interesting information to share.

I also wondered if, while under hypnosis, I would be able to visit my little feisty and lovable Scotty, a terrier-beagle mix that had passed away from cancer on his leg two and a half years earlier. It was a very difficult and painful parting and now my remaining beloved canine companion, an Airedale named Zachery, was getting on in years and I knew in my heart he would be leaving me soon too.

My appointment was scheduled for Sept 24, 2001, just a couple weeks after my appointment with a rheumatologist who had not uncovered any reason for the pain and stiffness in my hands and feet. I was a little disappointed to learn that my regression time slot was the last appointment of their long weekend in Atlanta. I kept thinking they will be all tired out. As the date approached, my excitement mounted, what possibilities lay ahead for me? Will my asthma improve? Will I uncover a rich history of exotic past lives? Will I learn to travel to another dimension on my own? Will the experience change me forever?

Needless to say, Sept 11th took the wind out of my sails and even made me consider canceling. The thought of driving down to an airport hotel a few weeks later for my appointment had me a bit on edge. It was a cloudy, rainy day and it seemed that doom and gloom was just hanging in the air. But then I thought, hey, this is probably just what I need to lift my spirit. A confirmation that life is continuous and what goes around comes around. So with that I found myself sitting in the lobby of the hotel waiting for a representative to call my name and invite me up for my appointment.

While sitting there waiting, I recall watching an interview process taking place, for a sales position I think. It struck me as disappointing to see how seemingly superficial the interviewing team was, not the least bit concerned for the feelings of the interviewees. The crass comments being whispered by the white shirt, red tied, blue suits just outside of range, yet close enough to hear their unnerving giggles. Ugh, I thought, I'm glad I am not vying for a position to work with these snakes. I saw one of the other regression participants return from their time upstairs and they were a full tilt emotional mess, tears streaming down their faces and wet tissues wadded up in their hands. Yikes, this might be a little more than I bargained for!

Then Linda Potter appeared and I couldn't help but be affected by her presence. It was the strangest feeling, as if she had just glided to the spot in front of me, like goodness personified. Any fears that had been bubbling up were immediately disarmed upon meeting her. Without hesitation and actually with sincere anticipation I followed her into the elevator and up to the hotel suite. It amused me to think that I was being so trusting. Here I was following this woman into a room and I had no idea what was really waiting for me. But I trusted the Sylvia Browne name and this woman had such an angelic presence about her that sure-ly nothing but a positive experience awaited me.

We chatted for a few moments and I confessed my disappointment in being her last appointment of the weekend, along with my concern that she would be exhausted at this point. She laughed and shared that actually she is energized by her work on the other side and that she is always operating at peak energy by her last appointment. She went on to explain that she is guided as to whom she books in each appointment slot and always finds it interesting who is to be given the last appointment in each location they visit. Well, I thought, that is a pretty good answer. Works for me. If nothing else I had to admire her diplomatic skills.

Linda proceeded to go over my paperwork and ask more in-depth questions about what I had written. She also asked if there were any other circumstances, other than what I had already listed, that I would like to cover while I am regressed. I thought for just a few minutes and then quickly added that as a kid I had always had this fear of falling down and smashing all my front teeth on the cement. I also had heard about two past lives from a fairly accurate psychic and I wanted to see if anything came up around them. They both involved my husband Slava, one being set in a Russian Czar's palace, and another in the lost continent of Atlantis.

Okay, I might lose a few of you on that one. I didn't say I was convinced of these past lives as of yet, but they had been brought to my attention during another exploration and they were an entertaining curiosity. What had kept them on my radar screen as a possibility were two things: One, that the information had come from a psychic I had known for a couple of years who had proven to be amazingly accurate on predicting business situations for me. And two, when I ventured into the past lives arena during one appointment, she had told me all sorts of entertaining scenarios that had made me giggle. But when she told me the most outrageous one, the one about a traumatic separation while on Atlantis, instead of getting the biggest laugh of all, out of nowhere I was flooded with overwhelming grief and became very distraught. Now how did that happen?

So we were set. Armed with objectives, it was time to commence the regression. Ah, but it wasn't to prove to be that simple. You see, for all the bravado I display from time to time in wanting to embrace something new and different from the esoteric chronicles, I have a heaping dose of skepticism to contend with. And so the challenge began. How to get past my disbelief into a place that would allow me to access information stored elsewhere.

Thankfully Linda wasn't one to give up on me easily and, fortunately by booking me as her last appointment, she had some flexibility. She stayed with me, gently and with good humor encouraging me to look further and deeper. She guided me in a way that did not force me to a place of discomfort, rather she helped me release the logical skeptic so I could find my way to the place of knowing, the place where I could find the knowledge I was seeking. I seem to remember counting backwards from 10, and feeling relaxed as I listened to the gentle music in the background and laid there on the couch with Linda sitting next to me. I actually felt a little silly because I didn't feel as though anything had actually happened. I was still awake, aware of my surroundings, and when asked.....

ME: Well I am still here, in the hotel right here. I just....I don't... I am trying to visualize all but I haven't....

LP: Ah, but you are not visual so don't try to do that.

ME: Or feeling it or....

LP: What I want you to do is tell me, when I asked you to go through the tunnel, were you able to do that?

ME: No. I don't like feel or nothing seems different

LP: Okay. I want you to get in your mind that there's a knowing. It's not like when I say that there is a tunnel, you don't need to see it (Yes) or you don't even need to feel it, just know that it is there. It is that simple. You don't have to have any sense of it all. And if I say to you that right now, I'd like you to step into the white light. What I'd like you do is to imagine it. Okay? (Yes) You don't have to feel it. You don't even have to sense that at this point. (Yes) I'd like for you to imagine that you are standing underneath a spotlight. Let's say the kind of spotlight they might use on a movie set. (Yes)

A really, really big one. And it is above your head quite a dis-
tance and it is turned on very bright. And imagine yourself
looking down at the floor where your feet are and seeing this
huge white circle where you're standing in the light of this
spotlight. Can you imagine that without seeing it, can you in
your mind imagine that? (Yes)

All right. Perfect. That is all you need to do.

Now. This spotlight is so bright and so powerful that if you
were to lift your hand up to look at it under that light, your
hand would actually appear white because the spotlight is
that powerful.

Now what I am going to do on the count of three is I am
going to have you step out of that spotlight. And right now
with your feet in the spotlight, there is nothing but darkness
around you. The only thing that anybody would be able to
see, or know, is that the spotlight is the only thing anybody
could see at this point. And so, here you are standing in the
spotlight, your feet are in the middle of this huge white cir-
cle and on the count of three what I want you to do is step
out of that spotlight even though the spotlight is in your
imagination, that's what I want you to do. What do you
think? Can we give it a try?

ME: Yes.

LP: All right. Exactly that. And what I want you to do is to
step out of that spotlight. Because I want you to take me back
to a lifetime, if you have one, that is related to the stiffness in
your hands and feet, the stiffness and the pain in your hands

and feet. I want you to take me back to that lifetime. Now when we step out of the light I don't want you to try and see anything.

What you are going to notice is an emotional shift. And that is what I want to look for. Okay? (Okay) Don't try to see anything. It is going to come to you in a knowing sort of way. So just answer my questions in a very relaxed mode. Okay? (Yes).

All right. On the count of three we are going to step out of that light, take me, if there's a past life where your hands and feet were injured or impacted in any way that's related to this life, take me to that life on the count of three. 1.2.3. Step out of the light.

Tell me what you sense. And let it come to you. Are you outdoors or indoors, which way feels better. It doesn't need to be clear. And if you think you are making it up, give it to me anyway.

ME: I just feel like I am in the dark.

LP: Okay that works. I want you to stay right there for a moment. Okay? (Yes)

Okay.

Now, were you able to imagine being in the spotlight and going from the spotlight to the dark? (Yes) Great.

Now here you are in the dark, do you get any kind of a feeling of being there. (No) Okay, just more a neutral like okay I am in the dark? (Yes) All right then.

Do you sense that you are outside or inside a dwelling. Give me which way feels stronger because you are starting to use a faculty that is brand new to you.

ME: Yes, it is just void, it's nothing.

LP: Okay. All right. What I want to do now, since we are working on going back to a lifetime that may be related to the problem you have had with your feet and your hands. We are going to try to move into that situation, into that lifetime. And I am going to push you along a little bit further after that. And what I want you to do, as if you were sitting back in an easy chair, and you are watching a movie screen and nothing is on it yet. And when I count to three, I want on the movie screen for you to be able to see, just like you got a flash of, a picture of or a knowing of that something had happened to your feet and hands before, I want that scene to be played on that movie screen. Are you ready to give that a try?

ME: Just what I thought before or what I am suppose to...

LP: What you are going to get right now. (Hmm) And whatever comes in your mind, don't analyze it. (Yes) If you analyze, you are going to put everything away from you. So don't analyze. Just give it to me. And you will feel like you are making it up. (Yes) But that's okay. Just give it to me anyway, because you can always say afterwards, oh, gosh I made it all up. And that is totally okay to think that for now. (Yes) All right, so, I want you to move in to whatever situation it was that you had that is related to the feet and hands issue in this life. Okay, so I am going to move you into that, on the count of three and I want you just to tell me what comes across your mind. On the count of three. 1.2.3. Tell me what you sense.

ME: (heavy sigh)

LP: Looking on the movie screen. Just sit there in the audience for a moment. If you think you start seeing something, tell me.

ME: It just remains blank. It's just like gray.

LP: Okay. The screen is gray or everything around you is gray?

ME: The screen.

LP: Okay. It's gray? (Yes)

What I want you to do right now, is put on that screen the scene that you got before that was given to you. Tell me when you have it. The one about your feet and hands. Tell me when you've got that on the screen.

ME: What I've imagined before?

LP: Yes, what you've been shown before and you can call it imagined.(Yes) Tell me when you've got that on the screen. Just throw it on up there.

ME: Yes.

LP: And put it into action, and I want you to show me a more complete picture then you got before, how it began, what happened, how it ended and the face of the players. All right, so it is rolling now, the film is rolling now, and I want you to tell me exactly what it was that you imagined happened to you. Give me details without analyzing it.

ME: But there are no details. It's the same as just what I've seen before. My hands being tied with ropes, (Okay) and I'm just hanging there and that's it.

LP: Okay. We are going to go for more detail right now, so bear with me. Okay? (Yes)

And, I want you to now see as soon as your hands were being tied were they at your side, were they at your front or were they up in the air.

ME: Above my head.

LP: Above your head. How many people tied you up? How many people did it take to do this to you?

ME: I don't see any people.

LP: All right. What do you sense? Do you sense whoever tied up your hands, was it a male or female? Young or old? Listen to the feeling that you get, don't try to see it all. You can almost feel them doing it. You can feel big hands, small hands. Male, female. Do you get a sense of it either way.

ME: No.

LP: Okay. All Right. And you also saw your feet. What did you see them do to your feet.

ME: Just take a stick and beat them.

LP: Ah hah. Can you tell from your surroundings what country you were in if you look at it now? And look around you. Did this happen inside a building or dwelling, or outside.

ME: Inside.

LP: It happened inside. What did the inside of the dwelling look like.

ME: Cement blocks. (Okay) Like there is a dirt floor.

LP: Excellent. Excellent. How many people were in there?

ME: I don't see people.

LP: Are you in there right now? Do you sense yourself in there?

ME: No. I don't know, I guess it is just kind of like feeling I am still looking at the screen and seeing....

LP: You are doing awesome. You're doing an awesome job. You are on a roll now. Let's keep it going. The dirt floor. Is that something you saw before or is that a new thing.

ME: No. It's a new thing. And the cement blocks.

LP: Can you tell me…. now I want you to take the first word that comes into your mind here because you are trying to audit and I want you to stop from auditing. I want you to tell me what country you think this is. The first thing that comes across your mind.

ME: South America.

LP: Excellent. I want you to tell me what year you think it is. The first number. Just say it.

ME: 16

LP: Excellent. I want you to tell me what do you sense you are wearing.

ME: Just kind of raggedy clothes.

LP: Okay. Now, for this kind of punishment to happen, do you feel that you were being accused of something?

ME: I feel like I am a man.

LP: Okay. How old do you feel you are?

ME: Not old. Like 20's or something, late teens, early 20's.

LP: Okay. What do you think the reason is that this has happened to you? What do you get a sense of that they are thinking what you did or are you being accused of something?

ME: Don't know.

LP: Okay. You don't get a sense of that at all. What I want you to do is back up in time just a bit to before this beating took place. I want you to go back in time, even if it's a couple of hours, or a day. I want you to back up in time, let's say a day or two. Move back to just before...

ME: I had black hair.

LP: You had black hair?

ME: Or, this scene seems like black hair.

LP: That's excellent. Do you know what your name was?

ME: No.

LP: You don't hear anybody calling you. (No) Okay. All right. What I want you to do is back up in time, just a moment. Just back up in time and tell me what it is you are accused of, back up to where you are told what you are being accused of and what is it they are accusing you of, why are they doing this to you. What is the overwhelming feeling that you get from it?

ME: Don't know. It's like there's a market or something. I don't know.

LP: Okay. Do you see the market or sense the market?

ME: I sense kind of a market with a little cart.

LP: Okay. And what do you have to do with that little cart and the market.

ME: I don't know.

LP: Give it a moment. It is going to become clear. What do you do to make your living, to put food on the table? What kind of job do you do?

ME: I don't know. Maybe I stole something. Maybe I stole some food.

LP: Okay. And why would you have stolen some food? What would have been the reason?

ME: Don't know. Look poor. Hungry maybe.

LP: That's very good. Now for a man in your twenties, do you sense that you had parents that you lived with or did you have your own family? What's your feeling?

ME: By myself.

LP: Okay. So you would be alone. Did you have any abilities that you can sense? Any kind of abilities, uhmm……..

ME: I feel like I was just like a farm worker or something. Just a laborer.

LP: Okay. Excellent. All right, and did you have friends? Do you sense that you had friends?

ME: No.

LP: All right. And what was it that you stole? Can you see it now? Can you sense what it was? Look down and see what it was they're accusing you of stealing.

ME: Just like, uhmm...I think of like squash and pumpkins and fall vegetables or something. I don't know.

LP: That's great. That's great. That's Excellent. Okay, so take me through the process now. You've been caught stealing. Who catches you? Let it come to you. Don't try to reach for it. It will all come rushing into you and you'll get impressions. Somebody caught you. Did they actually catch you with the food in your hand or were they told about it?

ME: I don't know.

LP: Okay. All right. They've caught you now and they want to punish you for what you did so can you see how it happened? Can you see the scenario? Look at it and take a look at what they did. I want you to look at it like it was a movie. And tell me exactly how they did it and what your reaction was.

ME: Oh it's funny [little laugh]. Because I think, it's like [laugh] there's a woman like Peru or Chile or something with the big hat (Right) and a dress and she has the cart with the food. (Okay) And maybe I took some food. (Okay) And I got CAUGHT! (Okay) It is like she caught me.

LP: Ohhhhhh, and she snitched on you.

ME: No, like she physically caught me.

LP: Okay she physically caught you. OH, she PHYSICALLY caught you! (Yes) You were going to run with it and she caught you?

ME: I think so, like she was holding me or something. I don't know.

LP: She was a strong woman.

ME: Right!! It was like strange. Big, she's big.

LP: Yes, she is probably used to people trying to do that you know. (Yes) It's her livelihood. So when she caught you, did she relinquish you to authorities?

ME: I don't know.

LP: Do you have a sense of it? Stay with it. Follow it. Stay with it just a moment. You see her catching you. I am going to turn down the air a little bit. You see her catching you. It'll come to you. Just sit there a moment and let it come in so you get a real good feel for what the process was. She had to have told somebody. She caught you....

ME: I think she just yells.

LP: Okay, so she yells and then somebody, somebody comes. Is that fair for me to say without me putting words in there?

ME: I guess. I really don't see from there to…the being in that….(That room) that room.

LP: Okay. Well you really don't need to see it all. It is all sensing, I think what you are getting. But you are doing an awesome job. All right. So, what I'd like to do, I'm going to take you a little bit deeper. I will do a really short count down, because I want you to, if you can, grab the moment where they took you and punished you for whatever it was so you can get a…..release that. We don't need to get right into it but we will see if we can get you just relaxed enough to where you get a little better feel for what happened. Okay, so listen to my voice, let's relax just a little bit deeper now. I want to take you down starting with 5 going a little deeper, 4 going deeper still, 3. 2. 1 deeper still. Okay, now, can you take me right back to where the injuries on your feet, if they came from that life, can you take me to that moment that you sustained any injuries to your feet and hands from that life. If you can, if you can, I want you to take me back to that moment on the count of three 1.2.3. And tell me what you sense. Give it a moment. Just a moment. Do you sense anything.

ME: No.

LP: Okay. Well it is not necessary that we see it. I was hoping to give you extra clarity on that. What I am going to do now is I am going to ask that you release that from this life, release it from the past life we are visiting. Okay, on the count of three, take a deep breathe and let's leave it back there where it belongs. 1.2.3. releasing it now, back to the past life where it belongs, freeing you up so your feet don't hurt. Letting it go, letting it go. What I want to do right now is I want you to take me into the white light. Where we just were. Tell me when you are there.

ME: Yes

LP: All right. Awesome. What I want you to do now is I want you to take me back if you have a life time related to your asthma I want you to take me back there right now. On the count of three, lifetime related to your asthma. 1.2.3. And tell me what you sense.

[long pause]

Do you sense if you are outdoors or indoors. Don't analyze now. Give it to me as you think you're getting it. Even though you may feel like you are making it up.

ME: Outdoor. In the light, but outdoors.

LP: Okay, so it was daytime?

ME: No, it's just that white light and I am outdoors.

LP: Oh, well that's wonderful. That's very nice. All right. What I would like you to do is take me to the place, if there is a place there where you first began the problem that you've brought in to this life with the asthma. If this is true, I want you to move right in to that situation and tell what's going on.

Are you able to sense anything. Remember not to try to see it all. There is so much going on around you, the telepathy that is going on right now, don't try to be visual, because you will block what the other is.

ME: *Well it is just like maybe like it is fog, like it's just... (Very good) The light kind of turns into.... you can't see anything really anything.*

LP: *Okay, so it is very foggy. What country are we...*

ME: *But it doesn't feel moist, it doesn't feel like humid fog. Maybe it's more smoky or something. I don't know. It is just white.*

LP: *Okay. What country are we in? The first thing, that comes to your mind.*

ME: *Well Argentina.*

LP: *Good. What year?*

ME: *12*

LP: *Okay that's fine. If you get any more on that in a bit, it's not that important. All right. You are sensing that there is smoke in the air, it is Argentina. Are you male or female?*

ME: *When you asked me that question it just said female. But I don't know. I don't see anything.*

LP: *Don't analyze. (Okay) Good. That's what you want to do. Give it to me as you see it or get it. We will analyze later.*

You are doing great here. All right so, there is smoke in the air. Where is the smoke coming from? What is creating the smoke?

ME: Like a roof burning, a grassy roof.

LP: Just one? (I think) A little bit of smoke or a lot of smoke?

ME: It is thick with smoke, you can't see.

LP: Are you standing there in it? How's your breathing?

ME: Well, I don't think I am concerned with my breathing as much as I just can't see.

LP: Are you with anyone? Any loved ones with you? Anybody at all? (No) Do you know what has created the fire? Do you get any sense about it? (No) Okay. Is it indeed a fire?

ME: It is just what I thought. It is a fire on a thatched or grassy roof.

LP: That's excellent. Trust it. Keep going with it. Get it going even more. You are doing a good job.

ME: It is like I am walking in a village and there is fire everywhere. Well, there is smoke everywhere. I don't know if there is fire everywhere, but you can't see, you don't know what to do, you don't know where to go.

LP: Other people having the same problems?

ME: I don't hear anyone or I don't see anyone.

LP: Okay, you are not sensing anyone else but yourself at this point and all you know is that it is hard to get anywhere. (Yes) All right. Are you breathing this smoke in, is it pretty hard not to? Is it surrounding you completely?

ME: I am just in the middle of it. I can't really see anything. I am like overwhelmed by it.

LP: Okay. And are you able to breathe all right?

ME: I don't feel any different. I am more concerned that I can't see.

LP: Okay and then what happens to you. Move a little bit ahead in time and tell me, do you get away from it? (No) What happens to you?

ME: I think I just pass out. I just think that…. (Okay) It doesn't feel burning or anything, it is just like overwhelming.

LP: Okay, but there was so much smoke that you couldn't see, is that right?

ME: Yes. You couldn't see what you were doing. Or where anything was. It was just all white smoke.

LP: Kind of like you were in a cloud. (Yes) That thick. (Yes) All right. What I want you to do…

ME: But it is white. (Yes) It is not ashy. It is not gray or black or anything.

LP: Right. Right. All Right. What I want you to do is take me to the moment you left your body in that life. You passed out, did you die at that point? Do you get a sense of that? Was that the last day of your life in that lifetime? Do you get a sense of that at all?

ME: No. I just don't know. That's all I just….

LP: ..that's all you just got. Okay. What I am going to do is direct you to take me to the very last day of your life in that lifetime. I want you to take me to the very last day of your life in that lifetime on that count of three. 1.2.3 it's the last day of your life. Where do you find yourself?

ME: I don't know.

LP: Do you get a feel for it? Give it just a moment and let it come to you like you have been letting the other stuff come to you. You are going to get a knowing or a sense. I want you to pass it on to me as soon as you get it.

ME: No. I don't see anything beyond the fire or the smoke.

LP: Okay. Do you believe the smoke that you were breathing in has a direct correlation to the asthma in this life?

ME: It could.

LP: Okay. Would you like to release it if that is the case?

(Yes) Let's do it on the count of three. I want you to take a nice steady deep breath and we are going to leave it behind you, freeing you up from the asthma problems you've had in this life because you don't need to hang on to that any longer. That was then, and this is now. On the count of three. Releasing. 1.2.3 releasing that memory right now.

All right. Great. What I want you to do right now, I want you to take me to a really special place on the other side that is called 'The Garden.' Do you think you can get there if I help you?

ME: I can try.

LP: All right. It's a very easy journey. On the count of three I want you to take me to 'The Garden' and I immediately want you to explain to me what it looks like. Go into 'The Garden' on the count of three. 1.2.3. Into 'The Garden'. Tell me...

ME: Pink flowers—pink flowers and purple flowers and yellow flowers.

LP: You are not messing around now. Great! Are you able to see them or sense them Connie? Is it more of a sensing?

ME: It is more like a picture.

LP: Okay. All Right. Good. And what else do you see around you?

ME: Green.

LP: All Right. Is there any place to sit?

ME: Yes, there is a little bench.

LP: Okay. Let's go have a seat on that bench right now for a moment. And I want to call in Raheim. Tell me when you sense his presence. He is a very strong male healer.

ME: I don't sense a male. It is more like a female.

LP: You sense a female. Ask her what her name is and it is the first one that you hear in your head. Pass it on to me right away.

ME: [Starts laughing] Oh well that is ridiculous BA LOU.

LP: BALOU?

ME: BA LOU!

LP: BA LOU.

ME: It is just ridiculous.

LP: Yes it is ridiculous doing this all day long I want to tell you. You are on a roll over there. Who is she? Now I want you to tell me exactly what you hear in your head, you are going to think you are making it up, but give it to me. Who is she? Is she your guide? What does she say? Yes or No?

ME: No.

LP: Who is she? I want her to…

ME: She has long hair, (Okay) a long gown.

LP: Does she have anything in her hair?

ME: Yes, a little crown of flowers.

LP: Is it Lillith? What does she say?

ME: She smiles.

LP: She has been doing this all day long. You've got her. The long hair and the flowers is her earmark. She is being silly. Lillith is going to help us, obviously. She must be smiling. She is having a really good time today. I want to ask Lillith if she can help you to understand the allergies you've had in this life. Did we uncover it in the past life. What does she say?

ME: No.

LP: Can she help us see a lifetime where it is related to.

ME: She is nodding.

LP: She is nodding yes?

ME: I guess so.

LP: Will she take you there now?

ME: Yes.

LP: Okay. Follow her. On the count of three I am going to give you a boost to go with her and tell me what you see 1.2.3 with Lillith. Where is she taking you?

ME: Deeper into her garden.

LP: Okay. Follow her. Keep me posted on where she takes you and what she is doing. Okay?

ME: We are going to go down, like deeper and deeper and you don't really see the garden anymore. It is kind of like going down a path and its maybe like dark trees overhead and it is ground underneath and soil, like you are walking on the soil.

LP: Okay.

ME: I don't see her.

LP: Is she still with you?

ME: I don't see her.

LP: All right. What is she showing you? Where are you at right now?

ME: Just like a, like reddish soil and its dark green trees that form arches.

LP: Okay. Does it feel like to you that this is a place you've been before.

ME: Yes. That is what is so weird, it made me feel like I was in, I guess it must be the Boboli Gardens in Florence. It's one of the gardens there. Yes it has to be that one. When you got to go down and the trees arch over. It is like that anyhow.

LP: Well she is taking you to a past life I do believe, she has very gently walked you into it. She is really working you. I want you to tell me, walking in there with her right now, seeing it right now, do you sense that you had a past life there? Does it feel right to you? I do not want to put words that are not true. In your best discernment do you feel that you have been there before. (Yes) In this life, or a past life?

ME: I assume a past life, but I don't feel one way or the other, but I don't not feel...

LP: Okay that's good. That's a start there. What I want you to do is look around there you said it's got the reddish soil, and the dark green trees that form arches. And I want you to tell me whether you had a lifetime that either frequented that place, lived there or went there for any purpose. What's your feeling, what's your gut feeling on that?

ME: I just strolled down, strolled through.

LP: Okay. Would this be a place that you frequented on a regular basis?

ME: Yes.

LP: Okay. When you go through there is it damp there or dry?

ME: More damp.

LP: More damp. Do you sense that it affected you, your breathing in any way shape or form in that lifetime when you would go there, possibly without you knowing it? You might have had some kind of breathing problem. Again, I don't want to put words in your mouth for anything that isn't true.

ME: Maybe. Just the dampness and the mold.

LP: Was there mold there?

ME: I am just guessing because it is damp.

LP: All right. Okay I want you to try to slip into the person that you were back then, try to slip into the person, can you do that?

ME: I don't know because [big laugh] I saw long blond hair. What am I doing in Florence with long blond hair?

LP: That wouldn't be so odd. Okay are you are seeing your-self with long blond hair?

ME: Or maybe its BA LOU or whatever her name is.

LP: Well take a moment and tell what it is.

ME: No, I think that is her again, because she has the long blond hair and the crown of flowers and the white robe.

LP: Lillith. Okay what is she doing with you? What is she appearing for? Is she showing you something?

ME: Yes, I think she is motioning to come follow her.

LP: Go ahead, go ahead with her and let me know what she shows you. She is trying to help you understand. It is amazing she hasn't thrown her hands up in disgust because she does do that.

ME: [Big laugh] Well she probably will quite soon.

LP: [Big laugh] But you are trying.

ME: Yes, I am trying. I don't know.

LP: Just stop editing so much. But we're moving. We are getting some work done here. Tell me where she takes you and what she shows you, because it could have great significance for you.

ME: It is kind of like now, up the gardens and up to the top of that plateau where you can look over the whole city.

LP: And what city are you looking over.

ME: It's Florence.

LP: Does Lillith, or BA LOU, whatever her name is, does she have anything she wants to tell you, to explain?

ME: No, she is gone again.

LP: Okay. She is trying to show you, she wants you to figure it out is what it is. She is leading and going oh, my god, you are still not getting it. So you went from below to now this plateau where you can look over Florence (Yes) Does it seem familiar to you? Does it look like the place you've looked out before?

ME: In past lives? I mean I have for this life.

LP: How old were you, in your twenties you said when your allergies started, in your 20's?

ME: Yes, late twenties.

LP: How old were you when you went to Italy in this life?

ME: A little bit before then.

LP: Did you travel, did you go to a place you have been to before? Did Lillith take you to a place you have been to before?

ME: In this life. Yes.

LP: In this life? (Yes) She walked you through. All right. I think maybe she is trying to show you that it came from this life, in something you inhaled (Oh) in this life. And I want her to appear before you and shake her head yes if we hit the nail on the head here. If it came from this life, if this allergy thing came from something you picked up from this life. Is it true? We want her to say yes or no.
Has she come back?

ME: Well I am getting yes and then no, and then yes and then no. I am getting confused.

LP: Geez. I am calling in Raheim. Let's get Raheim in the picture. He is Mr. No nonsense. A very strong male healer.

ME: Does he have a dark beard and dark hair?

LP: Very good. What is he wearing?

ME: I don't know but I see a gold earring in one ear. That can't be right.

LP: Yes. It can be right. That is Raheim. You've got him. All right. I am going to ask Raheim, the life, the place that Lillith just showed you, underneath the city in Florence, a place you have been to in this life, is that the reason, the whole reason for your allergies? Partial or whole? Now what does he say?

ME: He's not talking to me. He is just standing there. I can see his face actually, but I don't see the rest of his body.

LP: That's okay. [Heavy sigh.] They are not being very cooperative today. I don't know why they are not telling you. We know you went back to Argentina when you were around that smoke and that certainly could have an effect because in that lifetime you just remember passing out from that smoke. So it filled your lungs and so we know that smoke is a contributing factor to breathing problems so I assuming that the Argentine life may very well had something to do with it. But now they are showing you this Italy life from this time around and I want clear answers from either Raheim or Lillith, without any nonsense Lillith. If in fact…

ME: Yes, yes.

LP: All right. Who is answering, him or her.

ME: Her.

LP: All right. And what does she say.

ME: She just nods her head.

LP: All right. Thank you for stopping the nonsense. So it did come from your trip in this life. All right. I want to ask Raheim if there is anything else you can do to help yourself other than releasing, or is releasing going to be enough.

ME: I think he said yes.

LP: Releasing will be enough? Is that what he is saying? I'll ask him specifically. Is releasing from this life or past life enough? Does he say yes or no.

ME: I get the feeling yes.

LP: Okay that is what you go with. That is the best thing to do. Don't question that part. My goodness, that was a lot of work there.

I want Lillith or Balou, or BA LOU to show you, that's a new one, I want her to show you if she can do it without goofing around why you have a fear of smashing your teeth. What was it that happened to you?

ME: [laugh] Its funny, right away I saw a pumpkin, I don't know why but when you asked that question I saw a pumpkin with a pumpkin grin.

LP: So, is she going to help you find, is she showing you something? See if she shows it to you on a movie screen type thing. She may just show you exactly what happened, you may see the characters and see the whole thing.

ME: Just being pushed and falling.

LP: Okay, being pushed by someone. Where did you fall?

ME: On my face on the road. Hard road, stone road. Cobblestones.

LP: Okay and what happened to you? What happened to your face?

ME: Bloody.

LP: Okay. What happened to your teeth?

ME: Ching, ching, ching.

LP: [laugh] Okay, how old were you?

ME: Eight.

LP: Oh, you were a little guy. What country was this?

ME: I don't know. Spain is what first came to my mind.

LP: What year? The first thing that comes to your mind.

ME: It doesn't make sense but it is 16.

LP: Okay. You are just getting small numbers, but that is okay. I want Lillith to take you to a past life, if you had one, with Slava. I want her to show you how you knew him before, if you did. Tell me what she shows you.

ME: Well the first thing that popped in my mind is what I have heard before though. That we were little cousins in Russia, two little boys.

LP: I want you to see it if it's true. But I want Lillith to show that to you if it is true. If it's not true, I want her to show you what is true. And you will see more of it if it is true. You will get details. She will show you a scene, she will actually show it to you. Can you see it now?

ME: Red and gray granite. Hiding under the table.

LP: Why?

ME: Just playing.

LP: And who are you playing with?

ME: Another little boy.

35

LP: Are you a girl or a boy?

ME: Boy.

LP: And you are playing with another boy. Who is that boy? Is that Slava in this life? Or is it someone else?

ME: That's the feeling.

LP: Okay. Are you related or are you just friends.

ME: We are cousins.

LP: I want you to move ahead in time, moving ahead in time to an important time. Tell me how old you are now?

ME: 17

LP: Okay. And are you still friends with that cousin?

ME: Yes, I think so. We are dressed really fancy.

LP: What is your name in that life.

ME: Don't know.

LP: You don't get that then. Okay.

ME: But blue and gold fabric.

LP: Do you get a sense that you were wealthy? That the family was wealthy?

ME: Yes. White stockings. They had white stockings.

LP: What year?

ME: 17 is what comes to me again, but I don't know.

LP: Okay. All right. And do you have a mother and father in that life? Do you sense, you may not see them, but do you sense that they exist for you?

ME: Yes. I don't feel like I am alone or anything.

LP: All right. Okay. Is there anything else you want to look at in that life.

ME: No.

LP: Okay. What I'd like to do now, I'd like you to take me, if you have a lifetime in Atlantis, I would like you to take me there now on the count of three. 1.2.3 take me there. Tell me where you are.

ME: By the water. (Okay) Just little pebbles, just looking at little pebbles in the water.

LP: Okay. Male or Female?

ME: Female.

LP: How old are you?

ME: I'd say 17.

LP: Okay and where are you? What is the name of the place you are?

ME: It just looks like a normal place. Rocky cliffs and water, nothing unusual. Kind of more isolated like there is no one else around.

LP: Okay, All right. I'd like you to tell me, at the age of 17, do you live with your parents or do you live alone?

ME: No, I am alone.

LP: Okay. Take me to your dwelling. Walk into the front of your dwelling. Tell me what it looks like.

ME: I get the feeling it is more like a cave.

LP: Okay. What year is this?

ME: All I see is zeroes.

LP: Okay. How many zeroes?

ME: Infinite.

LP: Okay. And who lives in the cave with you?

ME: Nobody.

LP: And are you comfortable with that feeling?

ME: No.

38

LP: And how do you feel?

ME: Lonely!

LP: Where is everybody else?

ME: I don't know.

LP: Okay. I want you to move ahead in time to where you run in to someone, where you have an exchange of verbiage or a communication with someone. Moving ahead to that time now. Moving ahead to that time, okay moving ahead now. And tell me, who is it that you end up communicating with and how old are you?

ME: A man, he has a beard, funny hat.

LP: A funny hat, why is it funny?

ME: [laughs] Well there is a feather coming out of it. Screwy it doesn't make any sense for the time.

LP: Okay and what kind of exchange do you have with him?

ME: Kind of like an update of information, what's going on.

LP: Okay and what does he tell you, what kind of update does he give you?

ME: Kind of what happened to everyone.

LP: And what did happen?

ME: It just says a flood, but…

LP: A flood? (Yes) And how many people survived the flood? What's your sense of it?

ME: That they are gone.

LP: How many of you are left? There is you and this man. Are there others living elsewhere in this place, that maybe you are spread out, but that there is others or do you get a sense that you two are all there is?

ME: I don't know, for this area there is only us two but it doesn't make sense because he is all dressed up fancy. How could he do that?

LP: Yes. Ask him right now why you're standing there. I want understanding on that. I want him to explain so you can understand it.

ME: It is like he came by boat.

LP: Okay. And what's the name of the place he came from? What does he tell you? The first thing that comes into your mind?

ME: Well Spain again. (Okay) He looks I guess… because he looks like one of those old explorers.

LP: Yes. I got you. All right. And he said there was a flood. That is what he was telling you. And as you look around you, what does your terrain look like?

ME: It's these like black cliffs of stone and its like a beach and there's this water. That's it. There is nothing else around, it is like this isolated area. (Okay) But why he came by himself in a little boat is kind of ridiculous.

LP: And does he give you a reason why he has done that?

ME: No.

LP: Okay. What I want you to do is I want you to back up in time one year. Back up in time, go on back, go on back, all the way back. Backing up in time one year and now tell what is your situation? And tell me where you are living and what it feels like?

ME: Feels like I am being hurried away but I… I don't know, this kind of lines up with what I heard before so I don't know…

LP: Let's just go with what you are getting now and we can compare it later. But you feel like you are being hurried away. (Yes) And who is doing the hurrying?

ME: The one who doesn't like me being with, with…they want to break us apart.

LP: Okay. And the person they want to break you apart from is who to you?

ME: Would be my boyfriend.

LP: Okay. And who is doing the hurrying. Anybody who is a relative or friend, or different than that?

ME: Like a sister or mother. Kind of pushing me away.

LP: And what do you do?

ME: I get into this little boat.

LP: You get in a boat and where do you go?

ME: In this little place by myself.

LP: Okay and why did you go by yourself?

ME: Because they want to get rid of me.

LP: Oh, because they want to literally get rid of you. And this is your sister?

ME: No.

LP: Who?

ME: The boyfriend's mother's sister.

LP: Oh, okay. Look at her face for just a moment. Do you recognize her from this life?

ME:[big laugh] That's weird. It can't be. It is like this woman…this [said her full name] woman. It doesn't make sense. I worked with her at the Olympic Games.

LP: It doesn't make sense you are telling me?

ME: Well because she looks just like she does here, I mean that doesn't make sense.

LP: Sure it does, because they are trying to show you who it was.

ME: Well…

LP: Okay…

ME: [big laugh] She IS a mean old bitch, so that makes sense

LP: Well, there you go….well there you go. Truth is stranger than fiction.

Okay, so there she is and she wanted to get you apart from this boy and so they sent you or made you…how did they make you go in the boat? What did they do to make you go there? How did they do that?

ME: They just physically dragged me off and put me in this boat.

LP: And you were by yourself?

ME: No. Somebody took me in the boat. (Okay) I don't have a boat when I am there.

LP: Okay. This boat. Look at the person that is paddling the boat or however…

ME: Rowing.

LP: Rowing the boat. Do you recognize them from this life?

ME: No.

LP: Nobody familiar? (No) And where did they take you? Did it take you a long time to get there or short time?

ME: It didn't take maybe so long. I guess there was just no way to get away.

LP: You couldn't get off the place you were you mean? (Yes)

Okay. And the man that landed there, how long after you were on this place by yourself did the man show up? (Hmmm...)Was it a long time?

ME: It didn't seem like I was that much older. Maybe five years or something.

LP: Were you by yourself for five years on that place?

ME: I don't know how you would eat there because there is no food. (Yes) [big laugh]

LP: All right. So they take you away in a boat. Did you have parents? And a family yourself? Do you get a sense of that?

ME: Yes. I do.

LP: All right. Did anyone come searching for you?

ME: I say Slava, that's what I...

LP: Was he the boyfriend?

ME: That was, like I said, the story before and that makes sense now.

LP: Look into his eyes. That is how you are going to know. Look into his eyes. Does it feel like him?

ME: Yes.

LP: His energy?

ME: Yes.

LP: Okay. And this [woman from the Olympic Games] character, does she have anything to do with you and Slava now?

ME: [laugh] No.

LP: Okay. That would be an interesting reunion though wouldn't it. [laugh]. Okay. All right. There is a lifetime with him in Atlantis. That is very interesting.

What I want you to do is go ahead in time to the last day of your life there and tell me where you are? How old are you?

ME: I got 40- 42.

LP: And who are you living there with at this time?

ME: I am just kind of still there by myself.

LP: Okay. Take me to where you eat. Where it is time for you to eat something. Take me, move me right in to where you need to eat.

ME: [big laugh] A-ha, that is why I hate fish!! That's what I am doing, roasting fish.

LP: [big laugh] Okay and you are alone. (Yes) Okay. Take me to the moment that you leave your body in that life. We are going to leave your body in that life. We move up, up and out of your body. 1.2.3. Up and out of your body. You can look down and see yourself. Tell me when you are there, tell me when you are there. You are up and out of that body. Are you there?

ME: Yes.

LP: All right. What did you die from in that life?

ME: I think just boredom.

LP: [laugh] Okay. What was the lesson for you in that life? What were you suppose to learn by living like that? What is your feeling?

ME: Survival I think.

LP: Okay, very good. Anything else?

ME: Independence.

LP: Anything else?

ME: Self reliance.

LP: Do you see any parallels with that life with your current life?

ME: No.

LP: Are you in this life independent? (Yes) Self reliant? (Yes) Do you carry it too far?

ME: [big laugh] Yes!!

LP: Ding, ding, ding, ding, ding!!

All right. So that was good for that life, because you needed to be. But sometimes, when we've had such a severe life like that where it was just totally necessary (Yes) because all you had was you, in this life you may be pushing people away because (Yes) you got to do it yourself. (Yes) You may be pushing relationships away because you got to do it yourself. Be aware of that. (Yes) Use that knowledge to your benefit. Soften the edges of it. When you go to be so doggone independent, slow down a little bit, and say, I can let somebody do a little something, (Yes) try to feel good about it. Because we are in this soup together. And it is okay to have those qualities, in fact it is an asset, but it can be holding you back if you take it too far. (Yes) Okay, do you have that message now okay? (Yes, laughing)

All right, take me to 'The Garden' again please.

ME: I will try.

LP: All right.

ME: What's his name? Raheim is smiling.

LP: Raheim. Yes. He says come on down, so you've got the answers you needed there. Does he want to say anything at this point about...add anything to the discoveries we've had?

ME: No.

LP: Okay, I want to call in Lillith, the goofball there, and let her appear with her flowers. BA LOU, I've never heard her use that name. And there is somebody that is accompanying her and its Scotty. (Yes) I want you to see how happy and healthy he is, that is important for you to see that. Is he there? (Yes, overcome with emotion) Now the wonderful things about visiting our animals on the other side is that they can talk. So anything you want to talk to him about, any last words, anything, he will tell you. He will tell you anything you want to ask him. Please go ahead and ask him, because it is a wonderful time.

Let me know when you are done talking to him. You can carry on any type of conversation. Nothing? (Nothing) I think it is important to see how happy he is. And you see that Lillith is right there with him. And anything he did in this life, whether it is playing with a ball, running through the grass, his favorite things to do, his favorite toys, they are replicated. He has them over there.

Okay. I want to ask Lillith, right now, his name is Zachery and he is getting old, and getting close to going home, does she have anything she wants to tell you to help you deal with it? And please pass on to me what she says.

And what does she say?

ME: Basically he doesn't want to go either because he feels so connected.

LP: Okay. Is there anything you can do to help him? (No) And I want Lillith to reassure you that he will go when he has chosen to go. (Yes) It will be his decision. (Yes) Okay. Is there anything else you want to ask her about his well-being, about his care, anything at all because she is a wealth of information about that? (No)

I want to ask Lillith now if you will be having anymore animals in your life after Zachery joins Scotty and they play until you get over there. Will you have any more animals?

ME: I already do.

LP: You already do?

ME: Yes. But not by my choice.

LP: [laughs] They've chosen you and you've chosen them to be sure. All right. What I want you to do now is go right back into hmmm., you are in 'The Garden' and I want you to go there. And I want to ask Raheim if you need to go to the healing lab before we go back. Any reason to go to the healing lab? What does he say?

ME: He says c'mon.

LP: All right. Go with him. It is an awesome, sacred space. And I want you just to tell me what it looks like, where he takes you.

ME: It is like this bubbling water. (Okay) And it is all rocks. (Okay) And you just kind of get in. (Okay) [Laugh]

LP: [Laugh] What's he doing?

ME: He pushed me under. [Both laugh more] He didn't hold me under. (Yes) He just pushed me under and I bobbed up.

LP: Okay. What does he want you to do?

ME: He doesn't say anything more. That seems to be it.

LP: Okay. The healing lab is a really neat place. I think he obviously feels you have a pretty good handle on things. And know that you can go back there if you ever feel you need a break from this world, you can take yourself in the bathtub, and light a candle or two, close the world out and call on him to toss you into the water, your bubbling water.

ME: It is like springs, hot springs. Yes.

LP: Oh that's nice. But you can go back there on your own. And it really is, where you are right now, know that it is a real place. Where you have been visiting are real places and

*real events even if you feel at this point that you've manufac-
tured some of it, it will sink in with a little bit of time. (Yes)
Very wonderful healing you have done for yourself. Very
wonderful research you have done for yourself.*

*What I want you to do right now is step into the white light
to take a nice deep breath and we are going to ask that anything you discovered from a past life of a negative nature or
any past life that we haven't discovered, that you release
anything of a negative nature so you don't bring it into this
life. If any of the lifetimes you've had have a direct correlation to any of the pains, the asthma, the allergies, the pains
in the feet or the hands or any other place in your body, if it
comes from another place or another time, release it now. We
ask on a blanket command that it be released so that you
may get on to business in this life without all of that physical
manifestation.*

*Anything of a positive nature from another place and anoth-
er time, any creative abilities, any positive attributes, any
strengths we are going to ask that you pull that into this life
so that it will bring you up to optimum operating levels.*

*And with that I want you to feel the energy coming back in
through the bottoms of your feet, your legs, your lower back,
your upper back, down your arms moving yourself all the
way up on the count of three I want you to come all the way
back feeling absolutely marvelous 1 subconscious receding,
2 consciousness coming back to the foreground and 3 all the
way back.*

I quickly found myself fully awake and relaxed, surprised

and curious about what I had sensed, yet wonderfully peaceful like I had just returned from a coveted afternoon of sailing on a beautiful calm lake surrounded by trees and flowers.

My Fascination

I found the whole hypnotherapy experience really intriguing. I was not asleep, yet I was in a different place. My whole demeanor shifted in the beginning of the dialog. Normally confident and self assured, my voice was initially meek and apologetic for not being able to answer the questions. Yet later, once I was deeper into the session and I had accessed my subconscious, I returned to a more natural state of being, confident in my answers and what I was experiencing.

I was surprised that a number of the past lives I recalled were rather mundane experiences. I always fancied the idea that if there was some strange experience behind the image of being strung up by my hands and having my feet beaten, that it was part of some great drama for a higher cause. Surely it was because I was a spy, a political prisoner or the result of some sort of noble action. To discover that my mysterious recollection was the result of being a thief out of hunger is a far cry from how my imagination would play out the scenario.

I was similarly puzzled to find that my breathing problems related to picking up a spore in the Boboli Gardens in Florence. At that point, I had never even heard of such a thing, the idea that you could get a lung infection that could simulate asthma. Nine months later I was reading an article on WebMD that advised of a new study being undertaken to research the potential of people with a lung infection to have been mis-diagnosed as asthma. The study asserted that these individuals actually have a bacterial infection that can be treated with heavy antibiotics. The test to determine whether an infection exists is still too invasive, requiring a lung biopsy which can be dangerous, so the identification and treatment still remains in the research stage as of this writing.

I was also totally taken back to have a former Olympic Games colleague of mine appear in one of my past lives as a rather villainous sort. During my interactions with her in this life, I certainly had seen an evil side to her behavior, yet I never had that instant recognition you can feel when you sense you've known someone before. Interestingly enough, a few years later I ran into this person at an organic market and within the first five minutes of conversation she asked if Slava and I were divorced. Now this woman had never even met Slava and had no information to even suggest that that would ever be a serious consideration. When I questioned her as to why she would ask, she hurriedly and rather clumsily covered with that she had heard of other people getting divorced after the Olympic Games experience and named two couples who had. I just brushed it aside in the moment, but now it seems to have possibly been a query of deeper interest.

I expected Atlantis to appear more like the Hollywood version of the place, with a lot of visible space age/Jetson like technology. Instead, while it had a touch of mystical quality in the air, it mainly resembled a mixture of King Arthur's court and ancient Greece. My boat was a simple wooden row boat departing from an unremarkable dock.

Interestingly enough, a theme in my life has been to strive to avoid becoming bored and as a child I would often complain of being bored to death.

Finally, I was intrigued to learn that of all the trauma and turmoil being revisited the only experience that wrenched at my heart was visiting or discussing my beloved dogs Scotty and Zachery. I was literally moved to tears and almost speechless upon seeing Scotty in 'The Garden.'

And although frail from crippling arthritis, considerable loss of hearing and eyesight as well as a life-long heart murmur, my loyal Airedale Zachery remained with me for 18 months longer. Six of those months were on borrowed time, as he contracted a horrible tumor in his mouth; upon diagnosis the vet had given him only weeks to live. But at 15 years old, Zachery continued to live life on his own terms and never let any of his ailments dampen his spirit. On good days he still danced around and beckoned me to play with him. In his very last days, when his body could not hold his spirit any longer, he quit eating and drinking. He decided it was time to go.

I find the concept of choosing to live with my stepson's dog, Vassily, a rather wild assumption. I absolutely love dogs but Vassily tries my patience beyond belief. He is a special Russian breed....actually kind of good looking, a short haired, light caramel color with four white socks and a triangle shaped head, the only thing I don't like is he has the big old pit bull mouth! He is a dog that Slava takes care of and has come to love and I have to put up with. He's definitely a boy's dog, not a nice cuddly Zachery or Scotty. No, he is more of a sassy ruffian who likes to let you know he's there. He will wait until I am dressed up, then run over and knock his rear against me to leave his scent – and hairs – on my pant leg or skirt. Even worse, he slobbers on me. If he were a teenager, he would wear spiked black leather, have colored punk hair and multiple body piercings, and carry a big noisy boom box with him everywhere.

It remains a question in my mind why my emotional ties were stronger with my dogs than any other experience revisited. Was it because they were a more recent connection or because they offered pure, unconditional love and support?

My Belief

I do believe I received new information and insight into previously unexplained conditions and tendencies being experienced in this life. At first I was trying too hard to get there, but once I relaxed and let myself travel naturally to the state of knowing, it all seemed perfectly logical, that it was truth. I didn't get the sense of the fantastic, but more a calm sense of "and so it is."

This sense of innate truth I felt served to reinforce my belief that many of us have had other lives, that we can be impacted by them in our current lifetime and that we can access those experiences if we choose to do so.

I do believe I traveled to another place, real or imagined, but I was some place different. My tendency is to believe it was a real place and Lillith, Raheim and my beloved Scotty were really there.

I do recommend the journey to anyone who is open to possibilities and seeks to enhance their life through self discovery. Having gone through the experience, I now also believe it is critically important to carefully choose anyone you would ask to guide you in such a session. I'd approach my selection just like I would in researching anyone else I would ask to assist me in a vulnerable state. Just as I would evaluate a healthcare professional to whom I am entrusting my life, I would want to review their credentials and chat with them to get a sense of who they are and whether I feel this is someone I trust. I would want to make sure the session was taped and that I accounted for all my time while hypnotized.

Curiosity had led me to informal discussions about exploring past lives through hypnotherapy with others before, but it never felt right. Thankfully my intuition had guided me to connect with the incredibly talented and supportive Linda Potter for a truly amazing and healing experience.

The Value

Yes, I did say healing. When I first started listening to my tape, almost three years post-session, I was flabbergasted to realize that I had completely forgot that I had even ever had stiffness in my hands and pain in my feet!!! Not only had the symptoms completely disappeared, but so also had the memory of the experience. Aghast, I questioned my sister and other friends who could easily recall discussions around the physical discomfort I had expressed at the time. Wow! Now that is powerful!!

During further research, I located a follow-up note I had emailed to Linda nine months after the session. I had been excited to learn about the lung infection medical study and wanted to share that with her. I also mentioned that the stiffness in my hands had disappeared and that the pain in my feet had reduced by 50%.

While I received new information that would help me improve my breathing difficulties, I did not experience marked improvement as a direct result of my regression experience. However it served me well in providing hope and new direction in changing my situation. It launched me into a wellness journey that has introduced me to all sorts of new healing experiences and fascinating individuals who have successfully guided me in those endeavors.

In retrospect, it appears my lung ailments have served a purpose. They have caused me to seek out and explore external answers as well as those that can be found within.

Oh, and rather mysteriously now, I have acquired a taste for fish!

Healing Touch, Guided Imagery and Trauma Release

Ines Hoster, Healing Quest

Ifirst met Ines Hoster when I started attending the weekly breakfast meetings held by the Buckhead Business Association, a well respected business networking organization in an old, established, and economically accomplished area of metro Atlanta. A colleague of mine had recommended I start attending the meetings in an effort to expand my professional network. I originally balked at the idea of attending any meeting that started at 7:30 a.m., as I am not a morning person and am not particularly fond of premeditated networking. But Anthony's restaurant, the site of the meetings, is an old Southern tradition and a very pleasant place to start the day with its cheery meeting room, sun-filled windows and big bushy green ferns that line the ceiling from one end to the other. Each week, along with a guest speaker, a cast of characters young and old make up the changeable mix of attendees. Some are part of the Old Atlanta business network that includes bankers and real estate developers, others that are budding or established entrepreneurs and yet others that are chatty business development executives ticking off one of their many networking events for the week.

I was in between jobs and, deciding to kick-start my consulting practice, chose to give it a try over the next 12 months. A few meetings into my membership year, I remember introducing myself to Ines Hoster. Ines is a striking German woman with glowing tanned skin and flowing gray hair who is self assured and makes you think you wouldn't want to oppose her in a debate team competition. She is extremely well read, has a master's degree in sociology, and spends her time traveling between Atlanta and various towns and cities in Germany where she teaches and practices her energy work.

She started explaining something about an energy healing practice to me which just seemed to float in one ear and out the other since it was such a foreign topic. But she was making quite an impression and as a result I decided I needed to learn more about what she had to say. I exchanged business cards with her and planned to make it a point to meet up over tea one day soon. I am really unclear as to the why's and how's of us not immediately connecting, but I know that it was almost a year later before I actually did meet up with her. I was still hoping to have a fascinating chat with this engaging woman on a social basis, but when I called her and was trying to angle for such a meeting, it didn't seem to be going anywhere.

I finally acquiesced and decided I was going to have to book an appointment for an energy treatment if I was going to really find out what she was all about. As the name kept coming up in conversations with recent new friends, it appeared I was to do something. So I emailed her to set up a session.

Ines and I proceeded to connect by phone and set up my first appointment. She sent me the following form to capture my trauma history which was an interesting and self examining exercise in itself.

Trauma History

Please follow these guidelines in writing your history. None of this information is to be used in a judgmental way – rather to help me understand you better and the traumas I can help you release.

1. What brought you to me: Describe briefly your current trauma or health problems, if any.

Problem with lungs/diaphragm and breathing in general

Occasional pain in left knee (start of arthritis) and lower back-both injured in an accident when I was rear-ended with double impact.

2. Brief childhood history, including:
1. Type of birth; Cesarean
2. Traumatic occurrences;

None known other than had colic and pneumonia as an infant. Didn't like going to doctor, really felt at their mercy and knew pain was coming. Dentist pulled a molar when I was five without waiting for the Novocaine to kick in. Never hospitalized. Did not see a doctor from the time I was 5 until the time I was 18, I was petrified of going to the doctor. My mother tried to take me along once when my Grandmother was getting a checkup, but all my vital signs were going off the charts as I was too psyched out, so the doctor said it was not of any value since I was in such a panic. Did not see a dentist from the time I was 5 until the time I was 13, but then went regularly after that....to an extremely handsome and kind dentist, heh, heh.

i. Your relationship with mother, what mother was like;
Good, she was always concerned about developing my mind. We would visit a lot and she would allow me to make choices for myself early. Always made sure I had my three balanced meals. Was a 4-H Leader, Girl Scout Leader, helped out at school. The only real short coming was she did not indulge feelings that she thought were signs of weakness or needy...based on how she was brought up.

ii. Your relationship with father, what father was like;
Daddy's girl...he was very indulgent and could not stand to see me sad. He was emotionally supportive, always made sure he was there to watch any special school program, always encouraging, always trying to make special treats and life to be fun.

iii. The parents' relationship with each other;
Cordial, didn't openly fight or anything. Mom gave up her teaching career to be a stay-at-home-mother and she always regretted that as she valued her independence and her accomplishments. She put up with a lot of my Dad's irresponsible behavior in terms of finances and she always had to be the adult, the one to rescue the situation. It was a relatively peaceful family environment and always supportive of me. The one situation that was disruptive and puzzling, was when my sister and my Dad argued and she moved out while she was still in high school. There were strained relations until she finished university. Then after a year in

Minneapolis, she moved back home and taught school for a couple years.

iv. Your relationship with any other significant family member or important person in childhood, if relevant, with whom you experienced some trauma;

6th grade my grandmother had a stroke and we were very close. She lived 10 years beyond that, but was never able to be the active person she was which was very hard on her. She always appealed to me to please rescue her, but there wasn't anything I could do and the guilt was bad so I started avoiding her in the last years.

v. Any other trauma you incurred in childhood;

I don't know if it is considered childhood, but my father was in a life threatening accident when I was a sophomore in college and almost died...very hard as we have such a close relationship. He was in intensive care for six weeks.

vi. medical history: childhood diseases, vaccinations, and injuries;
3. What do I need to know that was hurtful or harmful in your adolescent years;

My sister moved out of the house when she was still in High School (I was around 5th grade) as she was not getting along with my Dad and I didn't understand what was going on, but assumed it was over her choice of boyfriend. I found out later in my late 20's that it was my Dad's fault.

4. What else was harming or hurtful in your adult life: describe briefly any relevant adult traumas and/or relationships;

Many work related. I have worked with many brilliant, near genius or genius type people, but often very unstable personalities that can be abusive. I am like a moth to flame when it comes to bi-polar personalities...dazzled by their brilliance and charismatic moments. Also several competitive women with that disorder that become paranoid and would go over the edge and become enemies with ceaseless energy. A number of serial liars too.

I often was the first women or one of a few women to work in particular business positions in the telecom company I worked at for ten years....lots of additional stress was put on to try and make me fail...but I just kept bounding along and proved them wrong.

At the Olympic Games I had a couple incidents where two individuals tried to make me out to be racist which was very sickening. It was an attack on my core being and that was very stressful. Both were eventually proved to be shams...but in the meantime it was difficult.

5. *Awareness of any past life experiences;*
Yes, several:

As told to me by a man who accesses the Akashic Records, or the book of life, my most recent past life was as an orphan in France and sent to live with very strict nuns. Escaped and then spent the rest of my life exploring and trying everything that I could.

Young man in Peru, caught stealing gourds due to hunger and was tied up by hands and had feet beaten. Later, in

Argentina was in a small village made of straw roofs that were burning and I passed out from the smoke.

Was a small boy of seven in Spain and fell down on the cobblestones and shattered my front teeth.

Cousins in Russia with my current husband and played in one of the palaces. Grew up in wealth.

Was romantically involved with my current husband on Atlantis as young people, but in different social classes. Was exiled by his family to a remote island to live and fend for myself like at the age of 16. Lived to be in 40's. Died of boredom and probably of grief as news that Atlantis had sunk reached me.

On a more informal basis, also been told that I was a WWI reporter and a theatrical dancer.

6. What is your spiritual life like;

I consider myself very spiritual and in touch with God, enjoy conversational prayer and arranged for a minister to marry my husband and I, but do not enjoy the structure of organized religion. I feel church based religions are often more about control, politics, power and greed than about living a spiritual life. I believe people should focus more on their actions then discussing church doctrines, especially ones that are exclusionary which I find reprehensible. However, I also believe the church provides comfort to many people who need something more tangible in order to believe and provides fellowship and support to members and others. It is just not for me.

7. Is there anything else I need to know?
No.

Thank you for taking your time to answer these questions. If possible type or hand print your answers, indicating your response to the right number. It may take about 6-8 type-written pages.

I believe now that probably just taking the time and thought to write out answers to these questions has a certain healing quality to them. They certainly make you step back and look at life in more of a big picture view then if you were just sorting through your day to day issues. It's a catharsis of sorts, acknowledging all the trials you have been faced with and overcome.

I faxed this form along with a medical history form off to Ines and began anticipating my "energy healing appointment," the thought of which tickled me down to my toes. What could this possibly entail?

Ines conducts her practice in a home studio. Her house is tucked into an old, heavily wooded neighborhood. To reach her home, you must traverse a very long and steep driveway and then make your way through what seems like a burgeoning field of flowers up to her door. She greeted me and whisked me off to her upstairs treatment area that looks over her living room and out onto her deck which is festooned with flowers and flowing fountains, radiating a real fairyland quality. All the sunlight and flowers and fountains immediately put me at ease and made me anticipate something good was going to happen. She had me take off my shoes and take a seat on the raised cushioned table.

We chatted for the first hour reviewing my trauma paperwork, medical history and expectations from the session. She explained to me the basic concept of Healing Touch Therapy.

Healing Touch Therapy

Healing Touch Therapy is an umbrella term for a number of energy based healing treatments. Practitioners either lightly touch or use their hands close to the patient's body in their energy field to influence and harmonize the energy system. These methods can restore any previously detected imbalances in the physical, emotional, mental and spiritual bodies to the desired state and allow individuals to access their full healing power. The therapies support a person's immune system and self-healing process, thereby enhancing the effect of other therapies. Healing Touch methods are recognized and utilized by health care professionals in hospitals and have been credited with reducing pain and anxiety, decreasing stress and tension, accelerating the healing process, preventing illness and activating mental clarity.

Ines then had me lay down and proceeded to use a sleek looking silver pendulum and a clear plastic measurement tool to start taking measurements of my chakras, aura and the balance between the physical, mental, emotional and spiritual bodies. At the time I didn't know what such things were but she explained briefly.

Chakras

There are seven main Chakras or energy points located in a line starting at the base of the spine and going up to the top of the head. Each of these chakras relate to a specific area of your body and specific emotions. When they are in balance, your life force flows freely. When they are out of balance, it can manifest in physical illness until you address the situation causing the imbalance. People who have learned to shut down their analytical filters can see the charka points.

Aura

The electromagnetic field around our bodies that express the true intention of your spirit.

As I lay there, my focus, hope and continuing goal was to find a way to fix my breathing problem. I believed I could improve and potentially eliminate the problem all together if I could just find the right door or sequence of doors to pass through. Ines may have looked a little bizarre standing above me with a pendulum and measurement tool taking notes and such, but hey, who was to say there wasn't something to this energy stuff. Just because I couldn't see it, didn't mean it wasn't there.

She spent sometime unruffling my energy field and clearing any blockages she detected, the whole time moving her hands slightly above me and then with permission, she lightly placed her hands at times on my feet, on my shoulders and on my head. Each time she touched me I could feel a warm, comforting sensation at the point of contact. This first session lasted 2 1/2 hours and when she finished she asked when we could book the next appointment. I was like going, whoa, hold on there. I was not sure what we did in this one. Ines proceeded to explain that she was a bit worried about my four bodies being so far out of balance. My mental body was going off the charts and controlling all my actions while my physical, emotional and spiritual selves were getting short changed. Well that seemed to make sense. All activity undertaken seemed to be focused on stimulating and entertaining the mind. Whether it was titillating conversation, exploring a foreign country, engrossed in the Internet, watching a favorite TV show, play or a movie or reading a book. In my life physical activity, baring emotions, or any kind of meditation seems to definitely take a back seat to other possibilities. Maybe she had something there.

She also had told me that she sensed a great influence from my paternal grandmother who had passed long before I had ever had a chance to meet her. She wanted me to investigate my grandmother's past history, in particular what might have been a source of the melancholy emotion she was picking up that she felt was currently impacting me. Ines went on to say that we inherit the emotional past of our ancestors, not just their physical DNA. At first I thought this was too fantastic to be true and I certainly did not feel like I was harboring some deep melancholy emotion. I considered myself a very upbeat, cheerful person and this just wasn't fitting with my self image. She went on to prove it to me while we did some healing touch work around this emotion. She was asking me about this sadness and out of nowhere, one tear appeared in my right eye and rolled down my cheek! How strange was this! Where did it come from? Maybe there was something to this emotional inheritance theory. I found this to be an interesting new concept and continued to think about how that might influence me as well as those around me.

This whole conversation had surfaced during a light touch session when Ines went to place her hands on my shoulders close to my neck. I had started giggling and she asked what was so funny. Although a mystery to me, I had always had an extreme sensitivity to anyone touching me close to my neck. In fact I had instinctively kneed a few University boyfriends in the groin who just had to test this theory even though I had warned them never to grab me close to the neck. Ines sensed that there had been an incident with my grandmother and grandfather when tempers had run high and that my grandfather had grabbed her around the neck and started choking her. Afterward, it was always a source of guilt for him and of power for her. I had never heard such a story, but then I knew very little about them, so I supposed it could be a possibility.

Over the next week, I did my research about Grandmother Siewert. Her name was Minnie and she had died in 1951 while she was in her 60's of liver cancer. She and her husband Adolf had grown up in Wisconsin and had not immigrated from Germany directly, rather their parents did.

Adolf had been married before he met Minnie and had a child. This was believed to be the love of his life and he fell deep into depression when they died. He later married Minnie and moved her to a farm in North Dakota where they had four sons and two daughters. All the children looked very similar except the oldest daughter which was rumored to have had another father. There was a possibility that this eldest daughter could have been born out of some trauma to Minnie or maybe even the child of Minnie's first love.

Although my mother had never had a chance to meet Minnie before she had died, she did have the opportunity to later meet with Minnie's sisters when they stopped to visit one year on their way traveling through town.

They told how their parents were mean and that they didn't get along with them. They also mentioned how Minnie was really sad to leave her family and friends in Wisconsin and didn't get back to see them with the possibility of maybe one time when she was older. She was very lonely on the farm in North Dakota. My mother said that at that time parents often still told their daughters who they had to marry so Minnie could have been forced to leave her real love behind in Wisconsin to marry Adolf who I believe was much older. I do have a framed picture of Adolf and Minnie on my shelves with the rest of my family pictures, but that is about the extent of my knowledge of either of them.

I had agreed to book another appointment and found myself back with Ines the next week. In total, I spent about 20 hours working with Ines over a series of appointments during the next couple months that lasted anywhere from a couple hours to as much as five hours. During the longer appointments, we would often surprise ourselves at how much time had passed as we became so involved in our explorations and energy work. I would tease Ines that I felt like I had just been abducted by aliens because it was rare that I would sit still long enough for this type of work without getting antsy. We would both wonder, where did the time go?

My Fascination

Ines used a combination of methods to treat me. Along with her healing touch therapy, she also used trauma release, guided imagery, muscle testing and her intuitive powers.

Trauma Release Therapy can take on a number of forms and was developed by Karl Nishimura, D.D.S., M.S. It is based on the assumption that a trauma to the body (either physical, emotional, mental or spiritual in origin) needs to be released from the cellular memory in order for the person to heal from the trauma. If traumas are not released, over time, the mind and body adjust and compensate to allow continued function up to a saturation point. An overload of the suppressed traumas can eventually manifest in the form of pain and deterioration of the body.

Guided Imagery focuses and directs the imagination towards a specific action of healing. It involves all the senses and calls upon you to not only visualize an act, but to also sense how it would feel. When you have a healing guide that you resonate with to lead you to the place of power in your mind and body, imagery has the capacity to deliver multiple layers of complex, encoded messages that will call your body into action. It is a right-brained activity and engaging in it will often be accompanied by other right-brain functions such as sensitivity to music, openness to spirituality, intuition, abstract thinking and empathy.

Muscle Testing or Kinesiology is a means of testing the body's knowledge about a certain topic. A yes or no type question is posed to the body and then pressure is applied by the person asking the question to see if the body's muscle supports a positive answer and therefore resists the pressure or folds to the pressure indicating a negative answer. Often the test is performed with the person being queried extending an arm out to the side while the person asking the question tries to push the arm down. The body's ability to respond is based on the electrical network it has within it and surrounding it. If anything impacts this electrical system that does not maintain or enhance your health, your muscles are unable to hold their strength when physical pressure is applied by an outside source.

Sensitivity to Touch Around the Neck

Her first focused treatment versus general balancing and energy clearing was to dispel the extreme sensitivity I had to being touched close to my neck. While I laid on the massage table, Ines sat beside me and raised my right hand up and held my right hand as we did a series of affirmations and request for release of this apprehension that did not belong to my lifetime. After a series of affirmations, she would check for changes through muscle testing which entailed me placing my third finger and thumb together and trying to prevent Ines from breaking my hold with her finger. If the answer was yes, it held. If the answer to her question was no, the seal would break. While the sensitivity is not completely gone, it has greatly been reduced by this exercise and I have a much better comfort level when I experience physical touch in close proximity to my neck. I also seemed to experience a lifting of a weight on my emotional heart through this exercise. This is more of a feeling, than a detectable change in my behavior so it is a lot harder to explain or describe some sort of evidence of change.

Arthritis Pain in Left Knee

The most dramatic results were from the trauma release performed on me during a visit where I mentioned the car accident I had had four years earlier. The incident involved being rear ended by a carload of teenage girls distracted as they peeled out of the movie theater parking lot. I was at a stoplight at a complete standstill when they had hit me rather hard. Although the accident had not caused me to be hospitalized, I was no longer in my 20's or even 30's at the time, and my injuries to my back and left knee did not dissipate quickly.

I received physical therapy at the time, but found those areas to continue to be weak spots years later, especially my left knee which ached when the weather became damp and rainy. Ines explained that energy can be trapped in your body from such incidents and suggested we try trauma release and then guided imagery. I thought it sounded a bit wild, but I am also game to try new things so I said, "Let's do it." She told me that we would start at the point of contact and the energy would move around my body and eventually shoot out my head or feet. I started giggling and asked Ines if I would see a flash of light or anything. I liked to tease her when she told me something that sounded ridiculous. She was good natured about it and let me make my jokes, knowing that allowing me to approach this healing adventure with humor made trying something that sounded pretty out there okay.

As I lay there on the table, Ines stood to my left, close to my injured knee. Once we began and to my surprise, I felt a slight pinging sensation move between the two main areas where I had received the greatest injuries. It started at the point of impact in my back, then moved around my back before it shot over to my left knee and moved around in that area. The sensation was very slight, hardly even noticeable. The only evidence I had that it was even really there was that Ines would ask me where it was and I could always tell her. She would move to the area I advised and perform healing touch and then ask me where it was now, and then move there and do healing touch. This process continued for about ten to fifteen minutes moving between my lower back and left knee area.

Then with a surprising turn of events, I felt it move towards my left elbow, an area that I hadn't even noticed an injury had occurred because I was focused on the strong pain in my knee and back at the time. But when I recalled the situation, I realized that I typically rest my left elbow on the driver side door handle. Sure enough, my left elbow would have received an impact during the accident as well. That fact really made me take notice of this exercise since an expectation of addressing an injury to the left elbow was not a conscious thought on my part.

Finally, without any warning and any discernible reason for it to happen, I felt a sharp pain surge through and shoot out my left foot. After this experience, Ines followed up with a combination of Healing Touch and Guided Imagery focusing specifically on my left knee. She helped me fixate on the injured area and envision a beam of healing white light to come and repair it. We did this work with my knee for about another ten to fifteen minutes that session.

My Belief

I have come to believe that the flow of energy through our bodies is key to our wellbeing. The work I did with Ines and then subsequently with other energy healers has significantly lightened my physical presence. Before I began this healing journey, I moved a lot more slowly, my breathing was deliberate and I felt a heaviness or burdened in general. I was attributing this all to my breathing challenges and the onset of middle age, but now I feel that it was caused by much more. Some of it perhaps related to inherited trauma from my ancestors, some from holding in emotional hurt and still other from trauma energy trapped inside of me.

I am sometimes frustrated by the fact that I can not see what others do in terms of auras and chakras, but that does not prevent me from embracing the concept.

The Value

The last time I saw Ines professionally, she had been pleased with the progress we had made in balancing my four bodies of mind, body, spirit and emotional self. Although not perfectly aligned, she felt much more confident that they were no longer dangerously out of sync. She had encouraged me to see an Iridologist, someone that can help uncover the mysteries of the body through the iris of your eye, for further clarification on my lung issues as she felt there was some complexity involved that she could not quite discern. She also finally convinced me to try colonics to cleanse my digestive track of the years of buildup she felt certain was there from an allergy to wheat products she had uncovered during our sessions and to continue managing my intake of dairy and wheat products going forward.

It has been about two years since the treatments and I have been sans any pain or stiffness in my left knee, even though the weather has been damp and rainy for a great deal of that period which had been a trigger for pain. Through the use of healing touch, guided imagery and diet, I've also made wonderful progress on my breathing dilemma which Ines felt certain had previously been misdiagnosed as asthma. She too sensed that it was some sort of lung infection and advised that I needed to stay away from wheat and dairy products which can cause the body to form a white mucus on the outside of the lungs and prevents them from fighting off disease or illness.

Sometimes it is hard to gauge changes in one's own appearance and wellbeing because those changes are so gradual and we always perceive ourselves differently from within than somebody assessing us from without. So to help me get an objective view of the actual changes I have experienced I have often turned to close friends who have watched my health fluctuate over the years. I always ask them, on a scale of 1 to 10, with 1 being the best and 10 being the worst, where do you think my breathing is today in terms of being labored and congested and my voice being nasal.

Before I started on my healing journey it hovered around an 8. Now, the response I get ranges from 4 to 6 depending upon diet, air quality and my exposure to specific allergens. I attribute the bulk of the change from my work with Ines and the Naturopath/Iridologist, Sis Sewell, whom she referred me to.

{3}

Reiki Master/Shaman/Earth Goddess
Jeanne Johnson

Jeanne is one of the most enigmatic individuals I have ever met. She has a mystical quality about her and seems to take on different physical personas at times when I see her. Sometimes she is a radiant person in her mid-thirties whose face literally reflects light. At other times she seems as much as 30-40 years older, as if she's walking under a shadow. And still others find her as to be expected, a sprite-like, highly compassionate woman in her early 40's.

Our first meeting was at an Eclectic Ladies Network party in April 2002. She was a guest of our group's co-founder, Cathy Horvath, and at the end of the party agreed to give our auras a look and share a little insight as to what we were currently experiencing or where we were headed. At this point, I readily admit I wasn't even sure what an aura was, but I was sure I had one and was anxious to hear what Jeanne had to say about it.

My rudimentary understanding of auras now are that they are vibrational responses that objects give off, whether they be conscious (people, plants, animals) or unconscious (stones, crystals, water), and that they contain some information about us. Auras around conscious objects change with time and circumstances, while auras around unconscious objects are believed to stay relatively fixed.

The auras of conscious objects, like humans, are made up of two parts: One that stems from the low level frequency of our body heat and functioning of our body based on our DNA, metabolism and circulation; and the other that comes from the high frequency part reflecting our thinking, creativity, intentions, sense of humor and emotions. It is the high frequency portion of our aura that can be seen by some people who are able to release the analytical side of their brain and let their right brain creativity take over. Watching someone's aura tells you what his or her true intentions are.

I can't recall exactly what Jeanne said about my aura at that time, but it did make me in awe of this magical power. If only I could do something like that it would be so helpful. I am optimistic when it comes to believing that people tend to have honorable agendas, and that can get me in to trouble at times. When you readily embrace everyone when you first meet them, you will get burned at some point by people who mislead you with their intentions. My husband has always cautioned me to give new acquaintances time to earn my trust. Watch and observe first, then embrace. While it is good, sound advice, it doesn't seem to work well with my nature. I like to jump in, feet first, to anything I do. This propensity means that sometimes I am rushing to jump out of the pool as alligator-type personalities start nipping at my heels, or, in the worst cases, have already sunk their teeth into my posterior with a ferocious hold as I anxiously try to shake them loose.

Jeanne and I decided to meet so I could learn more about her gifts and healing practice. As we were seated for our early afternoon lunch at an Italian restaurant called Maggianos, we each ordered a glass of wine and settled in to learn more about each other. Jeanne explained that, like many people who have found their way to becoming a healer, she had been suffering from problems that traditional medicine could not treat. Her doctor had advised her that she needed to just learn to live with the condition and be satisfied to manage it. This was not acceptable to her; she had four children and a husband to attend to and was sure there must be another option. As she researched alternative treatments, she became fascinated by therapies that focused on enhancing the flow of a person's life force through their body, working with a person's energy. She soon found herself drawn to two Reiki Masters practicing in north Georgia who performed an energy session on her and eventually became her instructors.

Reiki is made up of two Japanese words, Rei meaning universal or spiritual-conscious and Ki meaning life force. A Reiki practitioner acts as a channel for this life force that is spiritually guided to help the subject heal themselves emotionally, physically, mentally and spiritually. Practitioners do not direct the healing energy; rather they act as a conduit for it and gently place their hands on an individual's fully-clothed body in areas that represent their energy centers or chakras and other energy pathways. One of their responsibilities is to help their subject realize that they must consciously decide to improve oneself. In order for the Reiki healing energies to have lasting results, the client must accept responsibility for her or his healing and take an active part in it.

As I understand it, today's U.S.- based Reiki practice stems from a system developed by Dr. Usi after he had a mystical experience on Mt. Kurama in Japan. After Dr. Usi's discoveries formed the initial basis for Reiki treatment, he seems to have focused on further developing the spiritual aspect of Reiki. Later one of his students, Dr. Hayashi, developed standards for hand positions, something called the system of three degrees and the attunement process. A third individual of importance in U.S.-based Reiki is Hawayo Takata, a second generation Japanese immigrant who experienced the dramatic healing powers of Reiki when she was visiting her parents in Japan. She convinced Dr. Hayashi to teach her Reiki and eventually return with her to Hawaii to establish Reiki in the West.

Reiki is designed to be used for healing, connecting people to their spiritual path or for personal empowerment. For healing it invokes deep relaxation, strengthens the body to heal itself, and speeds up recovery. From a spiritual perspective, it is about learning to detach from the outcome and being present in the moment. It is not about a particular religion or belief system, rather it focuses on the basic values of unconditional love, caring, peace, and compassion for all. It is also about honoring each other's individual path. Reiki can also be used to enhance your natural abilities. Working with the Reiki energy will help you connect with your path and your skills, and develop your senses. With practice, it can enhance your creative, intuitive and business abilities. Reiki doesn't do harm and will not work if harm is intended. It cannot be used to control people or situations. It works to bring the best result or highest outcome for all.

While practicing and teaching Reiki has been a big part of Jeanne's life, it is not the only healing method she employs. She has also become very involved in Native American, Tibetan, and African mysticism and had the fortune to learn of the shamanic healing powers resident in nature. Shamanism is actually a world wide experience in all indigenous cultures. Jeanne is quick to point out that she doesn't claim any of these specific traditions, as she was not taught by native tribal shamans. Rather she uses some universally known techniques and has developed her own shamanic rituals. She believes that this mystical practice is evolving and advises that what she practices would not be the same as any tribe now teaches it. Jeanne begins with a traditional-looking shamanic journey, but uses Reiki versus drums or drugs to reach her meditative state. As soon as she arrives at the place needed and has seen and understood the situation, she again turns to Reiki which allows her to feel and see only the vibrational patterns and seeks to bring them into balance. It is truly an experience unique to the combination of modalities and not one that she has heard other shamans describe.

People become shamans when they have been chosen by a Spirit. They learn their powerful insights by communicating with nature and in fact Jeanne gained much of her wisdom from a tree. It sounds wild to those of us that do not communicate with the animals, trees, birds, rocks, wind and water, but yet who among us can say they have not been impacted by their time communing with nature. I suspect it involves letting go of believing you can't and embracing you can. Shamanic ritual involves sound, smell, movement and intent. It employs the help of power animals, yours and that of the shaman's, as well as herbs, minerals, crystals, feathers and other materials from nature.

One of my favorite stories Jeanne told me about her journey to become a healer was when she was experimenting with crystals. She had been drawn to one in particular that the storekeeper had told her was from Tibet. She kept handling the crystal, then putting it back in the belief it was outside her budget, but then she'd be drawn to pick it up again. Finally, with perhaps divine intervention, an acceptable deal presented itself and the crystal made a new home with her. Not too long afterwards, she found herself at home alone with the dog and decided to take the crystal out of its protective bag and explore it closer. Upon exposing herself to it, she felt her chakras break wide open with power bursts reminiscent of mini explosions. At the same time her mild-mannered dog got extremely anxious and started howling until she managed to put the crystal back in its bag and recover from the incident. She has since learned how to work with the crystal without its energy overpowering hers.

A third source of healing power that Jeanne draws from is Mother Earth, or the Earth Goddess, the female side to the God power. Much has been written about The Divine Feminine lately, including the popular novel, *The DaVinci Code,* and it is often a subject referenced in Sylvia Browne's books. This Feminine God Force seems to be slowly but surely re-emerging as part of a mainstream belief. Rituals center on the cycles of the moon and focus on celebrating and living in harmony with the earth and its seasons. Jeanne was drawn to her healing work in this area through Mary Magdalene, whom she channels frequently in healing sessions.

My Fascination

On the appointed day of my Reiki session, I followed Jeanne down her stairs to her healing room. I liken it to one of her Native American meditations, where you slip down a rabbit hole or other nature portal into the Lower World or womb of the earth. Her studio is dark and peaceful, candles are lit, incense is burning and meditative music is playing. I took off my shoes and jewelry and then hopped up on her massage table to settle in for my healing experience. While I was very comfortable with Jeanne as a healer, I have to admit, I was slightly uncomfortable in the setting. I always like to be in a light and airy atmosphere. I am not sure exactly why, maybe it is an unconscious concern over breathing, but that has always been my preference. So although I felt I was safe, I was not in as a relaxed a state as I would have been if the light was streaming in the windows. Nevertheless, I decided to open myself up to the healing power of the session as much as possible.

Jeanne started the session by placing her hands at the back of head and creating a sacred working space with one of the Reiki symbols. She continued to move around parts of my body and channel Reiki energy to the places in need. I soon felt like I was in a totally relaxed state of being, no worries, no particular thoughts, just in a place of complete rest. When she held her hands in a particular spot for any length of time, I could detect a distinct warmth radiating from her hands. It felt good and comforting.

The sounds she used to complement the treatment sometimes made me giggle. Some of her hand gestures and vocals could get pretty wild, and I suspect that they were a combination of some shaman-type rituals. She would tell me what she detected or saw and would advise me on changes in diet, exercise, releasing emotions, etc. that could lead to better future outcomes. Her advice to me, although gentle in nature, seemed almost foreboding. It was as if I were getting a message that said wakeup to your needs or pay the consequences. This made me feel a bit sorrowful, like I hadn't been doing myself justice. She indicated I was always so busy taking care of others that I might not be adequately addressing my own needs. That seemed perplexing, as I knew I always made sure I was engaged in doing something fun and interesting and that was for my own self-amusement. But on closer examination, I had to admit that I did spend a lot time worrying and taking care of the physical and emotional needs of others and tended not to give my emotional and physical self the attention they needed. These thoughts disturbed me, and oh, how I detest letting my emotions get away from me. I suspect that it stems from my early upbringing where showing emotions is a sign of weakness, and I don't particularly fancy weakness in myself. As the session drew to a close, she again used the Reiki symbol over the back of the heart and end of the spine to seal the energy in. Then she made some gestures to bring me back down into my regular energy pattern so that I would not feel disoriented. As with the conclusion of any energy type work, she handed me a glass of water to drink to hydrate myself.

On another occasion, I brought my stepson to Jeanne for Reiki the day before he was to have surgery. We were both highly distraught because he had a potentially serious abscess in his leg, and we would not know the extent of the problem until the doctor could actually see what damage had been done to his leg bone. Ruslan was not certain about the value of the Reiki treatment, but he was willing to give it a try, and he was open to me staying with him during his session, as I often helped him with language clarification.

Jeanne described the problem she saw but downplayed the visual, later saying she didn't want to scare us by telling us exactly what she saw. During the session, Jeanne kept asking us whether either of us had a headache. We both answered no, and I was rather puzzled why this kept coming up. When we returned home, I came down with the worst headache I had ever had in my life, to the point of being nauseous. It ended up being amazingly cathartic and was probably the result of a major release of tension.

The next day at the hospital, I was surprised to find myself completely calm, confident everything would be okay and in a position of strength for everyone else. In these types of situations it is very difficult for me not to become emotional and I welcomed the calmness, especially given the dire circumstances. Upon completion of the surgery we learned that, although there were extreme conditions, with the proper care and attention everything would be okay in a relatively short period of time.

A third occasion where I experienced Jeanne's healing powers was with a very dear friend of mine who lived in Minneapolis at the time.

She had been suffering terribly from a relationship betrayal by someone who had made many promises to her over a five-year period. Then without warning, he cruelly unveiled his ongoing infidelity and started attacking her character while she was in this most vulnerable state. It was an ugly and very devastating situation. I was at my wits end trying to figure out how I might be of help when I heard someone mention soul retrievals.

The theory is that, when faced with traumatic events, a part of your soul can be lost in time or even to a particular person. This leaves the individual feeling lost, disoriented and depressed. In a soul retrieval, the shaman journeys to another place of reality with her spirits, locates the lost soul part, brings it back, and returns it to the person's body and spirit.

The thought of this narcissistic personality stealing a part of my friend's soul was a visual I could embrace. I thought it was an interesting concept to explore and chatted with my friend about it. She was intrigued, too, and was willing to experiment given the dark state she found herself in. She had tried some traditional drugs prescribed for depression but didn't like the way they made her feel and didn't believe they would actually help her get better in the long run.

There just seemed to be one hitch – the geographic gap between Minnesota and Georgia. But Jeanne assured me that this was not a problem. By having a picture of my friend and being able to talk with her on the phone, she would be able to do both the soul retrieval and send her Reiki healing energy.

When a person does healing over distance, there are three laws in play: The universal law, the law of correspondence, and the law of similarity. The universal law states that a person attuned to the universal energy can call upon the energy forces around them to help send healing to a certain individual. The law of correspondence states that we are all connected in some shape or form since we have all been originally created from the same source. The law of similarity states that a photograph or even a memory of a person can be used for psychic purposes to direct healing at that person.

After their phone call, my friend retired for the evening as usual, slightly energized by the hope of the phone call, yet far from feeling like her old self. When she awoke the next day she felt a dramatic shift in her emotional and physical being. The incredible weight of her existence seemed to have been lifted, and she didn't feel the gnawing emptiness. In short, she was simply amazed at the change. When my friend caught up with Jeanne later that day, she was told of a wild experience wherein Jeanne mentally battled with three entities that were holding a piece of her soul hostage, two from traumatic childhood events and the third from this last experience. While it was a vivid and extreme image of the potential between worlds for her to comprehend, she could offer no other explanation for the dramatic shift in the way she felt. This day marked the emergence from the darkest point of this emotional devastation and set her on the path to recovery.

In late summer that same year, I was invited to an evening of drumming with Jeanne and her friends. I had heard that drumming was a meditative experience and was intrigued at the prospect of meeting the Reiki Master who was her teacher. Yet I was a little hesitant to jump into this experience because I have a horrible sense of rhythm, and the thought of trying to drum all evening seemed a little intimidating if not embarrassing. But curiosity won out and I found myself in an enchanting sunroom of one of Jeanne's friends who was hosting the evening. There were just five of us present: the hostess, Jeanne, her teacher, a man who was checking out this type of experience for the first time, and I.

The three veterans of the evening explained that the drumming helped them go on a shamanic journey into the Lower World and that it was important to keep the drumming going throughout the process so that they didn't get stuck there. That little bit of news was worrisome. Now I was on the hook as a matter of responsibility to do this drumming.

They had a variety of percussion instruments to choose from, various North American Indian drums and rattles. The other drumming neophyte and I exchanged glances from time to time, wondering what we had gotten ourselves into, but we tried our best to be good, or at least helpful, participants. We were encouraged to take our turn entering the Lower World by envisioning going into a lake and diving down deep into the earth or through a rabbit hole or other earth opening. I just couldn't get my mind around doing something like that. Going into the earth seemed frightening to me. Yet flying up into the heavens to reach the Upper World seemed like a journey I could embrace. As a result, the experience wasn't all that interesting for we novices, since we did nothing all evening but try to keep up the drumming and/or rattle shaking, even though our hands and wrists got extremely tired.

A month and a year after I first met Jeanne, I did have an interesting experience with Azna, the Mother God. At least I suspect I did. My sister and I were on the way back from a road trip visiting a friend in Jacksonville, Florida. The trip can get long, and she had her face buried in Sylvia Browne's book, *God, Creation, and Tools for Life*. Since she was consciously making an attempt to increase her water intake, we seemed to be making an inordinate number of stops at gas stations on our way back to Atlanta, to the point where all our stops had run together. We would both be hard pressed even to recall how many or where they were.

She was telling me a little bit about what she was reading and how interesting it was when I decided I wanted to get some Carmex out of my purse because my lips were feeling chapped. I reached behind my seat to find my purse and I couldn't seem to locate it. I dismissed it and continued driving. About fifteen minutes later, I started having a stronger compulsion to get in my purse and finally asked my sister to grab it for me. She casually looked for it and couldn't reach it either. But the compulsion to find my purse started gnawing at her now. I told her to forget it, I can wait until we stop, but she unbuckled her seat belt and made an all-out attempt to find it for me. Then she sank back into her seat and told me she didn't want to alarm me, but my purse was nowhere to be found.

Yikes!! I felt the ground drop out from beneath me. No purse? That means no billfold, no money, no ATM card, no credit cards, no inhaler and no driver's license. And we were still a good four hours away from Atlanta!!! My sister still had her purse so we would be able to buy gas to get home, but geez, that was an awful feeling!! Yet for some reason we both remained calm, and we swung our car around to head south again. I had to fight the urge not to put the pedal to the metal and speed our way back to where we thought I might have left my purse, but being stopped for a traffic ticket was the last thing I needed at this juncture.

We both hurriedly tried to reconstruct our last stop and determine where it was and what type of gas station it might have been. We were unclear as to the company name; we just remembered it had been a small two-pump station, and two men had been sitting outside in the heat having an ice cream bar in front of the station. The door to the bath-room was propped open and the stop seemed to have occurred just before we turned on to I-75, or at least 60 miles from where we were now. My sister decided to ask Azna for help and kept reassuring me that she felt quite sure that my purse would be recovered.

After a few trial runs, we finally stopped at the right station and I raced into the bathroom hoping against hope to find my purse hanging on the hook on the back of the single bathroom stall door. No such luck. I quickly ran to the inside of the station and approached the man sitting beside the single small desk and asked if by chance he had found a purse. Yes, he had. "Thank God, thank God!!" I shouted, elated with the news. He then proceeded to ask me to describe it, handed it over to me and asked me to verify that everything was all there…..and it was!! Unbelievable, over two hours later, and everything was still in tact.

The odd thing we wondered later is what prompted the man to go into the women's bathroom and close the stall door, the only way he would have found my purse!! He had said he had found it, not that someone had told him about it or brought it to him. I wish I would have had the presence of mind to ask him. My sister and I later reviewed the situation and knew that it wasn't to change the toilet tissue. There in fact didn't seem any conceivable reason for him to go looking in there, yet he had.

My most recent experience with the Goddess Spirit was this year when I attended one of Jeanne's Moon Lodge events. I wasn't quite sure this was going to be something that was an entirely comfortable experience for me. This was something relatively new that Jeanne was doing and it was important to her, so I wanted to be supportive. When I arrived at the clubhouse where the event was being held, I was relieved to find that the women were all still fully clothed. I had the impression that a lot of the Goddess events were done in the buff and that was going to be more than I was ready to experience. This proved to be a realistic expectation, but thankfully not one the women were embracing that evening as Jeanne did joke about us stripping down for the evening.

I must say there seemed to be very gentle spirits in attendance, full of laughter and a distinct reverence for the earth and all things living. The room was dark and glowing with candles. We went through various rituals involving singing, playing instruments, inviting spirits to join us and then sharing goals and objectives for the evening's activities. At one point, the energy in the room was said to be at peak, but I couldn't detect anything different than before. We ended with applying some special aromatic oils, each of us intuitively guided to choose one from a basket offered to us and then enjoyed trays of fresh fruit and mineral water. Jeanne asked me how I had enjoyed the evening and I confessed it probably wasn't my cup of tea, but heck, if it managed to banish the minor health problem I had focused on, I'd be back!

My Belief

I believe Reiki can help a great many people and is something everyone should try. Even more powerful would be the experience of learning how to call upon the healing powers of Reiki to help others as well as yourself. I have become increasingly more consciously aware of the fact that we live in a world of energy. I believe Reiki will help you become more attuned to the energy around you and help sense the flow of life about you.

I have always believed that the spirit world embraced by the Native American, Tibetan, African, Aboriginal and other indigenous cultures holds powerful wisdom and magic, something that has been greatly underestimated by the vast majority of Americans. I have the greatest respect for those who have learned to communicate with nature in this most intimate way and hold in high esteem their healing practices.

As for Azna, I have never really questioned her existence. I've always felt that she was there. But it seems to be a bit more complicated when we attempt to see her "as" or "part of" the supreme God power.

I think that stems from my childhood indoctrination that taught God the Almighty was strong and masculine, and reinforced during my adult life in a male-dominated society. At this stage in life I have come to believe God is really neither male nor female as they are but reference points we have created to help our minds get around the concept of God. I believe the feminine and masculine attributes both reside in God and perhaps we need to call upon these particular attributes that apply to the situation we are asking God to assist us with. That's my way of reconciling the male and feminine God power and I'm sticking to it, at least for the moment.

The Value

Jeanne has opened up a vast world of knowledge and wonder to me. She opened the door, and I have stepped through, but only in measured steps. There is a lot more to explore and in time I believe we will have many more experiences together.

One of the most valuable lessons I have learned from our friendship is the understanding that people react to individual healers and alternative forms of treatment differently. I thought it was just enough to trust the healer and be open to the possibility the treatment has to offer. But that is just the beginning. I've also learned that, for the most effective healing, one also needs to resonate energetically with one's healing guide. This is especially important to know for people who are planning to try an alternative treatment method for the first time. Understand that if you don't get the expected results, it doesn't mean that nothing will work for you. It may mean that you and your healing guide are not vibrationally compatible or that the healing method may not be right for you at that time. Don't stop there, please. Try something else, be an explorer. There are so many rich experiences out there that can enhance your wellbeing.

How do you tell if the energy will flow freely between you and your planned healing guide? Well, I haven't discovered a sure-fire method as of yet, but one thing that can help is to observe the healer's energy level when you first interact with them. If you are a bubbly type personality, do you see them as a high energy type too, or are they more sedate and perhaps vibrate at a lower level. Similar energy levels might be one clue to consider in helping you find the best match for a healing guide to assist you in your journey.

{4}

Iridologist and Naturopathic Doctor
Sis Sewell, N.D.

The first time I met Sis Sewell, I already had in my mind that she would be a feisty character. I had called the number Ines Hoster had given me to make an appointment and I reached Sis directly. She was not altogether pleased with the intrusion and told me I needed to call The Herb Garden, which managed all her Atlanta appointments. I dialed the number and was pleased to learn that I was now following proper protocol. The proprietor of the shop, JoAnn Roberson, N. D., (Naturopathic Doctor-physicians undergo a four-year training program that includes training in homeopathy, clinical nutrition, manipulation, herbal medicine and hydrotherapy.), informed me that Sis lives up near the South Carolina border and makes trips down to her shop in Cumming about once every two weeks to see clients. Her next availability would be the week after next and she proceeded to give me directions on how to get there.

It always amazes me the way life seemingly slows down considerably once you exit off the freeway and start making your way down roads weaving through the quiet communities just minutes from the thoroughfare. Small town camaraderie soon pops up everywhere and everyone seems to know each other's business. The directions were exacting and I soon pulled up in front of the little unassuming shop. Inside it reminded me of a little general store with boxes of medicines, food items, books and the like. The friendly proprietor greeted me and showed me a seat at the table in the middle of the shop. There she gave me a clipboard with several pieces of paper on it asking for a medical history and what had prompted the visit. My mission remained to rid myself of my breathing problems and I was quick to capture that information on my forms.

As I waited for my appointment, people wandered in and out, often with pets in tow. I later learned that both Sis and The Herb Garden shop were as passionate about treating our animal companions as they were about humans. It also became apparent that people stopped in for the conversation as much as they did for their purchases and it made the waiting time go by quickly as I eavesdropped on their lives.

Sis and her latest client emerged from a small room in back of the shop. She gave the man last minute instructions, scooped up my paperwork and then invited me in to her office. It was a tiny room with only artificial light, a desk, two chairs and an examining table. She seated me in a chair beside her desk and began reviewing my paperwork with me. By nature I like to have an upbeat disposition and feel most comfortable if those around me will crack a smile, but Sis didn't seem to be in the mood for any jovial behavior. She was very business-like and got right on with it.

Sis Sewell was certified in Iridology by Dr. Bernard Jensen, D.C. (Doctor of Chiropractic), N.D., Ph.D. (Nutrition). Dr. Jensen was an amazing man that had devoted his life to researching and uncovering

92

the recipe for robust longevity from various cultures around the world. While the information he has captured and shared in his many publications is vast, the essence of his advice is to focus on good nutrition and care for the organs responsible for the elimination of toxins. He encourages people to stay away from processed and fried foods, and to opt whenever possible for organic foods. Dr. Jensen pioneered the science of iridology in the United States and was considered America's leading holistic nutritionist up until his death at 93 in February 2001.

The science of iridology was first discovered in the early 1800's Hungary when 11-year old Ignatz von Peczely caught an owl and accidentally broke the bird's leg. During the struggle, the bird and boy kept glaring into each other's eyes and Ignatz noticed that a black stripe was rising in the eye of his captive. The boy nursed the bird back to health, but upon release the bird chose to stay in the garden for several more years. This allowed Ignatz to observe the bird and notice that the black stripe in the owl's eye had been replaced with white and crooked lines once the bird had recovered from the injury. Later becoming a physician, he never forgot the incident and continued his observation of the changes in the eye as a result of disease, injury and/or surgery. Von Peczely created the first chart of the iris based on his findings. At about the same time, Reverend Nils Liljequest of Sweden discovered the relationship between the use of drugs and the specific discoloration in the eyes as a result of his own experiences with illness in youth. Since this time scientists and doctors have continued to research iridology, improving upon the original reference chart created by von Peczely.

According to the booklet *Iridology Simplified,* by Dr. Jensen, a certified iridologist can identify inflammations in the body and what stage of manifestation it is in. Because the iris of the eye is connected to every organ and tissue of the body by way of the brain and nervous system, it acts like a mirror of what is happening inside. It is not designed to name diseases, instead it reads tissue and conditions, indicating the propensity for problems that potentially can be avoided by greater attention in nutrition and lifestyle. It is not a perfect science by any means. But we should keep in mind that the art of Western medicine does not reveal all the answers either.

My Fascination

As with many of the alternative healers I've come in contact with, Sis relies on a combination of healing skills and talents to advise her clients. I suspect there is a strong element of intuition at play as well, another familiar concept in traditional medicine. After all, addressing a human condition always requires a blend of art and science. We are complex beings, not widgets, and therefore unique in just how our bodies are reacting to an attack and how we will respond to defensive tactics. The most prized physicians are ones that can consider all sorts of possibilities, following their informed hunches based on years of study, their experiences and their ability to creatively problem solve, not merely consult a textbook of what is likely to happen.

Sis peered into my eyes and made some notes. She asked me if I had five little red blood moles appearing across my stomach. The question fascinated me and I responded I didn't know. But like a little kid wanted to find out in the quickest way possible, I lifted up my dress, and sure enough, there were five tiny red moles in a line across my stomach. Wow! That was amazing. She told me that it indicated a liver problem and that she suspected arsenic poisoning. All of a sudden I felt as if Angela Lansbury might pop into our room and that I'd become a part of a *Murder, She Wrote* episode. But Sis informed me that arsenic poisoning was often the result of direct skin contact with household chemicals. "Had I done any painting with oil based paints in recent years?" she asked. Amazed, I responded that yes, I had been repainting the trim in our house over the past two years.

Sis also told me that I had an infection in my upper left lung. Besides that, I had a much smaller problem in my right lung that looked like it could be an intrusion from a parasite, often attributed by traditional medicine to third world travel. Sis said that people in the United States could get it, too. She also told me that people who have received extensive vaccinations will end up with problems on the left side of their bodies. In my case, it was the start of arthritis in my left knee, infection in my left lung and then my liver problem.

She brought in a host of boxes and bottles and began testing my body to see which ones were appropriate. She began with the muscle testing or applied kinesiology, which is where a question is asked of your body and then a yes or no response is given based on the ability of your body to resist a measured amount of pressure from the person asking the question. Many people believe in this method of testing and have found it helpful. I personally do not like it because I believe there is too great of potential for either the healer or client not to be up to the task of paying attention and being consistent with their body stance. When I relayed this to Sis, I finally got the smile out of her I had been angling for. She said she understood and was going to use divination instead, which I believe is just tapping into her intuitive gifts, but not something she was willing to elaborate on. Anyway, we sifted through mountains of items she had pulled from the store shelves and tested against me. Out of thirty or so items, she ended up with five (and not the most expensive ones I might add!). There were two types of liquid cleanses, one for the lungs and one for the liver. There were also three bottles of capsules designed to detox my lungs, detox for yeast and restore the good bacteria in my digestion system which had been disrupted through heavy use of antibiotics. The latter capsules are called bifidophilus flora. I needed the yeast detoxification because I am allergic to wheat and unable to digest it properly, so now I had another reason besides the one given me by Ines Hoster to avoid eating wheat products.

As I was about to leave, it occurred to me to find out if Sis could tell me how long I have had this infection in my left lung. She peered back into my eyes with the aid of her magnifying glass and said it had been there a long time, about twenty years, which of course put me right back in the Boboli Gardens in Florence, just as Lillith during my past life regression had done.

My Belief

I find it interesting to visit Stephen Barrett, M.D.'s website, www.quackwatch.org, and see that he has maligned nearly all alternative sources of healing one might want to consider, including iridology. He is the ultimate skeptic, and surely as passionate about his beliefs as are those who reside at the opposite end of the belief spectrum. Personally, I like to make up my own mind about what works and doesn't work for me, and I encourage others to do the same. There are too many things we don't understand about being human, how life works, and how we fit into the planet. It is not as simple and cut and dried as Dr. Barrett would have us believe. It seems to me that the wisest warrior, when battling an illness, will seek out all sorts of information, consider it all, and make the decision that feels best for her.

At the end of the day, the adult person who is most affected by the decision should be the one making it whenever possible. Of course one should always get the advice of a respected physician in traditional Western medicine. But when time permits, you may also want to try alternative treatments that could prevent your body from having to undergo the severe trauma of surgery or the long-term upset of your delicate balance in body chemistry.

The role of nutrition in our health is often minimized or overlooked altogether when we approach illness or disease. We are a quick fix society and it is so much easier to take that little pill or go for surgery than to work methodically at changing our diets, physical activity and lifestyle in general. The latter takes a lot longer and requires a lot more discipline and commitment to be successful. The rewards are huge however. My husband had been suffering from indigestion for years with increasing intensity. He had been given prescriptions for several of the drugs advertised on TV as the cure-all, but they were not effectively addressing his problem and he had concerns over the long term effect on his liver. That's the trouble with so much of our treatments today. They address one problem, but can create many more long-term.

A year ago he traveled to Moscow and during the course of his two month visit, spent considerable time being tested and examined by physicians there. They advised him to quit taking pills and adopt a more strict diet that included a specific intake of raw vegetables each day. A year later and his problem is all but completely eliminated. He no longer experiences the debilitating pain and has reclaimed the spring in his step and his youthful outlook. He's even tried to convince me that his hair has less gray in it, although I am not sure I am buying that.

The Value

My visit with Sis Sewell was a real turning point in tackling my breathing problems. She convinced me to abstain from eating wheat and dairy products, and I did so religiously for six weeks while taking the various elixirs and supplements she had recommended for me. The change was dramatic and long lasting. On a scale of 1-10, with 10 being the worst, my breathing used to fluctuate around 8-9. After my six-week wheat hiatus, my breathing improved to around level 4. As a side benefit, I also dropped ten pounds which, I have kept off as well. Slowly I introduced wheat and dairy back in my diet, but I am always conscious of it and try to minimize my intake. As a result, my lungs operate anywhere between a 4-6 on the scale I described and I have found the swing to be directly impacted by changes in my diet. How much of Sis's advice was related to iridology, her naturopathic medicine knowledge or her intuition? I am not sure. I do know she is a wise woman who guided me to markedly improve my condition.

Colon Hydrotherapist
Mary Cote, Star Wellness Center

Getting a colonic flush? Sounds rather unpleasant and invasive doesn't it? Like something you wouldn't want to do voluntarily. Well, at least at first blush. I remember listening to some celebrity raving about their new-found treatment on a talk show several years earlier and I just chalked it up to some Hollywood fad. Then Ines had broached the subject and strongly recommended that I have it done, almost with a sense of urgency, to prevent the onset of future problems. She was particularly concerned since I had been such a big consumer of wheat products and it had become apparent that I was in fact allergic to them. The theory is that when you have a food allergy and you continue to consume significant quantities of those items, your body doesn't know what to do with it and merely sets it aside to decompose. As a result, this buildup ends up becoming toxins in your body and creates an environment that invites health issues down the road.

Ines and I continued to have several conversations around the idea with my resistance only slightly starting to waver. I kept suggesting that maybe I could just try working with enemas which seemed like a much more moderate approach. But she didn't buy that. It has been estimated that it takes as many as 30 enemas to equal just one colonic and an enema only reaches the lower part of the colon while a colon hydrotherapy session can cleanse the entire 5 feet of the large intestine. She had me about won over with that argument. I couldn't see myself going through the process of daily enemas for the better part of a year since Ines had suggested I'd need as many as 3-4 colonics. Yet I was still concerned about potential risks involved with the procedure.

In the past, a number of people had suggested to my sister that she have it done as well. Being the avid researcher she is, she had made several inquiries and had become convinced it could be risky. In particular, an internist friend had strongly advised against it, saying she had worked with a number of patients to correct a condition caused by colonics. The procedure had upset the natural bacterial balance in the digestive tract needed for proper absorption of nutrients and disposal of toxins. As a result, I too resisted colonics and wanted to avoid the dire trauma predicted by my sister's internist friend.

But I also had great faith in Ines, and when she encouraged me to call Mary Cote, a certified colon hydrotherapist, to discuss my concerns, I finally yielded. Mary had a warm and friendly phone voice that exudes a sense of propriety when discussing the benefits and perceived challenges of colon hydrotherapy. She explained her belief that 90% of all disease is directly or indirectly related to an unclean colon. The colon not only eliminates waste, but is also designed to absorb vital minerals and vitamins as well as conserve water. When it is healthy, it provides a home for good bacteria that helps the body absorb these critical nutrients. When it becomes coated with unprocessed waste, it can no longer assimilate nutrients properly. This unhealthy buildup is also quite toxic and can end up re-entering the body through the blood stream, making us feel tired and weak, even leading to illness. In addition, the buildup can cause our colon muscles to be sluggish and less effective in the elimination process. This all seemed to make sense so we proceeded on to examine my concerns around the perceived risks.

Mary informed me that it was actually the buildup in the colon that causes the intestinal flora, the good bacteria, to be overtaken by the bad bacteria resulting in an imbalance. This accumulation in the colon makes it impossible for the glands to produce the necessary intestinal flora you need for your digestive system to operate at peak performance. Without good bacteria, your digestion becomes sluggish and results in constipation. Cleansing the colon helps bring the acid-alkaline ratio back into balance, allowing friendly bacteria to thrive, while inhibiting disease-causing organisms. You also facilitate the rebalancing of your system by orally taking a good flora supplement to reintroduce friendly bacteria into the colon.

Mary also informed me that many people ask her about the effect on the body's electrolytes. "Electrolytes are the minerals in the body (mainly sodium and potassium salts) that maintain the proper electrical charge and pH balance (acid and alkaline balance) in the various organs and tissues of the body. Each one of these tissues, organs and body cavities has a certain proportion and balance of minerals to maintain the necessary pH balance. For example, the stomach should maintain an acid pH and the duodenum (first part of the small intestine) should be alkaline in order for proper digestion to occur. If this balance is disrupted, then digestion will be impaired.

"The pH electrical balance in the colon is very near neutral, ideally being slightly acid. A strong acid or alkaline environment is not necessary because digestion does not take place in the colon. Rather, a major function of the colon is to re-absorb the fluid from the unformed stool that is passed into it from the small intestine. After the fluid is re-absorbed and stool is formed, the colon moves the stool into the rectum and out of the body.

"The majority of material released during a colon hydrotherapy is formed stool that has already had the fluid and electrolytes removed from it, so the amount lost is very minimal and easily replaced by the body from the food and fluid we ingest.

"As an added precaution following your treatment, your therapist will give you a glass of purified water and a packet of Emergen C to drink. This product contains all the minerals you need to restore the small amount of minerals that may be lost during your therapy session."

She said that that at her Star Wellness Center, they use sterilized disposable hoses and speculums so there is no danger of viral or bacterium contamination. In addition, the Center also uses water that has been purified through a three step filtration process plus UV light.

Everything I was concerned about seemed to have been adequately covered so we moved along to questions that were more logistical in nature. Mary said that most people did not experience any discomfort during or after the treatment, in fact they typically left the Center feeling lighter and even refreshed. But occasionally some people had experienced nausea or became tired afterwards, so that was a possibility. I was also told that a session lasts about an hour and that I could go about my daily routine afterwards. For some, the session may trigger several subsequent trips to the bathroom for the next few hours, but there won't be anything uncontrollable or uncomfortable.

Feeling sufficiently informed, I made an appointment for the following week hoping I'd even have the added benefit of seeing my abdomen shrink!!

My Fascination

When I arrived at the Center, I was greeted by Mary and led back to a treatment room. It looked well scrubbed and sanitized and even a little high tech with the equipment viewing screen visible on the wall. Mary spent about 15 minutes or so showing me a book illustrating the different conditions that could be present in your colon and what signs she would be looking for when material passed through the glass viewing tube for a cursory analysis. I decided to approach this as an adventure in biology and became curious as to what we would discover about my colon during the ordeal.

She had me slip into an examining gown and then hop on the table and lie on my back facing the wall so I would have view of the equipment screen. She made sure I was comfortable and then had me roll slightly away from her and handed me the speculum to insert myself. I was pretty relaxed about it and I think that probably has a great deal with how easy the whole insertion thing went. No big deal, really. Then she started the equipment up and I felt like I could feel the slight rush of the water starting. She offered me mint to deter any nausea that might appear and I quickly told her that I am an anomaly when it comes to mint. It actually makes me nauseous, which totally surprised her.

I was instructed to tell her when I started feeling any kind of pressure, like I needed to relieve myself, and at that point she would reverse the flow and drain the water out of my colon. It wasn't too long before I gave her the signal that I was starting to feel like I needed to eliminate and immediately I felt the pressure dissipate and started to see the waste float through the little glass tube. I suppose some people would find this gross. I, on the other hand, found it to be a great science experiment and was anxious to see what we might be accomplishing based on the tutorial Mary had given me at the beginning of the session. Mary and I kept a keen eye on the glass tube and discussed what we thought was going on in my colon. As the session continued, she would massage my abdomen from time to time to help loosen any potentially impacted areas. When we were through with the session, Mary directed me to the bathroom for further elimination and after that, I proceeded to get dressed, drank my Emergen C and then we were done. I was impressed enough with the process that I made my second appointment and then was off and running to a social event that evening.

I was very pleased to find that I fell in with the majority of the clients Mary had referenced in our conversation and had no discomfort, upset stomach or tiredness as a result of the procedure. I actually felt like I was doing something really nice for my body and psychologically embraced the concept of gently scrubbing out years of sludge buildup. In fact I was so impressed by my feeling afterwards, I insisted on retelling my great experience to a group of my friends and they were all groaning like it was something nasty. Yet in my mind, it was just so cool to be able to clear the pipes.

My Belief

I believe our colons deserve as much love and attention as we give our cars and the plumbing in our homes. After all, we think nothing of flushing out our car engines when we've allowed oil to build up between oil changes or calling a plumber to work his magic on a slow-draining sink or tub. In fact the more I think about it, I suspect the typical American diet of highly processed and fried foods probably has many of us running around with a colon that resembles a toxic waste dump, full of gases and poisons that are just primed for an opportunity to cause some sort of health crisis.

Purification processes have been a part of healthy practices in many cultures around the world and in fact were part of our own mainstream culture early in the 20th century. In fact today's hydrotherapy equipment was actually developed at that time and used in physician practices and hospitals. As late as 1930, colon health was often a focus in many prestigious medical and scientific journals. Then the health profession started to move away from traditional holistic practices to the quicker fix of pills and surgery, causing the attention on preventive treatments meant to keep the colon healthy and vitalized to fade from common medical practice.

The Value

I felt a sense of renewal mentally, emotionally and physically after my two colonics. I felt good about taking the time to do something for myself that was apt to have a long term positive impact. I am further heartened to know that recent European studies report their belief that 80% of our immune system tissue resides in the colon. So by working on my colon, I actually was working to improve my overall breathing as well.

And now, to answer that question that is apt to be in your mind if you made it this far, "What type of toilet trip should you be striving for and what quality of paper works best?" Mary advises, "Once the urge to eliminate is honored by a trip to the toilet, the elimination should be easy and take nor more than 10 seconds. The stool will be long, large in diameter, light brown in color, without offensive odor and should float or sink very slowly. When the toilet is flushed, the stool immediately begins breaking apart by the action of water movement." As for the brand of toilet paper, I will leave you to research that on your own.

{6}

Angel Channeler
Cathy Horvath

It was during a networking conversation that I first learned that my friend Cathy channeled her guardian angels. I had invited my new friend to a meeting I was planning to have with a trainer who specializes in brain-based learning. The three of us met over coffee at Joe Muggs in Buckhead, a favorite social spot in Atlanta. As we were about to wrap up our conversation, it suddenly turned towards discussing the unusual things we had experienced.

I started us down that path when I shared that recently a strange event had happened to me when a white mist had shot out of a painting hung above my bed one night. It was so bizarre and yet so fascinating that I found the incident popping out of my mouth during the strangest moments, like now with someone I had just met. That tidbit had prompted our conversation to expand into all sorts of interesting arenas. Our brain expert mentioned that she even had a friend that could talk to horses and sense things that were other-worldly. Then Cathy surprised me with the revelation that she channeled her guardian angels and I just about dropped my jaw to the floor. I had been palling around with her for about two months now and yet I hadn't uncovered this little known gem about her. Even more surprising was that it seemed so incongruent with the buttoned up persona she presented to the world. I felt like I had just struck a rich vein of information and couldn't wait to get in there with my miner's gear.

I kept giving her a hard time as we walked to our cars and told her that I was anxious to hear more about her ability, how she invoked the communications and whether she could teach me to do it. My curious cat enthusiasm seemed to tickle her and we agreed to chat more about this over tea in the coming week.

That next week we met at Cathy's house and she brewed us up a big pot of ginger peach tea. We took our steaming cups up to her office and I felt like I was definitely entering her favorite space. A fountain provided a peaceful backdrop, and angels seemed to be tucked in and around each little nook and cranny that attracted the eye. There were pictures of her favorite spots in Sedona and shelves of books on subjects she had explored. She pulled one out to show me called *Angel Speak* by Trudy Griswold and Barbara Mark. She continued to tell me that she had learned to channel her angels from this book and that it was a tutorial of sorts. As far as she knew anybody could learn to communicate with their guardian angels by following the simple steps outlined in this handbook.

Cathy also told me that after first reading the book and trying her communication skills, she found herself frustrated with the process, that the information wasn't always accurate. As a means of venting, she wrote a letter to her guardian angels relaying her concerns and then decided she'd take the matter up with the authors of the book. She gave

Trudy a call and she answered the phone. This really came as a surprise to both of them as Cathy was hopeful, but not sure she would actually reach the author, and Trudy always screens her calls and never actually picks up the phone when it rings. They ended up having quite the conversation around circumstances happening for a reason. Trudy explained that she was leaving the next morning for San Diego to meet with her sister Barbara to collaborate on their next book. This next publication was to chronicle the experiences of those that had tried their hand at communicating with their angels based on their first book. Trudy instructed Cathy to put her questions in a letter and that they would ask their angels for answers to her questions.

Cathy pulled another book from her shelf and showed me her claim to fame, her featured correspondence with the channeled response from Trudy and Barbara. Their angels advised 'synchronicity of the events told to you by your angels is likely to happen, but the timing may be off. There is no timeline on the other side. Events may also change based on acts of free will, yours and others that the event depends on.' So, in other words, the information you receive is about how events are likely to play out in the future, they may change if you or those around you force a change. The angels also advised Cathy that her life lessons revolved around trust and patience.

Cathy went on to review with me that all you needed to do is to say the prayers in the book and then you could actually sit down at the computer and information would just start coming to you. You could type away as it came and then step back and read it for its full insight and value when you were through. That sounded easy enough. I could do this, I thought, and stopped on the way home at a bookstore for the key to my guardian angels.

This whole idea of communicating with them was of particular interest as I have always felt like I had inner guides watching out for me. When I would fall into one of those dangerous traffic trances where your mind wanders and all of a sudden you find you are miles further than your last recollection, my guides would start yelling at me to pay attention. I've been known to talk to myself quite a bit, a genetic disposition I believe I got from my mother. Her mother used to become exasperated with her and wonder, "Who are you talking to?" Given her predisposition for talking to herself, I was never chastised for it so I never believed it was anything to even concern myself with.

As I started to look a little closer at this tendency, I began to realize sometimes there seems to be new information about a situation that comes to me or even a debate that goes on. Maybe that is just a lively imagination and my brain's way of analyzing a situation or keeping me safe. Or maybe it is my guardian angels looking out for me on a daily basis. I liked that thought, and so it has become the one I hold on to. With that concept in mind, I was ecstatic at the thought of actually being able to initiate a chat and perhaps even learn their names, assuming there is more than one.

The next evening I was ready to make my angel connection. I had read my book and made my how-to notes. I had decided a tea party was in order, so I made a steaming pot of tea and prepared a plate of cookies to take to the computer with me. The excitement was mounting. What was I going to learn about my long-time friends? I sat down in front of the computer screen and said my prayer:

Angels of God, my Guardians dear
To whom God's love entrusts me here
Ever this day be at my side
To light and guard
To love and guide Amen

With great anticipation, I proceeded to take a sip of tea, a bite of a cookie and then put my fingers to the keyboard ready for their pronouncements………..and, and, and………nothing came to me. I waited and waited, impatiently taking more sips of tea and eating a few cookies, but nothing came. Disappointed, I gave up for the evening and decided I'd call Cathy the next day and report my lack of making a successful connection.

When I debriefed her the next day she started laughing and said, "Get out of here. You weren't really drinking tea and eating were you?" "Why yes," I said. "I thought a celebratory tea party was in order, after all it was going to be like old home week with my good friends!" She went on to inform me that eating and drinking, even if it's only tea, are too big of distractions when you are trying to communicate on another level. You have to be relaxed and totally open without any other activity engaging your mind. "Oh" I said, and decided I'd try again a few evenings later. Cathy also recommended that I try a pad and pen this time so I didn't find myself playing with the keyboard or surfing the net or something while I was impatiently waiting for someone to speak to me.

For my second attempt, I was in comfy clothes, sock-footed and relaxing in an easy chair with my feet up on the ottoman, paper and pen in hand. I went through each step carefully and then tried to still my mind waiting for new thoughts to come to me. Waiting, waiting, waiting….and again, a disappointed nothing.

My Fascination

In later conversations I learned that Cathy may consult her guardian angels on the fly for herself, but she mentally prepares herself for several days before she tries to channel her angels for someone else. She eats lightly, and stays away from sugar, chocolate, caffeine and alcohol to cleanse her body from toxins. She explained that some people can actually channel with a glass of wine in their hands, but that her understanding was that most people needed to concentrate on a purification process.

The intent is to mentally and spiritually prepare yourself so that intuitively you feel like you are in the right emotional state to communicate. You can't be worrying and have things on your mind if you are going to make contact on someone else's behalf. In essence, she feels like she has a much greater responsibility to make a clear connection. Without adequate preparation she says the connection feels more cloudy and hard to decipher. She can tell that she has entered her channeling state because her crown chakra, or top or her head, starts to heat up and feel like it is sizzling. She does not lose her state of consciousness; rather there is just a knowledge that the thoughts are no longer coming from her own mind. The phraseology is different and the insights are new.

My Belief

I believe when something comes naturally to you, we have a tendency to believe it is as easy for everyone else. I was disappointed that I didn't get the planned connection I had hoped for when I tried to focus on communication with intent to do so, but I am blessed to have my gifted friend Cathy who can check in for me if I need particular guidance. And she did just that in August 2003. The resulting letter to me was just slightly over a page, but right on target with hard-hitting insight. What we found interesting was that it dealt with issues that both Cathy and I were struggling with and it was a lesson for her as much as for me. So was it just Cathy's subconscious advising a friend? I don't think so, for the very reason I just stated, it was contrary to her own actions and conversations to date about our mutual challenges.

The Value

In late summer of 2003, Cathy channeled my guardian angels on my behalf and presented me with the following letter from them.

8/29/03

"We are responding to your request with pleasure. It is a joy to watch her grow and expand her consciousness to the awareness of more than the senses tell her at this time.

Her life will continue in turmoil for a brief period more; then she will be able to look back upon this time as a period of rebirth and renewal. For without this resting time she would not have come to know herself and her holiness as much as she does today.

She must endure the heartache that is to come as but a stepping stone on her life's path. She has much wonderment ahead of her and twists and turns she would never have expected.

Change is now part of everyone's consciousness and she must embrace and accept what is in store for her. She is a kind and just person but must not be motivated by guilt for everyone is responsible for themselves. We cannot be held accountable for another. We can be kind and loving and helpful but we cannot accept responsibility for the ultimate outcome of another's life for to do so would remove the ability of the other to continue their soul's work and lesson anticipated during their life experience.

Connie will move, she will expand into new business ventures—a departure from her past work experience and she will at times second guess her choices. Remind her not to do so. Her choices are valid and she has given much thought to her plans.......

....She will soon hear of an opportunity to carry her away from her home and she must not fear to accept. That is the start. More changes to follow. She will always remain your devoted friend. You bring much to each other's lives.

The God presence is with you both. She is being guided by day and by night as she rests her conscious mind. She is not straying from her path. This will all come about in the very near future, but we will not proceed with a timeline so as to dispel the belief in our words. Much depends on the movement of other lives as well as hers so she can slip into a role being vacated by one who is moving on. Like a domino effect, do you see?

Please give her our loving thoughts and tell her to ask for our guidance as we are there to serve her needs. She has only to ask. Go in God's love. Goodnight."

The words may be few, but they were loaded with extremely powerful and reassuring thoughts.

{7}

Astrologer
Toni Thomas

O ur resident Eclectic Ladies Network astrologer, Toni Thomas, came to our group through another member who has long since come and gone. That has been the case from time to time, a person finds their way to our monthly parties, brings another, and then eventually leaves for one reason or another but our newfound friend of a friend becomes one of the party regulars. Such is the case with Toni. She is a very petite woman, just shy of a hundred pounds, which always makes us all wonder how she ever learned to play the accordion growing up. She shared with us that her musical abilities were something she used as a key test to check out the viability of a long-term relationship with her dates. When a new beau took her home for the evening, she'd invite him in for coffee and then slip away saying she'd return with a surprise for him. Without much ado, she'd reappear with her accordion and play a little tune. How well he reacted to the surprise was how she determined the likelihood that they were a good match in the humor department.

Keeping with the theme of being Eclectic, Toni fills that bill to the extreme. When she first left home as a young adult, she went to live in a Catholic convent in upstate New York and studied to be a nun. She always says she values the experience, especially the lessons of discipline and compassion and the wonderful women she met there. Toni always knew this move was merely a stepping stone, a means for her to leave home and start making her way in the world. It allowed her to have the freedom from a father who didn't see a value in an advanced education for his daughter, and made possible her plans to go on to school and become an elementary school teacher.

Toni found teaching her new charges extremely satisfying, loving to inspire her students to learn and delighting in their enthusiastic discoveries. But as the school system began to change, establishing all sorts of boundaries that prevented teachers from personally connecting with their students, she became saddened by the resulting deterioration in the learning process. Another dramatic lifestyle change was in order, and she became a broker with Dean Witter and Associates. Being a people person, Toni again enjoyed forming relationships that gave her an opportunity to have lively and caring interactions with her customers, yet something still seemed to be missing from the equation. After much thought, she eventually decided to pursue her passion of astrology as a full time career, saying goodbye to the corporate world with no regrets.

Slowly, but surely, her business gained momentum, forming critical mass and now keeps her busy every day of the week doing charts, consulting with clients, keeping her customer base up to date with what they can expect for the month and giving talks about astrology to groups whose interest goes beyond their monthly horoscope. Being an astrologer still fulfills her passion for teaching and helping others make discoveries about themselves and those who influence their world.

Toni is always quick to point out that astrology has been around since the recording of time. From ancient primitive cultures to modern times, people have consulted the stars for guidance. Often people confuse astrology with the more commercialized horoscopes they read in magazines, newspapers or in online publications. While these horoscopes are fun, they focus only on your sun sign, or on only 1/30th of the information needed to really provide you with any sense of guidance around your specific astrological configuration.

Astrology is really not so much about prediction of specific events, it is more a lifeprint that can give you a lot of information about your journey and how best to navigate it. To identify and explore your individual lifeprint, you need to provide an astrologist your specific date, time and location of birth so they can determine the exact planetary configuration, or your natal chart, when you entered this world.

There are three groups of elements that your astrologist will target in order to identify their relationship at the time of your birth and create your chart:

- The Planets, which represent the energy affecting you;
- The Signs, which indicates the type of energy given to each planet;
- The Houses, which indicates when this energy is most likely to affect your everyday life.

The planets are represented by the position of Earth's eight sister planets (Mercury, Venus, Mars, Jupiter, Saturn, Uranus, Neptune and Pluto) as well as the Sun and the Moon. Astrologers interested in the relationships between the positions of all ten objects simply call them the Ten Planets. Their cyclical movements act like a giant cosmic clock that marks off past, present and future time and events.

The other key piece of information, along with what Sign/constellation the planets were in is what House these Ten Planets were located in at your point of entry. Houses indicate what areas of your life will be most influenced by the planetary movements. There are 12 Houses and they actually are more individually significant in your astrology chart than the Signs themselves.

First House: How you see yourself, physically and consciously, and how others see you

Second House: What you value and attract to you, outer possessions or what you are

Third House: Our understanding of information received

Fourth House: Sense of belonging and capacity to receive, need for family roots

Fifth House: Our needs for love and channels of emotional expression

Six House: Work and health, balancing necessity with joy

Seventh House: Ability to relate to others on equal footing

Eighth House: Evolve or sacrifice our ego boundaries for relation ship(s) to flourish

Ninth House: Expand our mind and form our philosophy of life

Tenth House: Our need to achieve and be recognized or have others dependent on us

Eleventh House: The kinds of energy we experience and friends we attract in groups

Twelfth House: Building inner strength to overcome limitations and that which is hidden, karma, enemies, confinement

Armed with these specifics, an astrologer can give you insight as to specific areas in your life that will require your attention and help identify times in your life that you should be prepared to seize opportunities, are apt to face greater stress and/or be prone to various types of life challenges.

My Fascination

Toni first developed my natal chart for me in June of 2003, shortly after my 46th birthday. At first I was overwhelmed with the wealth of information that came in my package and was sure that I would never make heads or tails of it all without Toni interpreting it for me every time I ventured a look. However, once Toni gave me a foundation of understanding, the more I study the information, the more I seem to be able to relate to it and see how it can illuminate some of my lifeprint.

For instance, I find the concentration or absence of planets in a particular house most intriguing. In my natal chart I did not have any planets in the 7th, 8th or 9th houses. The seventh house is about looking for fulfillment from others and the eighth house seems to invite change of the crisis nature, neither of which seems to be a pattern in my life. The ninth house deals with the ability to synthesize meaning from facts and experience and understand how everything integrates together which is something I come by naturally and does not seem to present a challenge to me either.

However, my concentration in the tenth and eleventh houses seems to ring true. I've always had a strong drive to achieve and have chosen paths that have led to recognition for my efforts which reflects my tenth house concentration. The heaviest concentration falls in my eleventh house, the house indicating that we live a large part of our life in groups. The earlier part of my life wouldn't seem to bear witness to this tendency, but as I've hit midstride my life has become the epitome of attracting group energy as evidenced to the many rich experiences that have occurred through my friendships with my ELN friends.

My Belief

I believe there is a lot of insight that can be gained about your self and others through the exploration of astrology lifeprints. I have found two books that are exceptionally insightful and often provide amazing profiles of people based on their date of birth or even just their sun sign.

The first book is called *The Secret Language of Birthdays*, by Gary Goldschneider and Joost Elffers. It was given to me as a birthday gift by one of my good friends and has always been a book I've treasured. It has a unique two page write-up for people based on the day of the year they were born. It has individual birth day taglines that encapsulate the person's likely personality and then highlights attributes and challenges for them as well as a recommended meditation. Further investigation into your sun sign will even tell you what age period of life your personality can be likened to and your mode and motto. We Gemini represent the third stage in life or 14-21 years olds, individuals who value personal freedom above all else. We have energy to burn and like being part of a group. We are typically in thought mode and our motto is "I communicate."

A favorite pastime of mine is introducing friends to this book and watching their eyes light up when they see themselves so plainly on the two page profile. I particularly remember having a fun conversation with an old friend from university. We would get on the phone and chat once or twice a year for an hour or so and catch up on each other's life. In one such call, I pulled out the birthday book and read him his profile. He could be characterized as an introvert, yet I felt through our conversations I knew him pretty well. As I was reading his profile, I remember chuckling and saying "Oh, this doesn't fit at all." Yet he didn't join in with my amusement and when I was finished told me that it actually fit him quite well. I was simply stupefied by that revelation!

The other book I'd recommend checking out is one that I recently was introduced to by Linda Potter called *Sun Signs,* by Linda Goodman. In this book Linda takes each of the twelve zodiac signs and gives an overview of how the energy plays out in women, men, children, employers and employees.

Of course the ultimate illumination is when you have your charts done and interpreted by a professional astrologer. Then you will have an illustration of your own personal lifeprint.

The Value

If you have never journeyed into the world of astrology and sought the knowledge it holds for you, and you have a curious nature, you are surely in for a treat if you decide to walk down this path. It is fun to look at the past and present and see how it lines up with what was planned for you from day one. Patterns start to unfold and events seem to make more sense when one looks back and views the relationships between what seemed like random activity at the time. It is also helpful to look to the future and learn how to plan the timing of activities and events in a manner that will likely provide the best outcome for you.

{8}

Medical Intuitive/Healer
Brent Atwater

I've always been fascinated by stories recounting the amazing healing exploits of Edgar Cayce. However, they've always left me with the impression that his diagnostic and healing abilities were a total anomaly, unlike any other being that had ever graced our United States.

The first time I attended a Mind, Body and Spirit (MBS) conference I became aware that there were in fact contemporary medical intuitives, individuals gifted with the same type, albeit perhaps not as strong, diagnostic and healing powers. One of my ELN friends was organizing the volunteer staff for a MBS conference and asked if any of the ladies in our group would be interested in participating. I thought it sounded like a fun and economical way to check out what went on at these events and signed up.

A half hour into my volunteer efforts it became clear that the price of admission was more than I had bargained for. I was assigned to the vendor check-in desk and the person who was in charge from the event company was completely disorganized. As a result, I was often taking the heat for her poor project management skills and it was downright embarrassing. On the upside, the spot did give me a good view of everyone going in and out of the tradeshow hall and a chance to study the market from both a customer and vendor standpoint.

One person that caught my eye was a radiant woman with long flowing hair and an infectious smile who seemed to come bolting out of the hall on a regular basis. We made eye contact a number of times, waved to each other and exchanged brief comments across the lobby. At one point she explained that she just was getting drained by the energy in the hall and had to take frequent breaks. I eventually caught sight of her name tag and realized she was Patti Conklin, one of the featured speakers. When I looked up her name in the program booklet, I discovered she was a medical intuitive, someone that could use their intuitive powers to look inside of you to identify health issues and their causes. Kind of like a human MRI machine.

Wow, that must be exhausting, I thought, and at times downright scary. I wondered if you can just turn off that kind of power, or if it is always on. I'd love to investigate this type of experience and immediately knew I wanted to get to know this woman better to learn more about her and her work. I made the connection and invited her to join our Eclectic Ladies group. She thought it sounded like a fun group and indicated she would like to participate. We began trading occasional emails and made tentative plans to go to lunch. Her work always keeps her in demand, traveling to speaking engagements throughout the United States and to different parts of the world and rarely leaves time in Atlanta. Such a hectic travel schedule has prevented us from making any in-depth connection as of yet, but I am always one to hold out hope when I feel that urge to make a new friend.

Our brief exchanges were enough to raise my awareness into the world of medical intuitives, however, and made me jump at the chance to meet such a person at a small dinner party a year later. Another of my ELN friends, a woman with her PhD in psychology, is forever exploring alternative methods of healing. Using an Internet search engine, she had discovered Brent Atwater, a medical intuitive/healer from North Carolina. After chatting with Brent by telephone, she became her client and was now arranging a dinner for a few friends to meet her when she was in Atlanta next. I was thrilled at the promise of meeting such an unusual talent and couldn't wait for the evening to arrive!

Our dinner was at a Chinese restaurant near Buckhead in Atlanta. There were four of us seated around a large round table in the middle of the dining room, our hostess, a yoga studio owner, Brent, and I. Brent is an elegant figure of a woman, and quite different than I had imagined. I don't think I had really pictured specifically what she would look like, but I was surprised to find her tall and model slim, tanned with a head full of long, magazine-worthy hair that she kept pulled back with a gold braided headband.

Ironically Brent appeared to be both open and closed in her initial conversations with us. While extremely forthcoming in answering any questions we had about being a medical intuitive, she was much more guarded about sharing who Brent was as a person. I later learned she had become cautious about revealing too much personal information to people in order to protect herself from those who were fearful of her unique gifts. At times there have been people afraid to even shake her hand or offer her regular business banking services. When I hear things like that I am always simply amazed that people can be so embarrassingly ignorant.

My investigative reporter persona was in full swing and I was delighted to have such a willing subject to interrogate. I wanted to know everything about Brent and her medical intuitive abilities – what it was like to be her, how did it work, how did she feel about it. Sometimes in my enthusiasm, I ask very penetrating questions, often oblivious to the potential impact they might have on someone. I process information rather quickly and even more effectively if I can keep a certain pace going when I am interviewing someone. I suspect it probably feels like my subjects have a big spotlight shining in their face as I continue my rapid-fire probe for nuggets of insight. Brent took heart in knowing that I was genuinely interested in her and her gifts and luckily did not take offense from my intense questioning. In fact, she later said she found it somewhat liberating. In the small community she lives in, she doesn't get an opportunity to talk about it often, and certainly not to the degree sought this evening. The three of us became a totally captivated audience as we were drawn in by our fascinating dinner partner.

Brent had been part of a group of young children identified with extra sensory perception skills and had been the subject of a study all through their childhood. Yet these gifts had not become a focus in her adult life. Rather she had chosen to pursue the study of law and eventually settled on using her artistic talents as an illustrator and painter. She had met the love of her life and they had been in a close relationship for many years when they had finally decided to get married. Hours after becoming engaged, he was killed in a tragic accident that sent Brent into a wild emotional and physical tailspin that left those around her fearful she would not recover. She was taken to the Duke Center for Integrated Medicine, where she had a long standing relationship from the earlier childhood studies. At first puzzled at what was causing her dramatic and dangerous shift in vital signs, the medical researchers eventually discovered that it was due to a rise in the accessibility of a high powered energy level which heretofore had been dormant. When they walked her into their MRI lab, all the equipment immediately powered down. When she stepped out of the room, the power came back on and all the equipment returned to full operation. Excitedly they performed other tests to validate their theory. They marched her into a room full of x-rays and had her tell them what she thought about them. Even though she had not been trained in the medical field, she was now spouting medical terminology reflecting the conditions she was viewing.

From that point, Brent began to expand her awareness of the new gifts she had received as a result of the cataclysmic event. She was evaluated by the Edgar Cayce Association for Research & Enlightenment, which further validated her abilities as a medical intuitive. She began to experience seeing inside the physical bodies of individuals, how their organs were working, or not working, evidence of past operations and emerging diseases. Often these new skills would be shocking when they made their initial appearance. The first time Brent saw a human heart pulsing inside of someone she became totally nauseous, finding it absolutely revolting. One can only imagine what that must be like.

Eventually the weirdness faded and gave way to awe at the ability to help people pinpoint their health issues when traditional means have failed. Her amplified powers show her gray looming around an area of a person's energy field indicating impending problems, gold sparkles where an infection and/or cancer is about to metastasize and purple sparkles where a person has an infection or cancer. A number of research facilities have documented her ability to detect conditions two weeks before they have appeared on the latest state-of-the-art medical equipment. She does this type of a body scan when she is specifically on a hunt to find a particular source of a problem.

Besides the diagnostic gift, Brent also received the ability to channel healing energy to either treat a specific problem or with the intent to have it do "its highest and best good" for her client which allows the energy to be attracted to areas in the most need. At the start of any healing energy session, Brent will do a high level scan that rebalances and energizes the chakras. During this process, she identifies areas that may be blocked, which she describes as being like causing your energy to try and attempt to breakthrough a football practice dummy or through partially clogged plumbing. With this knowledge, she sets her intent on where to direct the healing energy during the session. When she first was learning to manage the energy channeling process, she found herself getting hot, turning red and breaking out in a sweat, then turning ashen white, signaling the energy was running through her. As she has become more experienced with the process, she no longer finds herself overheating. Rather she now hears a low whistle in one or both ears, like a train is leaving the station, when the energy starts running through her. The whistling continues during the whole session, changing pitch as it makes its way through her client's body, finally quieting when the session is complete. She typically does this type of work in the late evening whenever possible because competing manmade energies are at a minimum then, as are the distractions that can occur during daytime hours. This also is an hour that allows her the freedom to relax and focus on her task undisturbed and if she so chooses, entertain herself by deciding to enjoy the kaleidoscope of colors that emerge from her body as the energy travels to her client's body.

Brent always chats with prospective clients before she decides to accept them for an appointment. She consults with her intuitive guides who advise her whether her powers are likely to help someone. Sometimes the sessions will work, resulting in visible progress and sometimes it will not. People theorize that a person will be able to use this healing energy to improve their condition if their life lessons, or the lessons for those around them, have been completed that relate to the condition they are battling. If not, or if this is their time to leave earth, then there is not likely to be a successful recovery. Much remains a mystery around this activity. But one thing remains clear; there have been a remarkable number of instances of amazing improvements and/or recoveries that have occurred as a result of Brent channeling healing energy.

Brent's first experience using her ability to channel healing energy happened when her beloved dog was in an accident. A major portion of his spine collapsed and he needed to be placed on a breathing machine. By working with him, Brent was able to help him regenerate his spinal discs and walk out of the North Carolina Vet School on his own ninety days after the accident. Another early incident happened to Brent when her finger was caught in the mower and she lost the bone structure there. She was informed by medical professionals that there was nothing she could do. Incredibly, with time and concentration, she was able to regenerate bone in that finger to the point that to the casual observer you would never guess that there had ever been an injury.

One of her most spectacular achievements was with a paraplegic who had been suffering from multiple sclerosis. When he came to Brent, he was in a wheelchair and been unable to move his legs and suffered with a numb arm for three years. She had been very hesitant to accept him as a client because she was unsure she would be able to help him and thought it would be cruel to give him false hope. But her inner guides persuaded her that this was in fact someone she could help and within five minutes of the energy work she was able to restore feeling in his arm and within fifteen minutes, he was able to move his legs. Four days later he was able to transition from being wheel chair bound to using a walker for mobility.

Other conditions she has been able to assist her clients in improving include Parkinson's, epileptic seizures, cancer and pulmonary illnesses.

Regarding turning the gifts off, that is something you learn to do in time. Eventually you figure out how to effectively control and manage your gifts, not intrude uninvited into the private world of others nor allow yourself to be drained by the energy of others. I kept thinking this must make you feel grand, so lucky that you had been chosen for this duty on earth. But Brent surprisingly revealed it made her feel "small, real small." The knowing that there is so much more beyond us, that we are but just small little lights in something much, much bigger, she finds very humbling.

By this time, we had finished our dinner and the restaurant was getting ready to close. None of us were really ready to end the evening just yet and when Brent shared she was just having too much fun for it to be over, we decided we would continue our conversation over coffee back at her hotel in one of the public areas. We found a table there and got comfortable. We continued our lively conversation and Brent turned the discussion towards health situations that our other two dinner companions were struggling with.

I happened to mention that I wished I had psychic powers. I was thinking out loud, as it wasn't really part of the conversation, but Brent heard me and said I did. I said I knew I had strong intuition, but not the kind of powers others enjoy. She still responded that I did and asked me what kind of shoes I was wearing. I pulled my feet out from under the table and she informed me that was one of my problems. By wearing shoes with rubber soles, my typical choice of comfort over fashion, I was blocking the earth's energy and my intuitive powers. She told me to remove my shoes, which I did without question, and sat there in my stocking feet. Brent went back to her other conversation, and I was left sitting there, mystified and looking rather like a chump.

As time passed, my antsy tendency got the better of me and I reached to put my shoes back on. Out of the corner of her eye Brent saw me and, barely breaking stride with her conversation, told me with a firm tone, "We're not done yet. Put your palms face up on the table." Brent can be rather authoritative at times, and when she told me to do that, I didn't question her. Rather, I continued on with the instructions hoping there would be some redeeming value in my actions. And were there ever! What happened next ended up to be one of the most extraordinary experiences I've ever had. And there's a lot of competition for that title. It just goes to show you that rich experiences await us when we allow ourselves that little leap of faith.

As I sat there I could feel the palms of my hands start to get warm and slightly tingle. I didn't know it at the time, but later guessed and Brent confirmed that she was channeling energy to me to amplify my own intuitive powers. The conversation at the table had turned to the Lost Continent of Atlantis and we all fancied that we had probably been there in another life.

Brent turned to me and asked me to tell her what the woman sitting next to me had done on Atlantis. I started giggling and said if I knew that I wouldn't be asking for her help. Well, this was serious work, and Brent sternly told me to be serious and to answer her question. I sat up a little straighter and tried to find an answer, but clearly I was no further enlightened than I was just minutes earlier. Finally Brent told me to look into her eyes, reassured me I did know the answer, and asked the question again. To my utter amazement, I could now see my dinner companion in an apron working in an apothecary type shop dispensing herbs and other elixirs to those in need.

Each time she asked me a question, I immediately pictured an answer and Brent would confirm I was correct. Then she asked me what her name was in that life and a pretty funky answer came to mind, "Esmeralda." I even kind of chuckled as I said it. Brent said she wasn't so certain about that answer, but as soon as I said it out loud it felt totally correct. In fact the rest of the evening I had to call my new friend Esmeralda. This was such a phenomenal experience. Nothing like this had ever happened before and nor has it since. It gave me an opportunity to experience what such powers are like and to finally confirm what I always believed to be true - that it is possible for people to have such visionary powers.

Next, Brent turned to Esmeralda, who had also received amplified power by resting her palms on the table with mine, and asked her what I did in Atlantis. This was interesting in that she said I was a scientist that worked in research and innovation. That revelation tickled me since I have such a passion to work with something new, yet curious that I am not an early adopter of new products and services, especially technology. Later in our conversations we discussed the theory that all those that lived during the 30,000-year reign of Atlantis and worked in the scientific community harbored tremendous guilt for the continent sinking as a result of their part in letting technology get out of control. That added some logic to my sometimes puzzling, ironic behavior: quickly embracing the idea of new, but forever cautious in its use on a personal level.

Finally Brent had both Esmeralda and I focus on our fourth dinner companion and the most incredible experience of the evening ensued. We saw the same vision of her in the same surroundings at the same time. In fact, we began asking each other questions and commenting about things we were watching in the room we both saw her in. Our friend then started spinning into other times and places, all the while we both kept seeing the same picture alive with moving detail, just like out of a Harry Potter movie. It was truly bizarre, wonderful and just absolutely fascinating fun.

While our late night coffee experience was certainly entertaining and one I truly will treasure, it is not what being a medical intuitive is all about. This was just a moment of play among new friends for a person who finds her life heavy with emotional situations on a regular basis. Imagine the pressure of having to often tell someone that their last hope of recovery is not going to work for them.

Brent is always mindful of how her actions might affect her ability to channel healing energy and follows a pretty strict regimen to avoid endangering her abilities. She is well aware that the true plan for these sacred gifts is to help people on their journeys whether it is to help them find the power within to heal themselves or to ease the pain along their designated path.

My Fascination

Months after our initial meeting, two friends and I made arrangements to have an energy session with Brent when she returned to Atlanta. We planned a dinner afterwards with several other friends interested in meeting Brent and then we'd introduce her to our ELN network at our monthly party the next day.

When Brent first arrived that week, she was the subject of a research study that documented her abilities. Two Atlanta researchers, a respected husband and wife team who do primary research in neurolinguistic programming, used equipment to monitor heart rate, brain waves, body temperature and other biofeedback statistics on one of Brent's clients to document the effect of the channeled healing energy. They discovered that her energy transfer, whether next to her client or across the room, smoothed out the subject's heart rate and raised her body temperature to a normal level to counteract a thyroid issue that keeps her temperature below normal.

They also made a discovery that amazed everyone in the room. Brent had recently started experimenting with channeling and painting a disease, then channeling and painting the healing energy on top of the disease picture. The catalyst to even try such a concept came about when a medical school that researches irritable bowel syndrome commissioned Brent to paint a picture of the disease for their annual report cover. She had brought five paintings with her that day for testing. Three were of a particular disease while two were specific to illnesses of the subject being tested with the healing energy painted over them.

In a blind test, they exposed the subject to all five paintings at once and all the subject's body readings that were being monitored became erratic. When they took the paintings out of the room, the subject's readings returned to their normal level. They further discovered that when a painting of only a disease was brought into the room, the subject's readings would drop to disease level, yet return to normal when the painting was removed. When a disease painting specific to the subject's condition and including the healing energy was brought into the room, the subject's readings actually improved above normal levels. Incredibly, the testing indicated that the healing energy stayed with the painting and the presence of the artwork actually changed the body rates being monitored! Everyone involved in the research was totally blown away and expanded research studies are planned. For the latest information, check out www.paintingsthatheal.com.

We have since learned that only a handful of medical intuitives around the world, who also have an artistic sense, have discovered this potential and create healing energy paintings as well. It makes me wonder whether the creative energies of the masters throughout history are also retained in their work and whether we can absorb some of their creative powers by just frequently visiting their art in museums. I know that there was a period of time in my twenties and thirties when I was absolutely compelled to visit every art museum I possibly could anytime I found myself near one. I also know that my creative talents have evolved over time.

As I neared the Saturday of my energy session, I was completely pumped at the thought of finally getting rid of whatever it was that made my lungs weak on occasion and ready to have it blasted right out of my system. When we started our session, Brent described my lung infection/scar tissue just like the other alternative healers. She believed we should be able to get rid of it but didn't want to do an energy treatment just then because often people feel under the weather when their system is flushing out the unhealthy cells. Given we had a lot of social activities planned for the weekend we decided to make an appointment to do the work long distance the following week. Brent did run some energy through me to clear my intuitive pipes and get me ready to be more receptive. I liked that idea and hoped I would notice some results.

At our dinner party that night, we explored all sorts of interesting topics. Brent showed us the difference in our life forces by having us look into a mirror and discovering how the light in our eyes shifted depending upon what we have a passion for. Some people have a passion for living, some people only have a passion for their hobby or work. And some people have a passion for it all. I am happy to say I was the example of someone that had a vibrant life force for it all! What a lovely compliment.

That Sunday at ELN, I started the story time off with finding a shell for Brent while I was in Ponte Vedra, Florida. When she had found out I was going to be at the beach for a long weekend, she had asked me to find a seashell for her happy board, the place she focuses on when she has to tell certain clients that she can't help them and often that they are dying. I felt a great responsibility for finding the perfect shell for this board and all the shells along the beach are about the same, 1-2 inches in diameter and either an apricot, white or gray color. Once in a while you find a piece of a shell that is brightly colored, but it is only a piece. After I picked up a selection of these shells, I started laughing to myself and said I think if I just stand right here facing the ocean, the perfect shell is going to come to me. Just then I looked about four feet out and under 12 inches of water, I saw something white peeking out of the sand. I waded out and investigated, reaching my hand down into the water and hoping the inhabitant of the shell wasn't alive. I dug it up and found it to be a perfect white hermit crab shell, 5 1/2" long and about 3 1/2" in diameter – in other words, a spectacular shell! When I pulled it out of the box to present to Brent, everyone who had been to that area of Florida was simply amazed that I found it there. A fun moment and a testament to what can happen when you start having more faith in your inner wisdom :-)!

Thursday of the following week we had our appointment long distance. In preparation, I had avoided eating heavy, greasy foods or drinking alcohol for the last 24 hour period, had not eaten for an hour before our appointment time and that evening had taken a 20 minute bath in a fourth of cup of sea salt. I was totally floored when Brent informed me that the whole session would be done telepathically from her home in North Carolina to mine in Georgia. I expected that we would at least be connected via telephone, but she explained that the energy she channels has actually blown out phone lines before and that she has learned that a phone connection is not necessary or really even helpful. We had our short call at 10:45 that evening. Brent said a Christian-based prayer and assigned me a prayer to be said after we hung up.

She instructed me to go ahead and get into bed and make sure I was alone, as another individual being present would disrupt the energy flow. She always planned an hour, but indicated it could be longer depending upon what she found once she began. In her experience, some people felt a slight tingling sensation while others described it as feeling a surge or buzz all over, and at times, in particular areas of healing concentration. Still others felt nothing the entire time. Some people have noticed different colored lights appearing in their closed-eye darkness.

One individual reported her experience as "First a purple circle that sort of pulsated in and out on the left-hand side; then some yellow edges on the lower back area; later a touch of red somewhere low in the horizon of closed-eye darkness.

"Later I felt a "surge" or awareness in my pubic area; followed later by an awareness around my troubled ankle. Around 45 minutes into it I felt a surge or all over buzz."

The purple light is said to represent a spiritual connection and the yellow/green egg like figure rising from the base of your closed-eye darkness signifies the energy entering your body.

Brent cautioned that I wasn't to be disappointed or alarmed if I didn't feel anything because the energy would still be working the same either way. We made plans to touch base in the morning via email unless she found something really unusual, then she would call me yet that night. That said, she told me she would begin in five minutes and I should scamper off to bed.

I hung up the phone and raced down the hall to my bedroom. I wanted to make sure I did everything possible to follow protocol. I said my prayer, hopped into bed and lay there with a big smile on my face, anticipation dancing through my body. I wondered what kind of healing energy Brent would be sending me. She had told me that when she sees blue it represents energy cooling, calming and shielding from pain, white brings peace and comfort as it takes away pain, orange is working on your immune system, red is burning out cancer and warming cold areas as its restoring the life force, a blue-purple is pain relief for deep tissue and bone cell work, green is general healing and balance, yellow clears a foggy head, black brings a state of grace, silence and peace with God, gold is charging and restoring the energy field and purple is healing a spiritual connection.

In my mind, I was telling myself I would likely feel nothing, because that would be just my luck. But as the digital dial on my clock rolled to 11 p.m., I, in fact, started feeling a slight tingling sensation on my left leg. It seemed to slowly travel up my left side and eventually down my right side like I had an energy field pulsing on the outline of my body. It wasn't a strong feeling, but it was a definite sensation.

I lay there relatively still for that first hour, eyes wide open, intent on not missing anything that might happen; besides I was completely flummoxed at the idea this was all happening across considerable distance. I understood that Brent had clients from all over the world that did this on a regular basis, yet until you experience it, it is quite difficult to fathom it is truly possible. By midnight the novelty had worn off and, although I still felt the tingling sensation, found myself drifting off. The next time I remembered looking at the clock, it was 1 a.m. Yet surprisingly, I still felt that I was receiving the energy. The next time I looked at the clock it was 2 a.m. and then 2:20 a.m.. Although I still felt the same feeling, surely she must be done by now. Then around 3 a.m., I was totally shocked to see the hour and yet continued to feel the sensation. Was this like an aftershock effect? She couldn't still be working on me, could she? Finally I awoke at 4 a.m., and no longer felt any presence. I drifted off. When I arose mid-morning the next day, I was anxious for a debriefing.

I shot off an email to Brent right away, curious to learn what she had seen and how long she had actually focused on sending me energy. Was it really into the wee morning hours? She was exhausted and I didn't hear back from her until late afternoon. Since we are close friends and have nicknames for each other, we relate informally versus her normal client communication. This is what she wrote me:

> *I'm a little tired CB Started the energy at 11 finished about 3:30. Your solar plexus/heart area was heavy, HEAVY!!!! So were the shins of your legs............thick feeling the lungs took some serious energy on the left upper side!*
> *For the second two hours it was working on your immune system and general healing. Mostly deep inner body core organs.......some blue for pain, although not much.....................I did the hemorrhoid last.*
>
> *SO let's see what it does! Have a great weekend, and keep me apprised!*
> *HUGS and giggles! Mostly giggles!!*
> *PS My shell says hello!*

I was perplexed at the solar plexus/heart area comment. Did that mean I had physical heart ailments? And what did she mean about my shins, I hadn't been feeling any pain there since my work with Ines. Brent clarified further:

> *Yo CB,*
> *I get no heart problems other than emotional,............ if you wish, I'll look "seriously" ie dialogistically next time I'm in Atl which will be May 20 –25+*
> *At the top of the shins under the kneecaps.... ie where they connect.*

Could be sludge from feeling like your future is "dragging."

Watch your lung responses, and keep me apprised............

See you soon!!!!!
Lots of bubbles and mischief! tee hee

In a recent follow-up session, my experience was somewhat different. Again I requested a focus on my lungs and also on a new ailment, a bladder infection I had been battling for almost a month. Brent informed me that when having trouble with the bladder, you should drink 1/4 to 1/2 cup of cranberry juice each evening. While employing cranberry juice as an assist with a bladder infection was not a new concept, the direction to drink it as the last thing you do before you go to bed was a new trick to consider. That way it stays in your bladder all night and does its work.

When the session began, I felt a dramatic surge of energy in both of my hands, perceptively feeling the energy enter each of my fingertips and then travel up my arm to mid wrist. I occasionally felt a slight tingling in my toes, but barely perceptible compared to that of my hands. Oddly enough, the sensation lasted less than an hour even though Brent continued to send me energy into the early hours of the morning. I also saw a brilliant purple star flash in front of my closed-eye darkness at the very start of the session. It was so clear and beautiful, but gone in a flash. Brent later informed me that it was most likely a spiritual connection as the energy began to enter me. During this session she now found my heart charka to be totally cleared giving me a clear energy path from my crown charka to my throat charka and on to my heart charka. But once it hit my solar plexus, there was a distinct slow down. Ah, my next area of focus identified. Healing orange energy was sent to work on my immune system and a slight amount of blue energy dealing with the bladder infection. This was followed by a general dose of gold energy to rejuvenate my overall energy field.

My Belief

I do believe Brent is the real deal and that she has been given extraordinary gifts to help people find a way to heal themselves where appropriate.

I am of the belief that the increasingly difficult pulmonary issues I have experienced over the last decade and a half have been by grand design, an actual help to me along the way. They have slowed me down, made me examine my life, the stresses I have accepted and at times contributed to, the choices I have chosen and made me ponder my greater purpose. If I had continued my fast paced life without pause, I would have never taken the time to look beyond surviving and managing my day to day activity to consider life on a larger canvass.

As if to encourage me and validate that I am on the right path, my journey to wellness has helped me continually improve my condition.

I also believe my condition has served its purpose and may be released if I just find the right method to do so. My intuition tells me that Brent may help me find this final solution. I plan to continue to work with Brent and have hopes that signs of my breathing challenges will disappear altogether.

The Value

The friend who first introduced me to Brent had been dealing with chronic fatigue for over ten years. During our last conversation about her condition, she was happy to report that she had experienced a 75% improvement in her energy level by working with Brent. Another friend who has been dealing with chronic back pain from a pinched spinal nerve was astounded when she felt her bones actually shift the night of her energy session. The next morning the pinched feeling was gone and was replaced to a much lesser degree with soreness in her bone in the affected area. Unfortunately it has not become a permanent fix as yet.

Personally, I have experienced many firsts through exposure to Brent's abilities. I had the chance of a lifetime to learn what it is like for others with highly developed intuitive powers. I also had the opportunity to experience and know it to be undeniably true that someone can in fact send you energy telepathically from great distances. These were beliefs I held, but now I no longer need to believe just from a leap of faith perspective.

Since our energy session, I have perceptively felt a greater calmness over me. The emotional intensity I had felt weighing heavily over me at times seems to have dissipated. I am more comfortable accepting that I cannot completely control future events, rather just do my best to influence them and leave the rest to the Universe. It's as if my heart is not as raw and susceptible to hurt, or at least not as worried that hurt was on its way. Perhaps not the healing I initially intended, but nevertheless one of great value.

I can't say as yet that my occasional breathing difficulties have markedly improved as a result of this healing modality, but I am of the impression that Brent holds the key and plan to continue working with her for the results I clearly believe are imminent.

For those of you that suspect you might be highly sensitive to the negative energy of others, here are some tips that Brent shares on how to manage your energy:

- To filter energy coming from your computer, keep a glass of water in front of your screen. Watch how fizzy it can become, almost like an Alka Seltzer has been dropped in there. Be sure to dump the water out.

- When you keep a glass of water or bottle of water on your nightstand next to the bed you sleep in each night, any negative energy that is around you will be attracted to that water. Pour it out!! If you later drink that same water, you are absorbing negative energy.

- Two tsp. of lemon juice in your water, one in the morning and one at night, will help balance your electrolytes.

- If you are feeling stressed and can't sleep, get up and soak your feet in water. It will act like a natural tranquilizer.

- Similarly, if you have just completed meetings with people who have seemingly drained your energy, go run water over your wrists. The negative or draining energy will run out your fingers.

- The hand you write with represents the hand you receive energy with, while the opposite hand is the hand with which you send energy. This becomes key when you think about the jewelry that you wear in that silver repels energy and gold brings energy to you.

{9}

Gem and Mineral Show
Wendy and Nancy

I first heard someone talk about the vibration qualities of minerals at one of our Eclectic Ladies Network parties. Wendy, that month's hostess, started telling me that rocks were alive and that they give off vibrations. She told of a conversation she had with her friend one day, "that peeled my skin back with her expression and nearly took my head off with her tone. My friend's words were, "Are you suggesting that rocks are not sentient?" That was my initiation into the world of mineral power."

That was certainly a fascinating thought. Rocks awake? They have a conscious? When she saw that my interest antennas were clearly visible, she suggested I get with Nancy and learn more about them. Nancy is a spirited woman with a twinkle in her eye, always looking like she knows something the rest of us don't. She is well versed in the subject of gems and minerals and loves to research their history and influencing properties. One of her greatest joys is finding a unique specimen to explore and lovingly add to her ever-growing collection. In fact it is rumored that her home is a virtual mineral mecca.

As we chatted, my mind continued to mull around the idea that minerals could be more than a cold, inanimate piece of matter. Granted a look at my jewelry drawer would tell you that I was drawn to minerals, much more than gemstones, but the thought that there was anything more than an attraction to the color of lapis, turquoise, amber, red and black coral, rhodonite, etc., was a new one to ponder. Making a mental note, I planned to explore this topic further at a later date.

During the next eighteen months, the subject came up briefly a couple times in conversation, but that was about it. Then December 2003 rolled around and these same ladies mentioned that one of the bigger shows, an annual event, was going on during the coming weekend and it was only a short drive from my home. Would I like to meet them there? It seemed like the perfect time to explore what they had been talking about and I agreed to join their hunting party. My instincts told me that I should walk the show floor with Nancy and Jeanne Johnson for the maximum experience. So I quickly talked to Jeanne, my Reiki Master/Shaman friend, and she agreed to go.

When I arrived I must admit I was full of anticipation. It was at the North Atlanta Trade Center and the parking lot was packed with cars. I was hoping this would be a magical new world I was about to explore. Would I actually experience a rock communicating with me on some level? With a big smile on my face and a bit of a muffled giggle, I entered the show floor and quickly became flooded with sensory overload. So many vendors, all of them were offering tables overflowing with colored stones that sparkled and sought my attention. Where to focus, how to begin?

Like a beacon of guiding light, my eyes immediately trained on the wide brimmed hat of my friend Wendy. She is somewhat of an Atlanta icon, a networking guru of sorts, and is known by her spectacular trademark toppers. She was busy studying her latest find with her husband George, both in deep conversation over a prospective purchase. It was a green sphere of some sort, quite large by my standards for purchasing a rock, as much as four inches in diameter. This alone was an intrigue to me. I could understand buying a rock that had been fashioned into a piece of jewelry to wear, maybe even some fascinating crystal formation to display in an office as a natural sculpture, a piece of art, but a mineral sphere? What would the attraction be?

She seemed to be concentrating on something as they held the sphere and then passed it between one another for closer examination. We chatted briefly and then I decided to leave them to their transaction and start milling around the place. By this time I felt I had found my bearings and was ready to set off and investigate on my own. As I perused the tables I found myself drawn to the same type of stones: a periwinkle colored opaque stone of the chalcedony family and a reddish purple stone called charoite. I also became spellbound by a unique stone that was half dark watermelon green and half ruby red. It was a tantalizing thought to think that these two stones, so markedly different in color, actually developed side by side without human intervention.

It wasn't long before I happened upon Jeanne and we had the fun of treasure hunting together. I quickly led her to a vendor that had jewelry fashioned in the shape of one of her totem animal spirits. It wasn't the type of creature you would often find as a subject for jewelry, so I felt like I had really uncovered something special for her to consider.

We continued to wander in and out of each vendor's booth, ooohing and ahhing at items of interest. I did not have one of those handy refer-

147

ence books my friends all seemed to be carrying called *Love is in the Earth,* by Melody. It describes the major minerals, where they are found and historically what they have been used for. But with Jeanne by my side, I had something that made the experience just as interesting. When we found a pile of interesting stones, she would hold one, meditate and then tell me what it would be good for. This was especially helpful when we circled around to the pile of stones that were the green and ruby combination. She held the flat, half mooned shaped piece that we both felt was the best specimen and declared its use was to dispel illusion. Now, that sounded like a handy companion to me, and was all it took to convince me that this two inch rock was destined to make a home with me, perhaps even adorning a silver cuff bracelet someday. That gave me a smile. With such a powerful bracelet, I would be able to make like Wonder Woman and hold my bracelet up to someone and repel untrue thought. Once this transaction was complete, it seemed like the activity naturally shifted and we were drawn our separate ways, as if our purpose of walking the show floor was now complete.

What seemed like within minutes, I found myself in the company of Nancy and a few others laughing and sharing their precious finds with each other. Most were holding just small little specimens, no bigger than an inch in diameter, of bloodstone or other common stones known for their healing properties. They had all seemingly been on a mission to find particular stones and were feeling quite pleased with themselves. At this point I was feeling that perhaps I had been remiss in preparing for the show. I hadn't studied any books and didn't come prepared with a shopping list. A small panic started creeping into my psyche. Maybe I am missing the whole point of this experience. I definitely felt like conversations and events had led me there that day and I didn't want to blow it. Sensing my need to feel like I had properly participated in this pilgrimage, Nancy smiled and led me over to one of her favorite vendors and offered to find me a good piece of bloodstone. She ran her hands over the box of stones, picking them up one by one, rolling them around her fingers, then putting them down and searching some more until she found the one she was looking for.

While waiting in line with my bloodstone, I showed Nancy the periwinkle colored stone I had been eyeing all afternoon. I picked up a small piece and decided I would get that as well. The lines were moving slowly which gave us more time to eye the beautiful rectanglar pendants of the chalcedony. Periwinkle is one of my very favorite colors and my eyes seemed to fixate on one pendant in particular. Nancy picked it up and examined it closer, remarking on what a nice piece it was. When I took it in my hands, I instinctively moved to hold it up to the intense light positioned over the case. To my amazement, shapes appeared in the now translucent stone and it looked to be the sun rising over a horizon. Wow! It was like finding a hidden painting. That exciting discovery quickly turned the tables on my planned purchase as I now felt a connection with this little piece of rock that I couldn't ignore. Once the transaction was complete, we hurried out the door to our cars so we could catch up with the rest of the group who were meeting for a late afternoon lunch at a nearby restaurant.

My Fascination

When we joined the others seated around a long rectangle table, I detected a lightness and sense of play in the air. Everyone seemed positively charged with the afternoon's activities and anxious to share their interesting finds. Wendy and George were sitting at the opposite end of the table from me and recounted their conversation and decision to buy the green sphere. It was fluorite, and Wendy had felt a huge vibration when she first held it – George, too. She passed it around the table and some immediately felt it and others, like myself, felt nothing. How interesting that we should have such extreme differences in our sensory experience. Ah, but that seems to be the nature of human energy. We each resonate differently with various vibration levels. That is a point distinctly made in Melody's book.

It was also interesting to note that Wendy had found herself drawn to fluorite many times and in fact her first introduction into the world of minerals was with a small gift of a purple and clear piece from Nancy. Upon further reading, the guide book explains that fluorite is used to discourage chaotic, disruptive and disorganized growth, something that I imagine came in handy as Wendy quickly grew her business. It is also known to help relationships and groups flourish in the realm of that which is beneficial to all. Again a seemingly perfect match to someone who makes their living helping others connect in the business community.

I had a notable moment of deja vu when I glanced down at Nancy, her specs perched at the end of her nose as she studied the book and then the specimen in Wendy's hands. As they both intently considered the situation, it seemed perfectly obvious to me that these two had been experts in this field of study much longer than the both of them were likely aware of. Let's just say for a slight moment in time, I seemed to picture them in another place, doing exactly what they were doing just then and thoroughly enjoying themselves.

My Belief

I do believe we are drawn to minerals that have properties that are beneficial to us in our current state of life. The chalcedony pendant I ended up with is from South Africa and is useful for balancing the energy of the body, mind, emotions and spirit, the exact activity Ines Hoster had been working on for me. It was used as a sacred stone by the Native Americans promoting stability within the ceremonial activities of the tribes and has successfully been used to provide a pathway for receiving thought transmissions. For years now people have been telling me that my intuitive skills are evolving to a higher level. Hmm.

The green and ruby combination stone, or zoisite with corundum, is thought to be quite magical, creating altered states of consciousness that can serve as a vehicle for reaching and utilizing talents and abilities of the mind. All of the psychic abilities can be stimulated and amplified by use of these consolidated energies. In particular, corundum is known to promote insight to the unknown. It provides for a "parting of the way" for all endeavors and acts to enhance ones intuitive awareness. Sounds like a good illusion dispeller to me!!

An even more spectacular demonstration of being drawn to a mineral designed to help what ails you is what happened six months later at another Atlanta show. During this May 2004 show I was attracted to three different pieces. My first was a pair of earrings made out of a blue-green mineral called chrysocolla. When I initially attempted to look up the mineral as just a matter to entertain myself as I waited for Nancy to join me at the show, I began reading that the mineral can be used to form a bonding action between one and the object of one's desires. That sounded interesting until I read on and learned, "due to the asbestos content," and stopped right in my tracks. Earrings made of asbestos material? No thank you.

In fact I was so shocked I told the lady in the booth why I was no longer interested in the earrings. She was horrified and asked to see my book and then quickly scurried over to her husband who had made the earrings. He came back over and explained I was looking at the wrong mineral in the book. I was reading about chrysotile. When my eyes correctly focused on chrysocolla, I became really excited. One of its healing properties focuses on the heart charka. Just one week earlier I had my first experience with a medical intuitive that had spent at least two hours working on my heart chakra. Now we were cooking. My mineral connection seemed to be back on track.

The second item that caught my attention was another pendant from the chalcedony family, this one an apple green called chrysoprase. It activates, opens, and energizes the heart charka, bringing the energy necessary to the physical body, through the loving energy of the heart.

And finally, I could not seem to keep my eyes off of several strands of beadwork in lime green, turquoise and black strung by Zulu women in South Africa through an industry development program. The actual beads are from Czechoslovakia. What a cool global economic partnership, beautiful beadwork, spectacular color and design and all helping women around the world develop a livelihood.

I believe it is more than coincidence that I kept having a thing for green too. Upon further research, I've learned that green symbolizes growth, abundance, prosperity and hope and helps heal the heart charka on an emotional level and the lungs on a physical level.

The Value

I think my friend Nancy puts it best, " . . . The sense of wonder and awe I feel when we are deluged with color, excitement, and anticipation. I always feel like a little kid before Christmas or Halloween. Actually, I can't wait for our next mineral experience.

"Have you read anything about feng shui, the oriental art of creating an environment which serves the physical and emotional nurturing of its inhabitant? According to feng shui, an individual would not wish to have objects around which hold negative or unhappy memories. Every thing in a person's environment should contribute to their physical and emotional well being. To me, the crystals and minerals serve this purpose. Each and every one reminds me of friends and good times, a wish to heal or find abundance.

"Minerals, crystals, objects of art, things that remind us of friends, stories that come by e-mail affirm our decision to be on the planet."

As for me, I can't say that I actually have felt a strong vibration from any mineral I've held yet. But I can tell you that I have felt a sense of greater emotional peace when I've worn these mineral adornments. Are they helping my heart charka and lungs heal? Are they bringing me growth, abundance and prosperity? Time will tell. But bringing me hope, that is something I can answer now. Yes, definitely they have the effect of improving my outlook at getting closer to my goals. And feeling you're on the path is definitely part of actually getting where you want to go.

{10}

Our Connection With Colors
Rochele Hirsch

Rochele Hirsch is an extraordinary woman who has enjoyed a dramatic international career that includes working on multinational corporation projects in both the US and Southeast Asia. One of the reasons I initially found her so intriguing was that her undergraduate degree was in physics and her masters in industrial and systems engineering. That has typically been an unusual course of study for any woman, especially a few decades ago. But even more interesting was the later discovery that her scientific foundation is blended with a real eye for design and color as well as other unique skills and talents that truly make her a Renaissance woman.

One of Rochele's passions is working with individuals to identify a palette of colors that will resonate with their body's pigmentation. When I first heard that this was something she did for people, I felt certain I knew what that entailed and had concluded "been there, done that." In the early eighties, my sister had gifted me with a wonderful

155

color analysis session for my birthday with a highly regarded colorist in Minneapolis. I delighted in the session where the woman declared me a spring and worked with me for hours to find just the right colors that worked best with the color of my skin, eyes and hair as a reference for wardrobe selection.

During the process she had sheathed me in a white cloth and placed me in a room rich with natural light so that nothing would distract her from her mission. She went to work checking hundreds of fabric swatches to determine what would make the final cut for my personal color palette which she assembled into a convenient wallet-size case. There were blue teals, yellow greens, blue reds, peaches and burnt umber, red purples, periwinkle blues, royal blue, gray, browns, tans, sunny yellows, off white and metallic gold. It was a fun adventure of something new and I've kept the colors in mind as I've updated my wardrobe with new purchases from time to time. When I explained that I had already had my colors done years ago, Rochele cajoled me into trying her method of color analysis, promising that it would be a different experience.

As if to signal this was a day for clarity, the weather offered up a nice bright sunny day as I made my drive towards downtown Atlanta. Rochele lives in a historic part of the city in one of those 1920s bungalows adorned with intriguing antiques and a welcoming, cozy charm. She invited me in to her sun-filled kitchen and offered me a seat at the table where she had set up paint brushes, glasses of water, paper and various tubes of paint. This was a surprise to me. I hadn't gathered until this point that she would be actually painting my personal palette.

As Rochele started dabbing bits of color on her painter's palette, I shared with her the excitement I had felt over attending my first gem and mineral show and proudly displayed my periwinkle blue chalcedony pendant. I continued to gush about my discovery that rocks give off different vibrations and that people react to them differently depending upon their vibration level. She smiled and said it is the same with color. "What! Color gives off a vibration, too?" I was beginning to feel like I had been walking around with a sock over my head for all these years. How could I have missed all this information for so long?

She went on to explain that the vibration from color she was referencing was the separate frequencies based on the colors. Just as in wave theory, we know that waves which add to the harmony, rather than those that are disharmonious, help BUILD the energy, the amplitude of the waves. It creates resonance. When you are wearing colors that are "off key" – they tend to block or inhibit the natural energy of your being, causing interference, rather than building resonance.

Rochele's approach to creating your personal color palette is like applying feng shui to your body. During the color selection process, she focuses not only on your skin tone and hair and eye color, but also your iris's pattern. She also informs you of desired silhouettes and lines of becomingness to work with the colors selected for you to complement your personal energy.

Following both her extensive training and her intuitive guidance, she selects and mixes the paint to develop the exact shade and tones that resonate with you. It's a curious process to watch as she considers a color and seems almost to do a quick meditation to see if the color is right. Sometimes the result is straightforward, using one or two pigment colors. Other times it takes a number of mixings to get the right hue. A particularly entertaining point came when Rochele was considering a purple color. Both she and I have an affinity for purple and, upon my urging, she was trying to work it in to my palette. But her color guides insisted it was not part of the plan. She kept going back and querying to confirm that it in fact it was not going to make the cut and ultimately accepted their guidance as the final word on my true colors.

A large part of her process follows the teachings of Suzanne Caygill, who developed the original color system for individuals, which she describes in her book, *The Key to Color Harmony*. It was Suzanne, a noted California fashion designer and milliner, who had the revelation in 1942 that "Human beings, the highest order of nature, carry information about their personality and style in their own natural coloration -- the pigments in their skin, hair and eyes – and these colors are related to the color harmonies in nature."

Suzanne went on to develop her theory of personality and style around each season, identifying 64 different personality types across the Four Seasons. She selected names to help her clients understand their relationship to nature. For example, Spring types include Early Spring, Golden Spring, Water Lily Spring, Apple Blossom Spring, Vital Spring and many others. While two Vital Springs would have similarity in style, energy, and personality characteristics -- their colors could be very different, depending on individual pigmentation.

Rochele had been fortunate enough to attract the attention of Suzanne and become one of only 40 students she accepted and graduated from her Academy of Color. Rochele went on to explain that the less complex, 4-part color systems that I was familiar with became popular in the 1970, beginning with Carole Jackson's book called, *Color Me Beautiful*. While this system sets people on the path to understanding that colors make a difference, it falls short of the in-depth knowledge and focus provided by Suzanne's method.

Rochele's use of a modern behavioral research technique called the Rayid Iris Identification system allows her to further hone in on your personality traits. The Rayid system seems to reinforce the old saying that the eyes are the windows to the soul. The structure inherent in the iris of the eye, the small, dark dots, light streaks or rounded openings in the fibers, are used as a means to identify behavioral, communication and relationship patterns. The markings, their precise location, and variations between the left and right eye are directly correlated with different personality traits. The four main iris types have been defined as:

Jewel: People with a predominance of dot-like pigments in the iris tend to be thinkers and precise verbal communicators.

Flower: People with a predominance of curved openings in the iris tend to be emotional, feeling-oriented and spontaneously expressive.

Stream: People with a uniform fiber structure in the iris integrate life through sensory experience, communicating through touch and movement.

Shaker: Those with both jewels and flowers in the iris tend to be dynamic, progressive, even extremist in nature.

Rochele used a magnifying glass to assess my pattern as a Stream and then flipped the glass around so I could actually look closely at my own iris and see the pattern for myself. For a mate-relationship, she said I would most likely be attracted to a Shaker. She further divulged that my eyes contained the markings of the Ring of Harmony and the Ring of Purpose.

Ring of Harmony individuals have high ideals about social and environmental issues. They dislike disorder and have a deep desire to experience the world as one big happy family. They often have a loving disposition, but are quick to point out negativity.

Ring of Purpose individuals feel they have a strong sense of special purpose. Constantly searching for their mission in life, many times unclear about how to achieve their objectives, they find that through diligence and commitment they are capable of anything.

As Rochele continued to paint the squares of color, I was still mystified how they would end up on something that was a handy reference. But about halfway through our three-hour session, a little miniature paper cutter appeared that she used to methodically size down the colors into uniform 1" x 1" rectangles. She then assembles these small squares of color onto two letter-sized palettes, one for me and one for her records. In addition she created a smaller 4" x 6" purse size version for shopping excursions.

Consistent with my earlier color analysis, I was declared a Spring with an impulse for renewal, rebirth, sunshine and easiness. Every Spring person is said to have an inner light, laugh readily and are happy-go-lucky, joyous people. Having enough rest is especially important for them. Springs harmonize best with "clear colors," and use round and petal shaped lines.

I love the description from Suzanne Caygill's book, *Color: The Essence of You* about the Spring personality: *The Essence of Spring*

> "*Spring ... the world suddenly sparkles into bloom. Spring flowers hold their heads up and reach toward the sun. The quality of spring colors is bright, fresh and radiant; there are no shadows, no darkness. Their harmonies are related to the yellow of sunshine.*

> "*Acting and reacting without laborious deliberation, re-supplying the sense of rightness, brings more affirmation into their lives and those of others.*"

As promised, I was declared more than just a Spring, I was a Floral Spring–Wildflower.

The Floral Spring identifies with the field of flowers versus the icy water of an Early Spring stream, or the sun beams of the Golden Spring, or the intensity of the Vital Spring.

The Wildflower Spring is buoyant … alive … untamed … and apt to show up in unusual places.

The resultant color palette was very focused and identified seven color families that I was to apply for specific uses. (Indicates my colors).

1) Skin Tones: the most appealing color one can wear and your most versatile color. It makes the woman look more feminine and alluring. (pale peach, white birch)

2) Basics: the neutral colors in your chart which form the backdrop for the other colors and accessories in your palette. (gray-beige, thrush brown and dark teal selections)

3) Primary: the most becoming color, meaning it "becomes" part of the person. It is the most passive color making you easy to be with, and doesn't raise or lower your energy. (jade green, grass)

4) Complimentary: the skin tone intensified. Exciting, it romanticizes and intensifies one's femininity in women or masculinity in men. (coral, apricot, peach)

5) Subordinate: subdues the personality, say "I'm here to help you," the soft sell approach. (blue-green)

6) High Shade: heightens your coloring. It dramatizes and accents the personality, saying "LISTEN to me!" (flax, golden wheat)

7) Pastels: Are the lightest value of each of the colors on the palette. For most people, they should only be used for linens, lingerie, wall colorings when the stronger intensity is not appropriate. (variations on the above)

There are also areas on my color palette for metals and patterns which are demonstrated through fabric swatches.

My Fascination

While most of us are aware of our attractions to certain colors and can probably name our favorite color, our understanding of how it can affect our receptiveness with others is typically basic at best. There is virtually a whole science behind how people react to color, but rarely is it brought down to the personal level of how color will work with your own vibration level.

If one looks at color without the benefit of having your personal vibration level considered, you can still consider the effect colors may have on yourself and others.

There is actually a practice called color therapy. Steeped in ancient tradition and ceremony, it draws on the way colors affect our moods, behaviors and surroundings. It can give us insight into our individual preferences since the colors we choose or avoid can be an indication of our current state of being.

The following is from Lisa Seelandt's article, "Mind/Body Medicine: Exploring the power of your mind to heal your body Part 1." on PlanetLightworker.com.

"Color therapists believe colors can be used to rebalance the body on both a physical level and psychic level. The theory is that as light is absorbed through the skin, it works on the nervous system to change the chemical balance of the body. It also is theorized that certain colors can be used to assist the body in healing by wearing certain colors and by calling certain colors of light upon yourself in meditations. These colored light rays as visualized can be sent to different parts of your body as healing light.

"Whether you are wearing these colors or meditating upon these colors for healing purposes, practitioners believe that the healing properties occur mainly because of the vibrational qualities of the specific color.

"Red is thought to destroy bacteria and raise body temperature. Red is also thought to create warmth, hence aiding circulation and raising body temperature.

"Orange is the symbol of the feminine aspect containing the energy of creation. Orange is believed to combat depression and transmute negative into positive. It is also believed that the color orange can affect mental, emotional and physical properties.

"Yellow repairs and heals, particularly beneficial for skin problems. Yellow is believed to improve judgment and stimulates mental processing abilities.

"Green is a cool neutral color. It helps balance and restores clarity of focus. Green is useful for conditions which surface from stress and tension, such as migraine headaches.

"Blue strengthens the immune defense system as it calms the body and calms irritations and inflammations. Many healers claim that blue is the most beneficial color of all for those with pain.

"Indigo is the soothing color that plays upon the mental and emotional bodies. Indigo restores free-flow and movement making it particularly helpful for cysts and tinnitus.

"Violet is the color of spiritual energy. Notice the color of vestments worn by Priests during high holy days. Violet strengthens spiritual awareness and heightens insight."

Below are some further insights about color from the intriguing book, *The Goddess in the Office,* by Z. Budapest, published by HarperCollins Publishers (www.zbudapest.com). The book was a gift from a highly creative woman I worked with at the 1996 Olympic Games.

"Blue Green (teal) says, "Step aside, I am here, and I can handle everything." Wearing it promotes trust. It makes people believe in you. It simulates your own practicality and helps you to maintain your spiritual practices.

"Turquoise (bright greenish blue) is the color with the highest feminine vibration, the creative principle proudly stimulated. This color makes you an eternal student of life, calms you down and reduces stress. Turquoise is good for workaholics, because it helps one to keep work in perspective; it increases analytical insight and even logic!

"Royal Blue is much like dark blue in its effects, but bolder. It is a color that suggests authority coupled with generosity. Wearing royal blue, you are perceived as energetic and powerful but not forbidding. It helps you to clarify your thinking and deal with organization and structure. It is a good color for an administrator, not quite so overpowering as purple.

"Light or Sky Blue is an ethereal shade that can temper the effect of the other blues. It suggests delicacy, clarity, and precision and raises the atmosphere to a more spiritual level. Wear it when you need to feel bright and youthful but remain fully in charge. It will make people want to be helpful without encouraging them to take liberties.

"Peach is a stabilizing color. It is seen as calming and affluent. It communicates that all is well. Peach is reassuring and safe. In peach you come across as trustworthy and prosperous.

"Red will make you stand out in a crowd, express your personal power or restore your physical stamina.

"Maroon will help protect you from draining people and ward off outside stress.

"Black is the color of authority, mystery, and the clergy. When you are wearing black you are saying to the world that your opinions are definitive: you are wise, trustworthy, and spiritual. You rely not on your outside beauty but on your inner strengths.

"Dark Blue helps you protect your emotions and repel personal and sexual comments. It helps inspire respect and create a certain distance. It helps prevent fatigue on the job and helps you keep focused and relaxed. When you wear dark blue, you will feel more authoritative, your wisdom will flow and you will be more aware of yourself.

"Yellow is a manifesting color. This color is good for enhancing your communications with others. You are heard better in yellow. Depression is held at bay, and you can present your skill and ideas with more success. If you are asking for a raise, wear yellow.

"White reduces muscular tension. It is a good color to wear when you have to meditate, mediate, teach or heal somebody. It suggests focus and purity of though and action, signals positive thinking, openness to new ways, but also a willingness to get rid of nonessentials.

"Silver stimulates self-respect and invokes the spirituality of the moon. This color reduces inner fears.

"Gold stimulates prosperity consciousness. It is a color of self-reward and enhances feelings of security. It motivates you to set high goals.

"Mauve helps us trust our feelings. It stimulates intuition, calms inner confusions, reduces over activity.

"Lavender is the ultimate in relaxation colors. Wear this, and everybody around you will feel that you are calm and collected. Use this color in high-stress situations when everybody is losing his or her grip. It stimulates intellectual thought and enhances inner beauty.

"Purple is the royal color of hard work, fame and fortune. You appear regal in this color and will get more respect when wearing it. Spirituality and power are associated with this color.

"Mint Green is calming. Green is the favorite color of nature; it heals the spirit. Green stimulates orientation towards the future and frees one from the past. It is also a money color; wear green and think green and you avoid being broke.

"Apple Green is a stimulating color. You accept challenges better when wearing this green. It helps you see new opportunities and perks up your interest in the world.

"Moss Green is the most subtle and nurturing color in the green spectrum. It is peaceful but strong and helps you maintain consistent energy. It is a supportive color, although in its darker shades it can convey an understated authority. The lighter and brighter tones, such as avocado, are more assertive and cheerful.

"Primary or Grass Green stands out when you wear it in a drab office. It communicates ambition, health and vigor, independence and calm emotions.

"Brown symbolizes security and stability. It calms down excessive mental activity and puts you in touch with your body. It is a good grounding color.

"Gray neutralizes outside stress, prevents too much involvement, and communicates a self-protective image. "This is a passive and calm person" is the message of this color.

"Pink helps you relax your mind and listen to your heart.

"Orange gives you more energy, helps heal yourself from depression, recover from the flu or other illness, bring in the desired results from projects, or organize and motivate yourself."

My Belief

Whether a means for healing or influencing, I do believe color holds power for us. As with anything, the degree in which it works with or against any one individual is, well, an individual experience. I have come to understand that influences on our energy are of great significance and the more we know about what to seek and what to avoid, the greater chance we have to garner the positive outcomes we work towards.

The Value

When I do wear the colors that have been personally selected to complement me as an individual, I always end up having people comment on my appearance. Friends and family will think I've lost weight or look particularly healthy that day. Even strangers will remark about my outfit or disposition. If you are considering starving yourself on a restrictive diet or going under the knife for vanity surgery, you may just want to consider working with color first to see what kind of results you get.

Acupuncture/Chinese Herbalist
Traditional Chinese Medicine Doctor Li Hua

My good friend and a favorite colleague, Linda Rosenbaum, was the first person to introduce me to acupuncture. She had mentioned her treatments in passing when we worked at the 1996 Olympic Games together and then later shared that she and her husband had sought pain relief for their aging dog Pluto as he became challenged with arthritis.

I was intrigued by the thought of it, but not sure how appealing it would be to actually have a treatment where you voluntarily had needles stuck in various parts of your body. I wasn't specifically adverse to the needle aspect, it just sounded like a pretty bizarre experience. But I also believe there is a lot of wisdom that has developed over time in Eastern medicine that is just now slowly gaining momentum in our Western culture. At the center of the movement seems to be acupuncture and the use of Chinese herbs. Case-in-point is my friend's sister-in-law who suffered for years from what the holistic community has accepted as heavy metal poisoning. She tried numerous avenues in traditional medicine to find a way to reduce the pain she felt and rejuvenate her energy, but nothing seemed to be effective. She also investigated countless holistic treatments and finally found the answer with a Chinese herbalist in Chicago. He advised her to bath in a mud that possessed unique healing properties so her husband built a special tub for her to try this latest remedy. She was amazed as large black spots surfaced on her skin during the process and then seemingly washed away. She had finally found the right door to walk through that changed the way she felt and that allowed her to physically lead her life!

As I started down the home stretch of chronicling alternative sources of healing, I began to feel that I would be remiss if I didn't include this important modality. I emailed my friend Linda and asked if she would make an introduction for me to Dr. Li Hua, her trusted Traditional Chinese Medicine Doctor who studied and worked in a hospital in China before immigrating to the US in 1994.

I traded phone calls with Dr. Li's assistants at first and then, after a follow-up call was made to my friend, Dr. Li took time from her busy appointment schedule to call me directly and tell me that she would work with me on my chapter about acupuncture. She made a point to caution me not to expect too much from one treatment however as immediate results will be highly dependent in each individual situation.

I was so tickled to get that call because after I researched her website, I knew Dr. Li was exactly the one who I wanted to experience acupuncture with. She had suffered from asthma as a child and was cured through Traditional Chinese Medicine (TCM). This is what prompted her to become a doctor in China and made me believe she would have first- hand knowledge of the type of symptoms I was dealing with.

I was curious about her training and she shared that her education in China included extensive clinical training with senior doctors, who imparted their wisdom from years of experience with patients, and medical textbooks that instructed students on the subtle art of observation as well as provided a strong base of Western medicine knowledge. She said that most people who try TCM for the first time are surprised at how quickly their condition can improve and that the results are sustainable with no side effects. People are also surprised to find that the price for individual sessions is very reasonable and that it is affordable even when a plan requires a number of visits. It is even covered by some health insurance plans. Dr. Li was quick to point out that you don't have to be a certain age before you can benefit from the healing properties of an acupuncture session. She has successfully treated those as young as newborn infants and small children with needle-less acupuncture.

Like Western medicine, Eastern medicine knowledge is under pressure to quickly evolve to address the change in our food supply and the resulting impact it is having on our health.

One of the major differences in approach between East and West is that TCM is more intensely focused on ongoing wellness through releasing stress and balancing energies for prevention rather than waiting until a problem physically manifests and becomes a health crisis.

Dr. Li is a warm, friendly woman who immediately made me feel like I was dealing with a highly knowledgeable and diligent professional. I already had an image of her in my mind from pictures on her website from an interview done in her office by an Atlanta television news personality. Dr. Li has also been interviewed by CNN, has been published in the International Journal of Integrated Medicine and has lectured on acupuncture to students at Emory Medical School as well as a number of hospitals offering continuing education programs. While she has impressive credentials and sets a tone of seriousness by wearing doctor scrubs, what struck me most about her as a healer who quickly earns your trust was her genuine interest in me and my health situation.

Before we met, I filled out a few forms that captured basic medical history and a chart that indicated the pain level and areas on the body where I had health concerns. Never one to be bashful when it comes to leveraging an opportunity to feel better, I made sure I listed all items that were front of mind: My lung infection/scar tissue; my digestive system/bladder that had been acting up recently and alerting me that something was out of sorts; night sweats/hot flashes; a painful toe from an overzealous home pedicure and of course the ever-present hemorrhoid that won't take a hint and leave. This was all relatively low on the pain scale at that very moment, with the exception of my toe which I indicated was hurting as a 3 out of 10 with 10 being the worst. The others were cause for discomfort on a sporadic basis.

Dr. Li spent about a half hour going over my paperwork and asking more questions about my general health. She indicated that she typically requests her clients to bring a copy of their medical records with them for her review so that she can have a comprehensive understanding of their current medical condition. She noted my age and mentioned that people in middle age tend to have four areas that are most affected by the change in their body chemistry: The heart, the liver, the kidneys and mental health. She recommended I focus on taking care of my kidneys and make sure to have them along with my heart checked by my doctor on an annual basis. She said she detected weakness in my Yin energy.

TCM operates under the theory that everything in the universe can be divided into two opposite sides, Yin and Yang, that must be in balance in order to achieve good health. When they become out of balance, the physical body becomes diseased. Water is the symbol of Yin and fire is the symbol of Yang. From a Western perspective, we can think of Yin being related to the emotional and mental bodies while Yang is related to the physical bodies, both necessary to form one unit.

From my discussions with Dr. Li, I learned that Tai Chi is the symbol of the balance of Yin and Yang. The circle is divided into half white and half black. There is black in the white part and white in the black part. Chi means vital energy and life force. The flow of Chi in the body has to rely on the entire body's meridian system to flourish. If there is no Chi, there is no life. If Chi is low, we feel low energy, sluggish, listless and tired easily. If Chi is too high, we feel anxious, anxiety, nervous and restless. Acupuncture can suppress the hyperactive Yang and nourish Yin; it can also strengthen deficient Yang and remove stagnation in order to balance the whole body to obtain optimal health.

Acupuncture is only a portion of TCM. Yin and Yang, the Five Elements, Organs and Meridians, Chi and Blood – are the main theories of TCM.

The Five Elements are an interesting way to look at the connections between our organs. To the right is a simplistic view of the five elements and their relationships with each other:

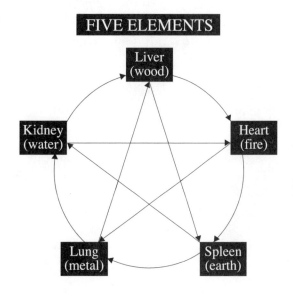

FIVE ELEMENTS

Liver (wood)

Kidney (water)

Heart (fire)

Lung (metal)

Spleen (earth)

First you view the relationship of the elements by moving clockwise along the circle. The liver, which is referred to as wood, builds the fire which is represented by the heart. The fire burns and creates ash which becomes earth or the spleen. From the earth, comes metal, or lungs. When metal is heated to a high enough temperature it becomes liquid represented by water which is the kidneys. Then you also look at the relationships between the five elements: fire causes metal to melt, wood holds the earth in place and keeps it from disappearing, water controls the size of the fire, earth controls water and metal controls wood.

When a Traditional Chinese Doctor first meets you to assess your condition, there are eight ways in which they will collect information from their observations to determine how well your organs are working synergistically as well as the healthy flow and balance of your energy. They will observe the colors of your aura, the physical condition of your body, the spirit of the person and/or energy field, the scent of the body, the physical coloration of your body (skin, eyes, etc.), your tongue, body temperature/ pulse/ circulation and what they sense overall about your wellbeing. For these reasons, it is difficult to tell a person what to expect in the way of a treatment until you have actually met face to face. It is also important that when this meeting does occur that you don't wear makeup, you don't drink caffeine, you don't wear cologne and that you don't eat any type of candy or food that will discolor your tongue. Interestingly enough, it is the tongue that gives the biggest clues as to whether your Yin and Yang are in balance.

As we talked further about concerns for people as they enter middle age, she noted that there is about a ten year difference between the peak of hormonal change in women and in men. Women generally start experiencing this change around 40 and finish around 55, while men start at around 50 and finish around 65.

During these times it is important for partners in a relationship to especially take more time to communicate, talk and pay greater attention to each other, be more caring towards one another. Work your emotions out of your body, don't hold them inside since that will be the seed for physical illness to manifest.

Addressing this life change from a medical standpoint illustrates the difference between Western and Eastern Medicine. In the West, medical attention will focus on the hormonal change and try and rebalance the hormones, a symptom, not the cause. In the East, medical attention will focus on the change in the energy of the organs and the overall flow of Chi, the root cause of the problem.

Returning to the example of hormonal changes occurring in midlife, I mentioned to Dr. Li that I had just started experiencing the dreaded hot flashes in the last few months. She explained that when a woman's hormones change, her Yin can become low. As you find yourself under stress, this burns Yin energy and takes it even lower. When the Yin is low, it is overpowered by the Yang which is fire. Thus you become overheated inside. By rebalancing the Yin and Yang, one should see this problem disappear and would not have to focus on products designed to control hormonal changes.

Another example of how the two approaches to medicine can be different was in addressing my bladder infection. I had struggled with a nasty infection over a month's time that seemed to be resistant to antibiotics. I was prescribed strong medicines such as Cipro and Penicillin, but each time I was about to finish the bottle, the symptoms would return and I would start feeling a pressure on my bladder like I was about to experience the excruciating pain and burning that can accompany such a condition. The first two times I took antibiotics and complained of recurring symptoms, tests showed that I still had traces of an infection. After the third set of antibiotics, my tests indicated the infection was gone, yet, I still felt the strange pressure on my bladder. When I explained my dilemma to Dr. Li, she said it was because I had not addressed the energy imbalance and that she felt she could help me with this too.

She was also concerned about my digestion system. We talked about diet and I confessed that I knew that I should not eat wheat or dairy products, but that I had been slipping in that area. I had experimented with the raw beet and carrot diet that my husband had found helpful to improve his reflux condition to see if it would help me, but it seemed to give me a peculiar, unpleasant feeling.

At this Dr. Li told me a story: Each person is different. In China we made experiments feeding a duck and a rabbit a mixture made of egg, cheese and butter. The rabbit got high cholesterol, the duck did not. You are like the rabbit and should not eat raw beets and carrots like your husband. A raw diet is too hard for your digestion system, which has been weakened by a lifetime of antibiotics, whereas your husband was not exposed to antibiotics early in life in Russia. Instead you should steam vegetables so that it is easier to digest.

I found it interesting that when I asked, she indicated that the Chinese do not use beets to analyze the effectiveness of your digestive system or as a healing treatment like the Russian doctors had with my husband.

She advised me to "use a warm soup or warm water to stimulate saliva and make sure to chew food well, again to stimulate saliva and aid in digestion. Don't drink iced tea or other beverages with ice, instead drink at room temperature. Ice or cold blocks saliva and makes your digestive system contract and have to work harder. For other people, the ducks, it's okay for them. Their systems can easily handle the effects of iced beverages. Also, do not take calcium tablets by themselves; they're hard on the digestive system. Instead take as a combination with magnesium and Vitamin A & D. Do not eat hot spicy food made with peppers like Mexican or Thai." At this last bit of advice I noticeably cringed, I absolutely love hot, spicy food, the type that makes my eyes water and clears my sinuses.

Dr. Li asked me whether I had difficulty sleeping at night and I was quick to report that I have always been a very light sleeper and had a hard time falling asleep at night. She said it was a problem stemming from my nervous system and from a propensity of having a low Yin energy. To improve this condition, I needed to focus on activities that will serve to calm my system towards evening and allow it to more easily enter a relaxed state. Our work to balance my energy would also support this effort.

When the topic turned to my breathing problems, Dr. Li said, "Lung is the only organ that is exposed externally. It is very susceptible to the air outside being too hot or cold or too moist or dry, just like it is internally susceptible. So, just like for your digestive system, don't drink ice cold beverages; don't drink them too hot, either.

"You have come to use your inhaler like a crutch to always open your breathing passages. Instead, in Chinese medicine, we would want you to work on strengthening your immune system with acupuncture and herbs. We would also want you to practice Tai Chi Gong, the meditation and breathing exercises to strengthen the lungs and make them strong.

"You need to focus on exercise for Yin and Yang. Yang is physical exercise or cardiovascular work. While Yin exercise is for calming the mind and emotions. Try mediation, yoga or Tai Chi Gong. Reading, painting and listening to classical music can also be effective."

My Fascination

We started our session with "cupping" after she explained that it would help open my energy flow or chi flow and I had confirmed it was okay with it leaving some bruises. Cupping is a natural therapy that is usually used in conjunction with acupuncture. Air is heated inside a cup and then it is placed on certain meridians, the fourteen major channels and/or pathways in which energy flows throughout the body, and acupoints, specific anatomical locations on the body that are believed to be therapeutically useful to treat and prevent health problems. The cup usually is made of bamboo, pottery, glass or plastic. Cupping does not break the skin or cause pain, only a feeling of suction and causes clients to have red or purple bruises the size of the cups. Typically Dr. Li uses one to ten cups during this treatment. I was instructed to remove my clothing down to my underwear and then lie on my stomach on the massage table, face down into the circular padded area designed to comfortably accommodate your face, yet allow for easy breathing.

As I lay there, it felt like Dr. Li was putting clips on my back, like the old metal clamps used in hair salons, not ones with teeth, just a tight clamp. I wouldn't say it really hurt, it just felt really strange and kind of uncomfortable, but then I got used to it as she proceeded to place seven clamps down my back along my meridians. Actually, the clamps were glass cups and the tightness felt was from the suction that the cup made when it attached to my skin. I have to admit I was laughing and commenting to myself in my mind, what have you gone and done now! I stayed that way for about 10-15 minutes. Dr. Li had very peaceful music playing with lutes and a lot of beautiful bird sounds.

When she returned she removed the cups and then massaged each area briefly as she took each cup off. When she was done, I felt a high-ly exhilarating whooshing throughout my body. I kept visualizing a scene where all of a sudden gigantic, wonderful high speed waves had appeared in the ocean and it was time to grab my surf board and catch a ride. Everything seemed to be surging through me in a great big pow-erful and very positive rush and I kept hearing myself silently exclaim-ing, "Wow, this is awesome, Wow!"

Next she had me flip over on my back and then adjusted the pillow up high saying she always liked it that way when she had a lung prob-lem. She proceeded to place the acupuncture needles in me starting with my forehead. First she would wipe the area with alcohol, lightly tap around with her fingers to locate the acupoint and then you would feel a slight prick as she inserted the first needle.

Then she moved to either side of my sinuses and inserted a needle. She made a slight joke that I looked like I had cat whiskers and that was a good image to keep in my mind as I now had three needles sticking out of my face. Next, she moved down to my chest to the end of my breast bone or my heart chakra area, inserted one there, and then further down by each kidney and one in my bladder area. She went back up to each hand, then down to my legs where she put one in each calf and then two on each foot. I ended up with fifteen needles in all as com-pared to the average range of three to twenty needles.

She covered me with a sheet and told me to close my eyes and think only about healing, to forget about writing for now. Dr. Li left me to fall in a relaxation state which I did, even though I had all these needles sticking out of me. I didn't actually feel them for most of the hour I was laying there. But after about 45 minutes, I started feeling a prickling on top of my head, then the sensation moved down to the one in my right sinus, next it went to the one in my right hand, following with the one in my right kidney, my bladder and finally my right calf then right foot. The best way to describe it is to visualize a little tiny gnome slalom skiing down my right side, slightly hitting each of the needles as he went so that they slightly vibrated from the contact. When I remarked about this later, Dr. Li said I started feeling the sensation when my energy became unblocked and was flowing freely. She didn't believe my energy had been blocked on my left side and thought my right side may have been blocked due to overuse since I was right-handed and tended to relentlessly immerse myself in writing projects. She likened it to my body going on strike until such time I gave it the attention it needed. Sometimes it takes several sessions before a person would feel this type of release experience.

When I returned home, my husband noticed I had strange circles, 3" in diameter on my back, seven in all. My sister remarked that they looked like some kind of alien markings. It may have looked strange at that point, but I didn't care. The sensation I had felt was a wonderful rush and the whole process put me in to a relaxation state that I hadn't been in for as long as I could remember. Dr. Li said she thought I would sleep well tonight too.

My Belief

Medicine in the West is left brain-focused, applying logic and hard analysis which is biased towards the science of healing. Medicine in the East is right brain-focused, observing and sensing subtleties in physical conditions and energy flows that is biased towards the art of healing. Together, integrating the two approaches, I believe we can achieve a complimentary medicine platform that gives us whole-brain medicine that balances the art and science of healing for more effective, overall results.

I believe sometimes it will be more effective to use one type of medicine over the other and sometimes a combination of both methods. Bell's Palsy, a condition where the facial muscles become weaken or paralyzed, is an example of a disorder that is most effectively treated by Eastern Medicine. It's caused by trauma to the 7th cranial nerve, and the onset is quite sudden where you can wake up with the problem or have it occur within a day of first feeling the symptoms. Utilizing acupuncture, 90% of the individuals with the affliction can realize results the first day of treatment. Shingles is another ailment that can be effectively treated with Chinese herbs to clear the virus and eliminate the pain.

A combination of acupuncture and Chinese herbs has been successful in treating ailments that have not been addressable with Western Medicine including open wounds that resist healing, removal of dead tissue and regenerating new tissue in extremities to prevent the need for amputation, removal of paralysis of unknown sources and detoxifications. An example of the two approaches of medicine working well together to provide a more effective treatment plan would be in the case of cancer patients going through chemotherapy. Western medicine will attack the disease and Eastern medicine can help boost the immune system, balance the energy and relieve the pain to help the individual make it through the treatment process. Another example is in the case of infertility where an individual seeks in vitro fertilization. As a standalone procedure, it is estimated to have a success rate of around 20-25%. When it is accompanied with acupuncture the success rate rises to 40-45% and when Chinese herbs are also part of the treatment plan, the success rate can rise to as much as 80%.

When time is on your side, I believe the wise move is to check with both types of approaches to medicine, review the logic and success rates behind the treatments and then, where it makes sense, first try the least invasive method with the least likelihood to cause harm or side effects in other parts of your body.

The Value

I am pleased to report that I experienced the deepest sleep I can ever recall having that night. The pain in my toe also subsided that night and was gone the next day, followed by a quick healing of the affected area.

That evening I experienced a sneezing fit where I had a series of about a dozen sneezes in a row that literally shook my whole body. I have had these occasionally throughout my life, but had not experienced one for over a year. Dr. Li suggested that it may have been caused by opening up the circulation in my nose and causing the sleeping guards residing there to wake up and expel the toxins. I also noticed a sudden appearance of a considerable amount of mucous in my stool the next morning, but then it was gone and when I inquired she suggested this could also be the result of eliminating toxins from the session as well.

It has been three weeks since my initial cupping and acupuncture treatment and I have not experienced a hot flash or night sweats during that time. The pressure on my bladder has only appeared once and only very slightly. All in all, quite an impressive run, from just one relatively short session.

{12}

Reflexologist

*Ko Tan, Nationally Certified Reflexologist,
NCBTMB, Certified Massage Therapist and
Instructor/Educator*

Just when you think you have learned everything you need to know about different energy modalities, you have an experience that helps you understand there is still a wealth of information out there to explore that you have yet to even touch on.

I had been chasing Ko Tan around Atlanta for a few months before I pinned down a time when I could meet with him to learn about reflexology and experience a session. He is a very gracious man and had agreed to work with me when we first chatted, but he often finds himself on the road teaching reflexology workshops across the country and our schedules made us continue to miss each other.

Reflexology is the science and healing art of applying touch to the pressure maps that are connected to other parts of the body. The reflexology body maps are found on the feet, hands and outer ears. I knew I had to include reflexology in my journey because my mother has had such great results from her experiences. My mom suffers from post-polio syndrome and has sought relief from various alternative therapies over the years for her overtaxed muscles which have been called upon to perform functions they were not originally designed to handle.

Mother's neighborhood friend Winky had researched and then introduced her to the world of reflexology. There are not a lot of practitioners up in North Dakota, so they would journey over an hour to Ada, Minnesota when they wanted a session. The reflexologist would methodically work on her feet which helped loosen up the tension in her neck and shoulders and ultimately restore her physical balance.

While Mother would not have any reactions to the session until the next day, she would always laugh at Winky who would fall asleep in the car on the way home. Mother's reactions were not severe; rather they just felt like she had experienced a deep tissue massage or chiropractic treatment that had given her muscles a real workout. But she always cautions that everyone reacts differently. When Mother first persuaded her friend Lucille to try out reflexology, she called my Mom up the next day and read her the royal riot act. Her legs were giving her all sorts of pain which she hadn't had before she had gone for a session. Mom smiled and told her, "Well that is because you haven't had the circulation going in your legs for some time. Give it a few days and see how it feels then." And so it was good. Lucille became a convert and booked a number of subsequent sessions.

When I entered The Harmony Learning Center in Atlanta for my appointment, I was truly surprised that I significantly sensed I had entered a different space. While most healers try to operate in a calm and relaxed environment, often employing feng shui to help them create this feeling, Ko Tan's success in creating a sense of peace seemed to far exceed every place else I had been. Yet it was a simply decorated room located in the lower level of a professional building. The small window had the blinds closed with barely any light seeping in. Most of the room was lit through a single sconce on the wall situated between two wall hangings, one of Koi and one with dragons. On the opposite wall were a couple of charts explaining the relationship between the reflex points and the rest of your body. There were a few bamboo plants in the corner and a few neatly arranged shelves mostly covered by decorative screens. The massage table in the center of the room was comfortably padded and had dark blue sheets and a lavender blanket with a pillow positioned to support the body under the knees and one for under the head.

I soon learned that Ko Tan might have an edge when it comes to applying feng shui. He has his masters degree in architectural design and practiced as an architect for six years before he was persuaded to become a full time instructor for the L.A.-based American Academy of Reflexology. While at first this may seem like a wild leap off a chosen path, with further discussion it seems the study of architecture was more the diversion from the planned journey. From the time Ko Tan was a very small boy in Malaysia, he was totally fascinated with the art of healing. His favorite pastime was to watch the local pharmacist prepare his magical concoctions. The kindly man was amused by this curious boy and would take the time to appease Ko Tan's inquisitive mind with answers to his questions, "Can you put this medicine with that one? Can you ground that into powder?" or whatever else popped into his head as a mystery begging to be solved.

When he left home to study architecture in the US, Ko Tan did not totally leave his passion for healing behind. During his six years of architectural studies, he also took massage classes. Then with just a year left of school, he traveled home to see his mother, who had become gravely ill. She had been bedridden for three years and the family was highly distressed that they were unable to relieve her excruciating pain through traditional medicine. They had tried everything offered to them, but nothing gave their beloved mother relief. A friend of Ko Tan's family had heard about a local man that was able to relieve pain with just the use of his hands and having exhausted every other avenue available to them, it didn't take a lot of convincing for the family to decide to give it a try.

When they arrived, they were shocked to see the long line of people lined up at the gate waiting their turn for the 30-45 minute healing session. The line parted as the family carried their mother through the crowd, everyone willingly allowing her to move to the head of the line in hopes of receiving some relief. She was very frail and the Healer was only able to work on her for 5 minutes, but in those 5 minutes he was able to do what others could not. Her pain was totally erased. Ko Tan spent the last two weeks of his mother's life at her bedside, finding her continued absence of any type of pain from just that one brief session to be a deeply profound experience.

When he returned to L.A., he decided to enroll in the professional reflexology program at the American Academy of Reflexology. Upon completing his masters degree in architecture, he proceeded to work as an architect and went on to study Traditional Chinese Medicine at the Samra University of Oriental Medicine. Later, he was persuaded to begin teaching reflexology for the American Academy of Reflexology and finally things "fell into place" as he became a full time reflexologist, massage therapist and an instructor.

Ko Tan has been a teacher of Traditional Chinese Medicine Theory since 1995. He was one of the few practitioners of the US invited to the

International Chinese Medicine Symposium in Shanghai, China, in 1994. As a champion for the continued growth and broadening acceptance of reflexology, he participated in the first US study conducted on the positive effects reflexology has on PMS symptoms, which was published in the Obstetric & Gynecology Medical Journal, December 1993. In 1998, he co-founded the Georgia Reflexology Organization (GRO) and has been the president since. In the same year he was elected to be a board director for both the American Reflexology Certification Board (ARCB) and the International Council of Reflexologists (ICR).

Reflexology has its roots in ancient healing practices from Asia, Africa and the Middle East and is considered a way to reduce stress through a process that releases tension and toxins and restores balance to the body. As a healing art practiced in the US today, it is based on the work of two American physicians, Dr. William Fitzgerald and Dr. Joe Shelby Riley, in the 1920s. Foot and hand reflexology is based on the premise that there are ten zones of communication passing vertically through the body from the head to the fingertips and toes. Along these zones there are also reflex areas in the feet and hands which correspond to all body parts. When you stop to think about it, the connection seems logical when you think that we all start from a single cell that multiplies and takes shape as the human form. Reflexology is also based on a number of other theories including the fourteen meridians and the twenty-eight pressure points in the feet and hands discovered by the Chinese and the thousands of nerve endings found in the feet and hands that can reveal body imbalances through the discernable blockages around those nerve endings. The physical act of applying specific pressures using thumb, finger and hand techniques to these reflex points, works to help restore normal functioning to organs and glands, improve nerve function and the flow of blood, and bring about a state of relaxation.

In 1957, the first ear reflexology map that corresponds to the shape of the human body was discovered in France by Dr. Paul Nogier. Later the Chinese verified this map and came up with another Chinese ear map. Then in the early 1980's, Bill Flocco developed the "Flocco Method-Integrating Foot, Hand & Ear Reflexology" in the US. It is the first reflexology program of its kind and Bill teaches it throughout the world.

There is an extensive scientific basis for reflexology as well. Ko Tan explains: "In the 1890's knighted research scientist, Dr. Henry Head, proved the neurological relationship that exists between the skin and the internal organs. Nobel prize winner, Sir Charles Sherrington proved that the whole nervous system and body adjusts to a stimulus when it is applied to any part of the body. In Germany, Dr. Alfons Cornelius observed pressure to certain spots triggered muscle contractions, changes in blood pressure, variation in warmth and moisture in the body as well as directly affecting the "psychic processes" or mental state of the patient.

"Currently research studies to further validate reflexology are being conducted in many countries including Switzerland, Denmark, USA and Australia. In Japan and Denmark reflexology has been incorporated into the employee health programs of several large corporations saving each company thousands of dollars annually. Over 300 reflexology research studies on over 150 health challenges have been conducted around the world."

Ko Tan practices the Flocco Method. He explained that reflexology therapies utilizing just the feet or the hands and feet are very effective, but by working with all three of the major reflex points areas (on all the hands, ears and feet) you will have the best results. While each area is connected to all parts of your body, they have an area where they are particularly effective in relaxing and creating balance during a session.

For the hands, it is the sinuses, headaches and digestive problems. For the ears, it is neck and shoulder stress as well as lower back pain. For the feet, it is internal balances such as liver blockages, assimilation of nutrients, coordination and cooperation between the internal organs, gland imbalances, sugar imbalances, etc. All three of the areas are considered equally effective in addressing pain. As the reflexologist touches each of these areas, he can tell what is going on in the body by the visual and tactile changes of the hands, feet and ears. As they change, the practitioner can tell when to move to the next area. Reflexology is not considered a massage; rather it is a reflex modality.

My Fascination

Before we began our session, Ko Tan had me fill out a brief form where I provided my contact information and answered a few questions about what health conditions were bothering me, what type of major surgeries and/or medical traumas I had been through, current medications being taken and the reason for my visit.

He then escorted me into the room where we were to have the session and instructed me to remove my rings, earrings and eyeglasses, shoes and socks and then lay down on my back. Ko Tan put on music and to my surprise it was not the expected Asian music or classical, rather a woman singing more traditional sounding folk songs. When I later commented on the music, he says he selects different types of music depending upon his clients.

He began by lifting my right hand up and putting his fingers through mine, gently rotating my hand on my wrist. With his other hand, he began applying pressure to my thumb, then other fingers, palm and top of my hand. I could feel my sinuses slowly began to clear. When he was through, he laid my arm back down by my side and slightly tugged on my hand with one of his as he put slight pressure on my upper arm with his other hand. It was at about this point that I remembered to mention that a mysterious pain had developed over the last month in my upper right shoulder, like something was about to erupt, yet there was no sign of anything surfacing on the skin surface. He suggested that it was likely a concentration of toxins that need to drain out of system and that he would be working on unblocking my lymphatic system in general to help aid in the release of body toxin buildup.

Next he moved behind my head and began gently touching the upper parts of both ears. I was surprised at how soothing it felt and was thinking I should learn how to do this magic. Later he moved down to the base of my ear lobes and applied pressure to them. He asked if I felt stress in my neck and upper back and I said I hadn't noticed any. It was during this part of the session that I started seeing purple energy blobs appear in my closed-eye darkness. I am always entertained when something like this happens, but this was even more unusual than what I had experienced before. Typically I would see little purple blobs changing shapes and coming towards me indicating little spirit guides coming to aid in the healing process. But this time, the purple blobs were big and coming from behind my eyes and then disappearing into a yellow blob of energy.

I mentioned this to Ko Tan and he indicated that it was a good sign, I could be releasing something I had been holding on to. Later as we talked more about reflexology, Ko Tan explained that at the heart of the practice is the intent to release and balance so the body can help heal itself, and that was exactly what was happening to me.

When he moved to my left hand and repeated the same routine as followed on the right, something unusual happened when he was finished. I was still feeling the pressure of his hand on my upper arm, yet I could see him through my half closed eyes as clearly at the opposite end of the table at the base of my feet, out of reach of my arm. When I asked him about this after the session, he told me that it is important to keep a physical or energy contact throughout the session to keep everything flowing as he worked inside my energy field. When he had physically released his hand from my upper arm, he consciously kept his energy presence there as to not break the connection while he walked to the end of the table to began working on my feet.

By this time I was in a full state of relaxation with my eyes fully closed, a stillness that does not come quickly or easily to me without being asleep. As I was lying there, I started to feel a prickly, tingling sensation in my head, and when asked what part of my body Ko Tan was working on, he confirmed he had in fact just completed working on the reflex points between my head and right shoulder.

That night I felt a strong tiredness across my shoulders and upper back, like I had over exercised those muscles, yet amazingly the only physical movement I had was a light touch and slight pressure on my hands, ears and feet. By morning, most of the tired muscle feeling was gone. I also had slept very, very deeply. So much so, that I was told I had made an incredible snoring noise that night like a Mack truck was making its way through the bedroom. Thankfully that is not my typical nightly routine, yet it evidences the deep relaxation that ensued post session.

My Belief

I definitely felt like there was a shift in my body as a result of the session evidenced by the workout felt by my neck and shoulder, the clearing of my sinuses and the deep sleep I had experienced that night.

Through my journey, I have also come to value the appearance of the purple energies that appear in my closed-eye darkness. The fact that they were moving out and away from me further validates the releasing and balancing effect of reflexology on me.

The Value

I have a new-found respect for my hands, feet and ears and the connection they have with the rest of my body. It makes one think about the wisdom in taking the time and giving the attention needed to better care for these areas.

I would like to learn more about this modality and how I can apply some of the theories to help myself relax and keep in balance. I am especially intrigued by the effects of touching the ear points and that might very well be the result of that reflex point being the preferred contact point for relieving tightness in the neck and shoulders, the point where I hold a lot of my stress. Ko Tan offers a 28 hour course for those who want to learn how to apply reflexology for self care and I am putting that on my list of things to do. Those interested in pursuing reflexology as a career should anticipate 200 hours of study to become a practitioner.

{13}

Sounds and Vibrations
Spiritual Songs

The healing power inherent in sound is not something we seem to focus on as a society, yet the results can be quite remarkable. Something as simple as listening to classical music has been known to have healing qualities beyond basic relaxation and relieving stress. In fact a French Doctor named Alfred Tomatis developed an electronic ear where he takes classical music and enhances the higher frequencies to promote the healing properties. When listened to via headphones for several hours a day, people have been known to improve their hearing, reduce or eliminate tinnitus and boost their energy levels.

I found that the world of sound therapy offers a broad range of possibilities and am certain that my explorations have only merely scratched the surface.

A Journey Through Music

For several years I had been hearing about the wonderful sound chair at The Dallas Center. The raves were so passionate, I knew I had to make it a stop on my healing journey at some point. I also find Carol Dallas to be a fascinating person to talk to so I felt certain that a sound therapy session with her would no doubt be memorable and most probable give me a valuable part of my healing puzzle.

Carol has her masters in music and has been in an innovative counseling practice with her husband and practice partner, Robert Dallas, for 15 years. Carol specializes in brain balance and integration help for children and teenagers with a special focus on intuitive teens. I met Carol back in 2002 when we first started ELN. She is a friend of Cathy Horvath, who had invited her to attend one of our parties. Carol came and we were delighted to have her company. Unfortunately she packs a very full schedule, including church organist, so our weekend soirees do not fit in her calendar on a regular basis. I did manage to snag a lunch with Carol though which gave me a taste of the type of stimulating conversation you can have with this deep and introspective woman.

True to form, I had a hard time catching up with her once I had made a mental commitment to experience sound therapy. But I felt certain she was meant to be part of the journey and continued my faith that all things that were meant to be would happen. And so it was mid-afternoon on a day in early October that our schedules finally clicked and I was ready to have my sound experience.

When I arrived at The Dallas Center, I found a lovely scent filling the air. Not a heavy perfume-filled one, but something warm and inviting, that made you think of a cozy, comforting home. Carol called down to me when she heard me rustling around in the main floor waiting room and told me to come on upstairs. Her office is sunny and painted with a warm, light brown tone called water chestnut. They had just moved into this office a month before and through Carol's sense of design, it had already taken on a calming and relaxing energy. I remarked about the striking array of antique ceramic pots lined up on the window sill of her office, all different shapes and textures, one a dark green, the next a light green, then a blue and a yellow. It looked so perfect, like a picture out of a magazine. She was pleased I noticed. They were pots that she had collected over the years and now had found a perfect place of daily prominence in her work space.

I took a chair in front of Carol's desk and we began chatting about how physical ailments have a spiritual source. Carol explained that the root or problem will always grow, even if you manage to lop off some of the branches with some sort of healing modality. She is a firm believer that for 99 % of our health issues, we need to participate in it in some way or another to try and reach a place within so that they can really effect long lasting change.

We talked about the physical conditions I was hoping to address. Of course there was always the lung infection, the hemorrhoid and more recently the sporadic feeling of pressure on my bladder. Carol commiserated about the hemorrhoid and said her mother had always said that "it is a major thing in a minor place".

We reviewed what I thought the issues were that I was dealing with presently that may be part of the root cause of my ailments. We also supported each other's notion that for effective healing, you need to look introspectively as well as go through the modality. By looking for deeper issues that need to be addressed, you can avoid having the same problem physically manifesting someplace else if you manage to address the physical problem that has currently surfaced. We also agreed that stress is at the bottom of most health problems since it suppresses the immune system and makes you extremely vulnerable to whatever potential physical problem is hanging out there ready to attack.

I reviewed my healing journey to date in abbreviated form and shared that the cross validation I had experienced between modalities has led me to a point where I feel confident in knowing what is likely going on in my body.

Carol inquired, "If you would walk out of here today with one thing in your life put back together, what would it be?" My answer was quick, "Get rid of that hemorrhoid! I don't want to end up having surgery over it."

Carol further shared that she grew up in a family that made her feel the need to be constantly on guard, and when things went wrong, she was thought to be at fault most of the time. Her whole childhood was spent striving not to make a mistake.

CD: If you missed sweeping the floor in this corner and left some crap on the floor, it was on the same level as killing someone. There was no scale of worse or not so bad. It was all the same which makes one operate constantly in a state of hyper-vigilance and put enormous criticism upon oneself. It causes a sort of free floating anxiety, if it hasn't gone wrong yet, it will. And what can I attach it to? My state of health is a wonderful thing to worry about. These attitudes, thoughts and feelings are pervasive in the cells of our body. The cells of our body are always listening and reacting. Vibration is an important part of this process as everything in the body is vibration, to me it is like one big tapestry.

ME: Carol, can you see it, what is going on in your client's bodies?

CD: Not instantaneously for the most part. It depends largely on their state of mind and my state of mine. But the answer is yes, but not immediately and not necessarily right now. I do not consider myself a medical intuitive, but part of it is visual, since I am a visual learner. And then there is an energetic sense of it. I ask to be shown in my body where the person is experiencing their problem. I will always say if the person is in tremendous pain, I don't want that because it will be too distracting. But show me where it is, I usually will start getting something then. I am feeling right now, on your behalf, your left lung. Then it is going on up on the left side of the body.

ME: Do you believe the cells think on their own like an independent processor or does all the processing take place in the brain?

CD: Each cell is a universe onto itself. It contains all the subtle bodies-emotional, spiritual, physical and mental, and the bodies of the chakras.

The cells have some commonality since it has to know and have an understanding of the whole body, but also they have their own uniqueness. How it manifests, how it fits in, like knowing it is an ear cell, so it doesn't show up like a fingernail.

Our physical conditions are symbolic representation of an emotion, or thought process. The body in its complexity answers or is the spokesperson for a lot of different systems that are going on inside us.

Why does yours manifest as an infection that stays in the lung and does not manifest someplace itself? People may try and answer that question with a book. But my advice is to beware of labels, especially in the alternative fields. New Agers are prone to applying labels. We can't fit into a box, no more that you can interpret dreams from a book. We are too complex of beings.

Your lung is continuing to speak to me on your behalf.

ME: Is there a standard vibrational level for everyone?

CD: Everything vibrates as one thing in the spiritual realms. I believe when scientists get their microscopes small enough, they will be able to break through to that level, to that place and see where everything is one thing. I call it the godiment, or god element, the static level where everything looks the same. Then everything starts vibrating and rises above the static.

When we are talking about vibration, one of the things we are talking about is leaving the static spiritual world and coming through the veil into the world of flesh. This is when we have come into a world of duality. God, whoever that is, has cre-ated two poles of extreme in the flesh world, black and white, hot and cold, masculine and feminine, yin and yang, etc.

As a being of flesh you move between each pole as you put your life into what you want it to be, to create your grays and your colors.

Even in the spiritual realm we were starting to gather at the two poles, some a little more optimistic, some a little more pessimistic, some more feminine, some more masculine, a little more to left, or a little more to the right, every individual has a different mix of the two poles. Each coming into the flesh world with a piece of the puzzle of reality.

Everything in us is vibrating. The vibration starts with sound, then it turns into color and finally physical matter.

Emotion is how we understand the planet, because the emotional body vibrates things sympathetically with everything around us. Vibrating to the color of the walls and sending it into the brain and then things start to happen in the brain we see it as a certain color. Back in the 60's and 70's, a woman taught blind people to repair telephone wires based on the vibration of the color of the telephone line; they could feel the differences in the color of the wire.

Each of our physical, mental, emotional and spiritual bodies vibrate at a different level, like a different note within a single chord, yet part and parcel of the same body.

My Fascination

I took my place in the sound chair, which looked just like a regular black leather recliner, and Carol began the music.

CD: What sound is used for here is to relax you. Relaxation is a complex thing which goes all the way from sitting by the pool with the margarita in the hand up to giving the brain and body what they want in ways of opening up and connecting with each other.

The latter is what you need to really relax and get your-self out of that state of beta where you spend all your time paying attention to the outside world. The music lets yourself began relaxing inward so you have more contact with your inner self and can start an exploration that goes down deep.

This particular sound chair was created by Barry Oser, a nationally award-winning concert pianist and composer, and his partner, Dr. Larry Schultz. The chair is outfitted with transducers that turns sound into a vibration so you can feel it through your skin and deep down into the bones. The sound will actually hit you in the different chakras, it is all very coherent. It plays through an eight-channel sound system and fills you with deep relaxation and allows you to be mentally quiet.

Now the chair has other components. You can lean all the way back, you won't slip out, but it elevates your legs above your head. It can also rotate you slowly in an orbital motion. But I can tell by your face and your energy that you find this alarming so we aren't going to do this today.

ME: I'd like to experience that part as well, but I get motion sickness.

CD: Working with motion sickness is another thing, we can work on that another time if you want.

ME: I really like this chair! Now I know what everyone is talking about. This is just really cool. How did you decide what music to play?

CD: I did some intuitive checking on you with muscle testing to decide what music I should select as I put you in the chair. I had another piece picked out to start, but when you got in the chair, something in my head said, oh, you better check that. I ended up selecting el-Hadra The Mystik Dance *(Aquarius International Music).*

All healing really starts with you becoming cohesive in yourself –going to a place where you can contact your body, your higher self, and the cells of your body. The cells of your body and everything else going around in there stand ready to work on your behalf.

The overriding intelligence of it all is sort of a combination of your mind and your higher self, or what we might call the higher mind. When you come into contact with this part of you, you can start floating through your body and talk to any part you want. When you start doing things like this, your body becomes more your friend then your enemy.

This will work better if we can both get into a state, part of this is to help me get into your energy field and see where we want to explore. Let's begin by working you into a slightly deeper state. Close your eyes, be with your breathing for a minute. You don't have to change it, pay attention to the rise and fall of the breath in the body. Add the color of sunlight to the breath so as you breathe, the chest and the lungs are filled with the color of sunlight. Fill it with sunlight and then as you exhale send the color of sunlight all over your body. Don't push it, just let it go where it wants to go.

Put your attention on your hands, filling your hands with light, filling your hands with the breath down into your hands and fingers. Put your awareness on one hand and let yourself be at peace with that one hand. Let that hand be like a pool that you can fill with water, cool or warm, whatever you need. Every time you exhale fill the pool with water, and with your next breath, as you exhale, pick up the water and pour it into the other hand. Now began the process of paying attention to the other hand. Fill it with breath to fill it with water and then began sending the water from one hand to another, however you want to do it, letting it be in the flow of the breath.

Then settle into both hands and then relax. Then very gently open the chakras on the palms of the hands and the pads of the fingers and let the hands feel so soft that they seem to disappear and are no longer part of your body. Return your breathing to your heart and chest, send your attention to the place in the lung, that area of the body that bothers you, just let your attention be over there. Let yourself know that you are here for exploration and particularly for listening. Inform that part of your body that it has your permission to speak, perhaps call to mind the visual of the Buddha speaking to the one who sits at his feet in the temple. Please speak of yourself and then just let it go, keeping your attention on that side of the body but not forcing it to do anything, seeing what comes up, feelings, vibration or anything at all....do you notice anything in that left side of the body?

ME: Well one thing that is interesting is when you were doing the pools of water visualization; I kept seeing a white orchid with red on it, when you mentioned Buddha, the orchid turned into a white lotus flower with red on the tips of the pointed petals. Also my palms and fingers are definitely humming.

CD: Now let's teach you the use of your healing hands. Think about the area there on the left, ask for the color of it at this point. You don't have to have a real clear visual. See if you have a sense of color.

ME: Yes there is a little line that goes across my left lung that is black, not as big as it used to be.

CD: Touch that side of your body with your hand, left or right, whatever seems natural. And see what color is associated with the healing energy.

ME: I already have a suggestion in my head, I have been told that I have blue violet healing energy. I can really feel the heat.

CD: You are using the intelligence of your own body to work on it. The black line is probably symbolic, it is interpreted to you as a black line that has meaning for you somewhere.

Think of your blue hand as the hand of the goddess, laying on your body and that the blue charges the vibration coming out of the hands and just let it go down into the body. Visualize your body becoming very loose and very pliable there, the cells of the skin and then the muscle, and the bones of the ribs absorbing this healing energy of the hand, sending it further and further down into the lung itself.

And the very cells of the lung, taking this blue energy and utilizing it for whatever they need to become strong and healthy and capable of throwing off anything that is not of benefit.

Know that the blue energy is sort of a medium through which the mind flows sending its wisdom and its power into that section of the body. You can do several things now, you can visualize the lung taking the healing energy and utilizing it for its own purposes.

ME: *I feel a very strong heat in my lung from my hand, I felt like the line dissolved almost like a circle and got smaller and smaller until it is barely there.*

CD: *Oh, excellent.*

ME: *But my mind is interfering. At least that is what I feel is going on, but my mind keeps questioning how can it go that quick, yet that is how I feel. That is how I sense, but my mind is battling that, saying it's crazy.*

CD: *You are just moving into a more complex way of dealing with life than perhaps you have before. On the surface a simpler thing is to go someplace and they give you an antibiotic. But when you start dealing with the profundities of life, that is when you start using your own power for whatever purpose you want to use it for. When we speak to the body or the body speaks to the brain and the brain speaks to the mind, whoever is talking to who, whatever is going on in there in reality comes into a place in the mind where we can interpret it in a way to make sense. If you are seeing a line dissolve and it becomes smaller, first of all just trust that there is something beneficial going on in there and that you are understanding it in a way that makes sense to you whatever the reality may be. Some of these things are coded into symbols, symbols of color, symbols of sound or symbols of feeling in the body.*

Now, you can stay with that, or you can say bless your body and then let your hand go back and rest. If it feels good, you can keep it there.

ME: It felt good, but I feel like it has done what it needs to do. I still feel the heat over here though.

CD: This is one of the things you can do to help yourself with it. The more you do it, the more you program what is going on in there. Now I am going to do a little exploration here.

ME: I want one of these chairs too!

CD: The lung is speaking to me of fear, insecurities, self-doubt, and of a decision made early in life. Go back with me to the Boboli Gardens. Where were you in your life, and what were you up to?

ME: I was working for Nortel Networks, and I was an operations auditor. I was working on a project over in Europe, and I was vacationing afterwards after the project.

CD: What was happening in your personal life?

ME: Not much, I was spending all my time traveling.

CD: The word religion is coming up, religious or spiritual beliefs?

ME: It wasn't a focus at the time.

CD: Talk a little bit about receiving, allowing yourself at the stage in life to receive, whatever you needed from life, to allow yourself to have love.

ME: This doesn't connect with me.

CD: Was life happy then, were you content?

ME: No, I was not content. But I also had extreme highs with the extreme lows I had to deal with.

CD: Was there within you someplace a sorrow?

ME: Maybe, probably from someone who I had a relationship with in college, not as deep as I wanted. It's hard for me to find someone that is a good match for me intellectually, physically and emotionally.

CD: Whatever got into your lung at that time got there because there was a place of vulnerability and life not working out in some way.

ME: Maybe because I was working in finance and it was typically an adversarial role, I don't like to fight.

CD: That probably had something to do with it. I am getting a beige color here, blah-like, and that has to do with the emotional import of your life at that time.

I am also getting some connection to a past life as well, maybe more than one. There is some religious order that you are a part of where you are expecting to receive from your religion something that would make life seem really pro-found to you. That didn't work out and set up a deep sorrow in the heart, which began manifesting in the lung and then follows a line from the lung down to the colon.

I am looking at some of the spiritual causes of the pressure in the colon that led to the hemorrhoid. It is not just the part peaking outside but for a lot of the tissue inside, there is a weight descending upon it that builds pressure as it tries to leave the body and come out spiritually through the root chakra and physically through the intestinal system. This energetic weight is settling itself down there at the bottom of the body and is not able to release it. That's the pressure on the bladder. It is connected a lot with your root chakra and also with the second chakra which to me is the holding tank for unresolved emotions and unresolved thoughts, the things we have not dealt with.

In our loving kindness towards ourselves, we just stand there with these things in our hands waiting until the time we decide to deal with it. It is never thrust upon us, we can deal with it in any lifetime at any point, but it stands there patiently holding all these things in its hands. When we are ready to resolve an issue, we will go back there and get it out of the pile. It will still be there, just like it was a half a million years ago, or whenev-er it got setup or whenever it happened for us. The reason it is doing this is because we want to see the truth about something and that will set us free. The judgment and the heartache that we carry from one lifetime to another is what we put on our-selves. We want to resolve those feelings, and that critical judg-ment that faults the belief that we are wrong, that we are being punished or that we somehow have to pay for it.

Even though it may actually be just a page in the chapter of our book, we hold it patiently until we are ready to forgive ourselves and let it go. What you are looking for is a way to move your energy through your body, through your emotional and mental systems and through your spiritual body and let it flow on out without holding on to things.

There is an image here of things trying to flow through you like a river and you keep reaching in the flow and grabbing out things, little rocks or things floating in the water and asking, is this something I am suppose to deal with? Is this something to take care of, something I need to fix? And that is actually where the hangup is, in the belief system that something needs to be fixed or dealt with or made right so that you will no longer be wrong.

Imagine now that you just sit back on the bank and relax. Watch the water flow through with all the little rocks and all the crap floating in it, yeh, there's a shitload, isn't there, and just watch it flow. Now on the surface when we deal with this in visualization it is easy to do, but you have to put it into some places in the system for it to actually work. The more you remind yourself that this is one way to do it, it starts having an affect on your energy system as you turn yourself from constantly having to fix that which is wrong to just letting it flow on out without having to fix it.

One of the ways to do this is to go into meditation with the area of your body that is affected. Just like we did with your left lung. And the way you will talk to yourself and receive answers is not necessarily the way I would or anyone else. As you go in you ask to understand in a way that you can understand. And then just let it be. I would invite you to go into meditative conversation with the colon and with the tissues of the colon that have lost their tone, the walls of the cells that have lost the ability to hold themselves together with strength. Begin your conversations with talking to this area of the body and exploring the emotional reasons why this is affected, the spiritual reasons. Not in judgment but in sitting quietly like the Buddha and listening, giving yourself permission to speak and then just letting it go and knowing that answers will come to you in different ways.

Usually there is an insight, it may happen then or it may happen next week. As words spoken out of another person's mouth, out of a book you read next, out of the feelings you have about yourself. Using the breath to help to heal the body and just like a healing hand, put your mind to work in tandem with the breath going into the colon area and just breathing there.

ME: When I was working on my lung and then on the colon, could you feel it at all?

CD: The lung was so prominent in me, now let me go down into the colon.

ME: Can you feel any heat in the lung?

CD: Yes, the lung is just like bright yellow and burning in me. And the colon has done the same thing. Let me send myself down there and ask to feel that. Anger pooled is right at the sphincters, the anus opening. A ring of anger, it is actually protective anger. Don't go there and don't hurt that one. Protective anger.

Do things that will help to clean the lymph system and strengthen the cell walls. Try rebounding, a mini trampoline, very gently in the beginning to help clean the lymph system. Also try dry skin brushing with boar bristle bath brush from the health food store. Brush towards the heart, brushing all the places on the body but your face in order to stimulate the lymph system.

And the exploration of what the protective anger is all about, someone else has hurt the small one, could be a specific person to life in general. Little person hurt and the little person angry.

As you are in conversation with an area of your body, talk to it about dealing with yourself in a way that is not so physical, releasing all that dense energy that is going on down there and spreading it around to different parts of the body so that other systems can take care of it.

As it comes up, your emotional body wants to deal with some of it because that emotion wants to be expressed. When you express emotion, you bring it into your mental body for understanding.

You can deal with emotion just by being angry, or afraid or whatever the emotion is you see, but then when you bring it into the mental body, then you have awareness of it, ahhhh this is what my anger is about and you can give voice to it. Talk to it in ways that balance the emotion with cognition, lets look at this and lets do some rational looking at it.

What I want you to do right now, I want you to be a very sweet and kind, higher mind and I want you to go through your body and give a blessing to these places that are disturbed and tell them that you are going to be in conversation with them and you are going to come to an understanding and to healing. That they always have permission to speak and you will lay hands on them as often as you can and send in the goodness of your own energy.

And draw yourself back into your heart. And then let your breath bring you up to the surface and let each breath make you feel more aware of being in the chair, hearing the music rising to the surface so that it feels very natural for your eyes to open of their own accord.

ME: I can still feel the comforting heat inside my lung in my chest.

CD: Breathe into it. Breathe into the area and have the intent that the breath is healing.

Relax the cell walls and communicate with each other, expel any toxins and become strong and strengthen the immune properties. Go to the colon and do the same thing.

ME: That wasn't as strong, it doesn't stay as long. It was there for of some of it, but not all of it. And for awhile it was moving between the two.

CD: Go with whatever comes up.

ME: It did for awhile, didn't stay as strong or as long. The lung feeling is still going on. What is also interesting on my little journey, I have always said my intent and focus was on my lung. This time I said my intent and focus was on my hemorrhoid and where is the energy going, it is going to the lung.

CD: Sometimes you have to take care of some other things first.

Vibration Devices

In addition to my session with Carol and the sound chair, I also explored how vibration can be used with electronic devices.

Feeling The Vibe

I first heard about "The V.I.B.E." or Vibration Integration Bio-photonic Energizer when Bhimi Cayce brought an open house flyer to one our Eclectic Ladies Networking parties. She is always one to be involved on the cutting edge of products for your health and wellbeing, so of course it warranted further consideration. Bhimi explained that when our cells and organs operate at their optimal frequency, it creates a feeling of balanced wellbeing. Alternatively, when we vibrate at a lower frequency, our body becomes susceptible to disease. We can feel sluggish and overtired, or we can become irritable and unfocused. The frequency, or the vibrational movement of our cells and organs, becomes lower than our optimal state mainly because of toxins from foods, pollution from our water and air, electromagnetic interference from cell phones, computers, microwaves, radios and televisions as well as those generated by our exposure to our processing of stressful situations. When this happens, our immune system becomes compromised and over time, our cell's energy is too low to fight disease.

The V.I.B.E. is a relatively new patented energy device developed with the objective in mind to create the optimal model of healthy resonance, much like a tuning fork, so that when used, the device allows your cells and organs to remember how to operate at optimal frequency. Once an individual is exposed to this tuning fork, their body recognizes the optimal performance level and begins resonating and shifting in an effort to emulate this desired frequency state. The change can trigger the release of toxins and signals the body to start healing damaged tissue.

Introduced to the marketplace in 2002 by inventor Gene Koonce, a Colorado-based electronics engineer, The V.I.B.E. is based on pioneering theories and techniques of Lakhovsky, Tesla, Rife and Clark. There are currently 200 devices in use in 38 states and 9 countries around the world. Controlled clinical studies have commenced at nine universities, some of which include Harvard, Stanford, Arizona and the US Army.

Bhimi had just started offering sessions for clients and I thought it looked and sounded interesting, albeit a little futuristic. I had every intention of attending the open house event and then my schedule got swept up in another direction and it didn't get to be. It was over a month later when a phone call with someone on the opposite side of the continent again brought The V.I.B.E. to my attention and suggested it could be an interesting exploration during my healing journey. I try to pay attention when information seems to circle back around and face-off with me again in a relatively short period of time, so I decided a follow-up was in order.

When we chatted, Bhimi shared that in the short four months she had been offering 2-10 minute sessions, she had already booked 200 clients. The reasons for coming to use the device varied, some were making it part of their cleansing and detoxifying regime, some pursuing an opportunity to rejuvenate and reprogram their cells towards a youthful state, some using it as a complementary modality in their healing plan against serious disease, and yet others seeking a sense of spiritual wellbeing. There was even an amazing experience where one woman's brain tumor disappeared after two months of daily sessions. But no claims of miraculous healing for every individual are being made. Each person's experience will be different based on their specific circumstances and journey. It is offered as a means to help you improve your wellbeing, the breadth of that change being an individual experience.

When I arrived for my appointment, I felt I had entered a New Age dimension. The lighting was very soft, with recessed sconces, and there was calming music playing in the background. A note on the door advised clients to please power down their cell phones before they entered. Bhimi handed me a form to complete that asked a few questions about my health issues and also encouraged me to put down other thoughts I might want to focus on that would help imprint my intent at the cellular level.

She led me to a private room and there in a place of respect and prominence it stood. The bottom of the device enclosed a laser with a copper-looking material; next there was a cylinder that housed a Tesla coil, and last there were twelve glass tubes that contained inert gasses, with a Plexiglas six-sided star on the top and bottom of the tubes. Above the top star is the image of the Tree of Life, a symbol of healing and ascension, and finally a glass circular coil wrapped in wire. Bhimi pointed out that there was also copper tape running along the baseboards of the entire room as a means to hold the energy within the confines of the room. I'm sure you get the picture, it looks like you have just stepped into another time dimension well off into the future, or perhaps even well into the past on Atlantis. I even learned from the website that one of the gases is krypton.

Before we started, Bhimi explained that my session will last four minutes. During that period, The V.I.B.E. will send out its tuning vibrations eight times. I will know it is happening because I will hear a humming sound and the glass tubes will light up. I am advised to focus my intent on a healing or on something I am trying to manifest in my life when the humming commences each time. I am to remove anything with a concentration of metal such as my watch, ring and glasses and then place my palms open-faced on my knees. She shares that some people will feel a slight tingling in their palms, some feel a stronger vibration all through their body, some feel a warmth and yet others feel nothing. The energy can also be felt where one has a weakness or imbalance. Bhimi leaves the room as I break out in a big smile and giggle in anticipation, wondering what I will feel when the first hum signals the start of the session.

At the first sound of being V.I.B.E.ed, I noticed a bright orange color in one of the tubes and lavender and yellow in others. I later learn that there were actually light green, aquamarine and blue colors that appear too, but they were too faint for me to notice at the time. The colors are the result of the gases becoming activated in the twelve glass tubes. I had decided to spend four of my eight focused intents on healing and the other four on other pressing personal issues. Nothing seemed to be occurring on the first three, but by the fourth time, I started feeling a little tingling in the very center of my palm. It continued to get stronger and then lasted a minute or two longer after the session was over. Bhimi and I discussed the session and talked a little more about the device before it was time for me to leave. At first I didn't seem to have any discernable changes in myself, but about a half hour later I felt a distinct tingling in my crown chakra that lasted about 20 minutes. I didn't feel energized, but then I had been operating at a rather hyper-speed lately, so that would have probably been counterproductive. Six hours later, I found myself rather sleepy, and since typically I would not turn in for another five hours, it appeared my session had put me in a state of relaxation.

Feeling the Fear

Well, okay, I have to admit I felt a little nervous on this particular healing outing. An individual that was experimenting and learning on an energy device powered by software on a laptop made me feel a bit like a lab rat in a 1960's sci fi movie. The device is the QXCI and is based on quantum mechanics. It was developed by Professor Bill Nelson over a 20 year period and works to balance your energy through biophysics which in turn allows your body chemistry to naturally adjust to this energetic shift. The QXCI device resonates with thousands of tissues, organs, nutrients, toxins and allergens for one hundredth of a second each and records how the body reacts. During this testing, it is looking for viruses, deficiencies, weaknesses, allergies, abnormalities and food sensitivities to determine the energetic state of your body. Once it measures the frequency of all intended variables, it then compares it against an established norm and identifies areas at risk. Depending upon the assessment, it may send electronic impulses that raise or lower the frequency to effectively move towards a healthier energy balance.

The irony is that the system designed to detect and reduce stress actually seemed to cause me stress. That is because the subject has to wear sensing monitors around both their ankles and their wrists as well as a headband that encircles the entire head. Again I needed to remove any jewelry with a heavy metal content as well as my glasses. This experience lasted over 1 hour, the first 30 minutes or so consumed with detailed questions and then another 30 minutes seemed to be consumed as we slowly transferred between software modules. The real stress came to bear when the practitioner told me that she had used a probe to treat a wart that had been menacing her on her face for quite some time and, ignoring the program messaging that told her the session was complete, continuously ran the program until she managed to burn her face. Of course she was pleased that she was able to significantly reduce the size of her wart. This same practitioner also kept having trouble moving between assessment and treatment modules and would offhandedly jest, "Whoops, hope I didn't fry you with that key stroke," or something to that effect, which is not so funny when you are hooked up to a piece of equipment that sends you electronic impulses.

To be fair, I don't think this was an accurate portrayal of the capabilities of the QXCI. And I am most appreciative that the person generously took the time to show me the breadth and depth of the device's ability to assess different body systems, sent me balancing energy for a few selected body systems and let me experience the device in action. My caution would be to anyone looking at trying this device or any other device run on a PC, to make sure the practitioner has a healthy respect for the system's capabilities and that their software and hardware are running harmoniously without a tendency for the screen to freeze up.

That said, I will say I do believe Professor Nelson is really on to something with his invention. There are a number of fascinating diagnostic reports that can be run and I was impressed by the ability of the program to pick up on known ailments. When the QXCI device scanned my lymphatic system, the main area of concern was my upper left lung, which is exactly where I have my lung infection, albeit significantly in better shape than it was a couple years ago. When we ran the module that assessed my spinal column, everything looked pretty good except for two areas of concern, one of which was the last vertebrae of my neck which showed inflammation, the same problem area picked up by reflexology a week ago. It also properly identified my most significant allergens.

Another interesting possibility, and one I only heard second hand, is that the practitioner located in the southeast is doing virtual healing sessions with an athlete up in New York. Virtual healing is the term given to distance healing when it is done through the direction of a software program. On mutually agreed upon days, the practitioner has been sending healing energy to her client at unspecified times. She just sets the computer to run at a randomly selected time once she leaves the office for the day. So far, her client has always been able to report back when the virtual healing session took place.

Dean Voice Analysis Program

Vickie Dean is self assured and highly confident in the abilities of the Dean Voice Analysis Program (DVAP), as she rightly should be. Vickie appears to be without any sort of physical disability when only eight years ago she was told that she could be spending her life in a wheel chair. Hers is the old story of necessity being the mother of invention when she found herself suffering with excruciating pain after what was the fifth automobile accident of her life. In this last incident, she had suffered herniated and compressed discs, nerve damage down her left side and damage to her pituitary gland.

Vickie had run out of options through traditional medical channels and yet was not satisfied to accept defeat. She began studying alternative modalities to facilitate her own recovery and became particularly fascinated with sound therapy when she experienced a session that allowed her to go home that evening and actually sleep for four hours straight without awakening in pain. In her research, she found that we each have our own composite frequency of every individual resident frequency of all the substances housed in our bodies. Numerous studies have proven that when one of these frequency vectors becomes injured or weakened in any way, the voice looses the ability to produce that frequency. By scrutinizing the response frequencies emitted by the voice, we are able to get a very clear picture of what is going on in the physical body in terms of nutrient deficiencies, toxicity and biochemical imbalances.

Armed with this knowledge, Vickie began her quest to develop a voice analysis application that would help pinpoint the low frequency and/or weaken areas of her body so that she could develop a specific sound therapy to repair and restore her physical condition. Through her disciplined study and rigorous testing that correlated her findings with those of traditional medicine, Vickie was able to develop a software program that not only helped pinpoint specific problems that could help her regain her health, but also that of many of her clients. One of the doctors with whom she conducted research, Dr. Haltiwanger, found her program so reliable, he started insisting that his patients get a voice analysis first before he started ordering testing so that he could treat them faster and keep the costs of tests to a minimum.

She gets excited when she starts recounting the stories of the many people she has helped. One recent amazing episode involves a good friend that had broken her foot in three main places during the holidays. When the friend went to emergency, she was told that she had to see a specialist to repair her foot and one wouldn't be available for five days. They sent her home telling her to return at a later date even though she was in terrible pain. Upon hearing about the incident, Vickie quickly made a trip to her friend to analyze the situation and develop a custom sound therapy CD to assist in her healing. By the time the friend returned to the doctor's office, the specialist told her that she didn't need surgery, there must have been a mistake since there was only a small fracture in her foot that needed to be wrapped. Yet clearly the original x-ray showed her foot had been broken in three places just five days before, even the new x-ray showed evidence that she had broken her foot in three places earlier.

Vickie also recommends her clients utilize color therapy in conjunction with sound therapy for the best and fastest results. She has found that color therapy will first go to work on the emotional body while sound therapy first works on the physical body and then addresses the emotional body. In tandem with traditional medical therapies, they can work to cut the recovery time necessary in half.

When we began, Vickie had me speak into a microphone three times to capture a voice print. Each time I was assigned a different type of 30 second speech to deliver. The first was to be a factual response that didn't hold any emotional attachment for me. The second was to relate to something I felt passionate about, and the third was to cover topics I found stressful. At first I thought the easiest thing to do would be to grab something out of my notebook to read. But she quickly informed me that wouldn't do. When someone reads, their voice frequency ranges are cut in half as people always enter a rote mode. She said it is particularly hard to get a good voice print from someone who has been professionally trained to create a stage voice because they don't use their full range of octaves. I was also advised to avoid any repetitive sounds like "ah" or any pauses. Once my voice print was captured, Vickie showed me the results, and she found them to be quite interesting herself, as my passionate and my stress voice prints were almost identical, representing little to no stress response going on at this time. I suspect that my previous sound therapy treatments may have contributed to that result.

She also noticed that my emotional and mental bodies appeared well balanced, emulating a nice even scalloping pattern. My physical body showed some issues, but nothing dramatic, and then she paused as if not sure how to address my spiritual body. Finally she just blurted out, "Well, your spiritual body looks to be in chaos!" That made me laugh, as I certainly did feel like my view of our world and our spiritual nature had dramatically shifted over the last couple years with the result being, the more you know, the more you realize you don't know! As we chatted about this a bit she commented that a chaotic pattern often will show up when someone is in a period of transition.

Vickie next looked at something called markers and showed me where I had 3,500 areas pop up with low frequency ratings. At first this sounded like something I should be alarmed at, but Vickie was quick to point out that the average is between seven and nine thousand with most of her clients tending to have upwards of fifteen to twenty thousand. She further explained that often the people that come to her are ones who have exhausted traditional channels and are looking for new answers as they deal with very serious and tough issues. Vickie examined the results and looked for patterns. She told me that I should be pleased that I only have one of the top six toxins present that she typically finds in cancer patients. Her experience indicates that a person is highly susceptible to cancer if she finds four of the following six toxins present: mercury, tin, lead, nickel, antimony, and cadmium.

What I found particularly fascinating is that she put a scientific name on my left lung infection: *Streptococcus mitis.* She also confirmed earlier findings of Sis Sewell, the doctor of naturopathy and iridologist I had visited two years earlier. Sis had told me that I had a lung fluke and arsenic poisoning, both of which I had yet to address. Vickie's findings also collaborated that of Ko Tan and the QXCI vibration device that had identified a weak vertebrae in my neck area. Yet, the most critical item she found on her voice analysis radar screen was that of the bacteria content in my digestive track. Her recommendation, like that of Carol Dallas, was that I needed to focus on healing that area.

My next step will be to have Vickie develop two CD's for me. One that will help me detoxify and another that will be supportive in my healing. To detox, one typically has to commit to listening to the CD 3 hours a day, 5 days a week for a month. Then after that, you need to listen to it 16 hours a month as a maintenance program. The detox CD can be used for years to come to eliminate any new buildup of toxins. The supportive CD will become ineffective over time as your body balances out in that frequency range.

The Ghandarva Meditation

Another interesting vibration experience I participated in is a mediation developed by Tom Kenyon called The Ghandarva Experience. Kenyon is an accomplished therapist, author, mystic and lecturer, who, through his own extensive research, designed a meditation to transport participants to the realm of divine music.

He based the ceremony on the ancient Indian text called Vedas, which was written by the sages/intuitive seers of the time. The Vedas speak of an inner realm of musicians called Ghandarvas with the sole purpose to sing and play music to God the divine in all its aspects. A realm such as this appears in many traditions and religious practices throughout the world and is referred to as the Angelic Hosts in Christian traditions.

Tom began making a conscious effort to tune into this realm. He found through his experiences and that by toning and repeating the chants and mantras of the Divine, with the pure emotion of love and gratitude, we are able to elevate ourselves to the Ghandarvic realm and join them in singing praise to God.

The Ceremony begins with chanting the names of the Gods and Goddesses, the Deities of the major religions and traditions around the world and throughout time. Based on this invitation made out of a love and sincere thanks, the energies begin to come in to the space where the meditation takes place. Because participants ask for nothing for themselves or the world at large, rather they simply express unconditional love through sound, the celestial realms are drawn from all dimensions of consciousness. The communication of this unconditional love occurs on a cellular level and our physical heart literally opens up, responding to the vibration created. As the toning continues, the vibrations elevate our own beings. When the toning of the vibration of love is complete, a sound is made to signal the end of the Ghandarva Ceremony and a blessing completes the experience. The actual ceremony only takes about 20 minutes or so and follows a CD created by Kenyon.

My Belief

I have long been aware of the power of music to evoke great emotion in myself, whether it's a group of Kenyan children singing in a field, a Broadway production of The Lion King, a private performance by Belorussian pop star Lenoid Bortkevitch, or enjoying an evening listening to Atlanta-based singer/pianist Benjy Templeton. I don't even need to understand the lyrics, but rather the tones themselves will open a floodgate of emotion within me that can be almost overwhelming at times.

I now understand that there was a lot more going on inside me than just admiring the beauty and passion of the notes being expressed. The vibration of their sounds was also speaking to me on a very deep level, uncovering that which I generally kept well hidden.

I believe sound and the related vibrations do have the ability to greatly impact the state of our being by virtue of balancing and restoring frequencies that have become weak or skewed in our bodies. I am further convinced of this by the sensations I felt when I was exposed to these therapies and by the ability of these experiences to confirm what other modalities had told me in the past about my health print.

The Value

I am delighted to have uncovered a non-invasive way to address health issues that gives me the flexibility to work on healing by virtue of listening to sounds in the convenience of my home or during my commute. It also offers new hope for those people that are faced with complex energy imbalances that traditional medical practices are unable to satisfactorily address.

{14}

Equine Assisted Psychotherapist
Gary Kimbrough, M.DIV. and EAGLA Certified

During the last year I had the good fortune to meet Gary Kimbrough, an accomplished therapist who has helped a broad and diverse client base through some of their most challenging lifepoints. Some of his more high profile crisis management experience includes guiding executives through high profile mergers and being called to the Pentagon after 9/11 to help train the counselors on how to deal with post-traumatic stress. Until recently, what many people didn't know about Gary was that he also has an unusually strong connection with horses that has been honed since he was a young boy on his uncle's farm. Over the last couple years, Gary has worked to combine his two passions of guiding people through transformation and introducing people to the magical qualities of horses into a practice that offers equine assisted psychotherapy and corporate team building retreats.

On two different occasions Gary had enchanted me with stories about horses; how they mimic the personalities of the humans they come in contact with and how they offer a unique means for self-exploration through emotional and spiritual healing journeys. The latter practice is referred to as equine assisted psychotherapy and uses the relationship formed between a client and the horse to illuminate behaviors through the use of metaphors. This differs from the hippotherapy that many people are familiar with that has demonstrated a phenomenal healing quality for both children and adults suffering from physical ailments that often involve the loss of motor skills.

Given the spiritual "chaos" I was currently experiencing, further confirmed by the voice print analysis Vickie Dean shared with me, I decided I should follow my curiosity further and arranged an equine assisted session with Gary.

Gary and his wife Linda have a picturesque country home north of Atlanta. It's a very peaceful place with a gorgeous view of the hillside just beyond the pasture, but it takes a bit of driving and focused concentration to reach it from the main metro area. I felt like I was making good progress on the appointed day, when I found myself at a loss as I tried to find Whitlock Road off of a town square in a northern suburb. I circled around the square for about 15-20 minutes, stopping to ask people if they knew where I could find Whitlock. But everyone I stopped to ask was just visiting the town square that day and didn't have a clue how to help me.

As I continued circling, a man who appeared to be in his mid-thirties was laughing and joking with his older friend as he made his way across the square and up the street. He was quite the character and a little voice in my mind kept encouraging me to ask this man for directions, but his highly animated antics kept me from approaching him the first two times he was within earshot of my car. Finally the third time my car met up with him, I gave in to my intuition and asked him if he could tell me how to find the elusive street. He smiled and laughed, then politely and with great efficiency told me how to get where I wanted to go. It was a strange moment when we had this communication because I almost felt like it was a setup by a greater power. The man's eyes seemed to twinkle knowingly, as if to say, I was wondering when you were going to get around to asking me how to get where you needed to go. Hmmm, I thought, this certainly is looking like it is going to be quite a mystical day.

I arrived at Gary's about a half an hour later than planned. Being intuitive, Gary shared a laugh with me that he knew just before I turned up into their driveway that I was about to arrive. He was in jeans, a t-shirt, boots and a big white straw cowboy hat, cutting quite the image of an American cowboy with his tall 6'4" frame. We walked into the barn which was sporting a fresh coat of red paint and took up two chairs in the middle of the building. We settled in for a chat as we listened to country western songs, complete with yodeling, being sung by Wiley Gustafson, a horseman and rancher from the state of Washington.

Gary had first developed his love of horses when he spent his summers on his Uncle JH Smith's cattle farm in Madison, Tennessee. He and his brother thought they had died and gone to heaven whenever they found themselves on the 100-acre property that was anchored by an old Victorian farmhouse. As soon as the sun rose, they would be fishing in the river, riding the tractor or exploring the countryside, enjoying their freedom like two young colts.

Although he was relatively young at the time, Gary clearly embraced his uncle's message on the proper way to relate to a horse and form partnerships out of mutual respect. His Uncle JH was a horse whisperer and was one of the first men at the time to develop a natural horsemanship philosophy. He always told his nephews, "You don't break a horse with ropes or whips, you gentle a horse by learning the psychology of the horse and by viewing the world through the horse's eyes. You need to learn how to communicate with a horse in a language you can both understand." The movement for this type of kinder, gentler view of horsemanship has been lead by such pioneers as Ray Hunt, Tom Dorrance, and Monte Roberts who taught others the techniques and whole psychology of the human and horse relationship.

When he was around six years old, Gary became drawn to a little black and white Shetland pony called Beazelbub. The pony was high strung, temperamental and downright wicked at times. His uncle had warned both Gary and his brother not to go near this pony because he had bitten their cousins and had terrorized the other horses so badly that he had to be separated from the rest of the dozen or so horses that they had on the farm. Although normally compliant, Gary decided one day that Beazelbub just didn't look all that vicious and warranted a closer look. Beazelbub sniffed his hand and licked it, egging Gary on to investigate further. His brother was horrified as he watched in disbelief as Gary climbed over the fence to go pet the pony.

As soon as he was in the fence, Beazelbub took a dead run at him. But when Gary showed no fear, he came to a screeching halt and started nuzzling him. Gary proceeded to pet him all over and then followed him around mimicking the pony as he ran and bucked. He kept this activity secret and faithfully visited his new friend each day for a week until he was inspired to try and take a ride on Beazelbub. He grabbed the pony's neck and swung his leg over. With a firm hand on his mane, the two of them took off in a nice jog, loping all over the pasture, Gary grabbed his hat and started waving it yelling "yee haw" emulating the 50's westerns that he watched on TV. All of a sudden he caught sight of his uncle viewing him from the road and Gary started crying, figuring he was in big trouble for his secret escapades with Beazelbub. When he got closer to his uncle, he noticed he had a big smile on his face and yelled to his nephew in an admiring yet astonished tone, "Damn, if that don't' beat all!"

Gary was thrilled to find out that his uncle was not mad at him when JH declared, "How could I be mad at you, watching someone have so much fun!" Later when his uncle asked him if he would like a saddle, Gary decided no, he didn't want a saddle; he didn't want to break the connection. He continued riding Beazelbub from dawn to dusk, until his feet would drag on the ground. Three to four years later, Beazelbub died. Gary felt such a grievous loss that he no longer wanted to go back to the farm. His uncle kept encouraging him to return, saying it would be very good if Gary came back and got out there running and bucking and carrying on again. When he finally managed that first trip back, JH took him by tractor down to the river where he had buried the pony with a little memorial plaque that said "Here lies Beazelbub, a close friend to a boy who lived to buck and run. May you both buck and run forever." He told his nephew to go talk to his friend and to come back home when he was through.

It was his special friend Beazelbub and his Uncle JH that began Gary's long connection with horses. His uncle taught him to ride, to communicate with horses, respect them and to watch for how they would mirror what was going on with him if paid close attention. He taught Gary how horses relate to the world around them and that his attitude would determine how horses respond to him and other people. That you could get a horse to do anything if you did it in a manner that feels natural to them. To always keep in mind that horses are rhythmic in everything they do, even when they walk. And that one should always spend more time with a horse on the ground before you ever try to get on a horse's back.

Horses live in the moment, they don't look back or forward. They taught Gary to be really okay with who he was and to live in the moment too; to be present and tuned in to what was going on around him.

Horses have three primary needs that need to be met before they can learn to do something:

1) They are prey animals and humans are considered predators. Thus they have to feel safe or their instinct to flee will kick in.

2) They are a herd animal who likes routine and they must feel comfortable with their surroundings.

3) They like to play and if they are having fun, they are more receptive and can learn to do difficult maneuvers more easily. They are very similar to kids this way.

As Gary grew older, his family moved and he didn't get a chance to spend time at his uncle's farm. Oddly enough, he still found himself always in the company of horses whether it be dating someone who owned horses or just staying near a place with horses. He always seemed to have an opportunity to hang out or ride as a means of stress relief as he went on to earn his to earn his bachelor's degree in history and his master's in divinity in clinical pastoral training.

Once he completed his studies, Gary began working with the chronically mentally ill with thought disorders, such as schizophrenia and bipolarity. He enjoyed his clients very much and learned to communicate with them by not being afraid or intimated, to be still, breathe and learn to reach them by finding a common ground, the very same approach his Uncle JH had instilled in him when forming a relationship with horses. During this time, Gary met his wife Linda and they decided to move to Atlanta in the early 80's. There he found himself working with adolescents in a residential home program for those dealing with ADD and ADHD. His new clients were highly troubled youth that struggled with conduct disorders, often having been expelled from school and unable to function in a normal home setting. In parallel, Gary also worked as a family therapist with patients that suffered from eating disorders. He often found that these clients were angry and eating their anger through overindulging or not eating as a result of perfectionism.

Gary followed this experience up with work in an outsourced Employee Assistance Program (EAP) for corporate clients, working for such Atlanta icons as The Coca Cola Company, Georgia Pacific and a number of banks and law firms in the metro area. In this role he coached managers on how to deal with job performance issues by being supportive while confronting the issues and by developing respect, keeping your focus, taking care of yourself before you confront employees and always coming from a position of safety and security. Interestingly enough, these were again the same issues he had learned to address when working with horses. Gary also found a significant part of his client base in the EAP program were dying of AIDS. He used his pastoral background and the Beazelbub plaque to help them understand that their spirit will never die; that it will always be a part of who they had touched. Gary would help his client and their families create rituals to communicate their acceptance of the situation.

In the early 90's Linda, who had always been very driven and active, was diagnosed with multiple sclerosis. At times she was unable to walk without a cane and would have to go to bed due to the unbearable fatigue. Gary became her caretaker and eventually the stress started taking its toll. He became aware of the imbalance of giving and giving without being in a position to receive and started asking himself what was missing and how was he going to go about getting it. Around this time, he had a dream he was out on a prairie, totally naked, frightened and exposed, not knowing where he was or where he was going. Then he heard the thunder of the horses' hoofs, he stood straight up and as the stampede approached him, they parted and circled around Gary, encouraging him to run and play and buck like the old days. That was the answer; he needed to find a way to play again, to help relieve the stress of his job and caretaker role.

He found a stable close to home and drove up there in his suit and BMW telling the stable owner he needed to be reunited with horses. April, the barn manager, looked him over a bit dismissively and told him to pick out a horse. After work, Gary returned in jeans and boots and proceeded to pick out the biggest quarter horse he could find, one called Rusty who shook his head at him as if to say, "Been looking for you. It's about time". Everything his uncle had told him came flooding back and he began working with a number of horses at the stable that had developed behavioral problems.

Linda continued to be symptomatic, having difficulty walking and balance problems, and Gary's revived interest in horses had her taking a closer look at their healing power. They had an upcoming board meeting in Wyoming and Linda suggested they stay at a dude ranch while they were there. Gary thought it was a great idea, but encouraged Linda to learn to ride first. As part of her Christmas present that year, he gave her riding lessons, and her first antique rocking horse that became the catalyst for her passion to collect them. Linda fell in love with an Arabian horse named Dee and took lessons from April at the stables near their home. Within months, her balance improved, her muscles got stronger and her MS symptoms disappeared.

As Gary continued working with challenged horses at the stables, he began to get into the mysticism of the Native Americans, their relationships with animals, the paths, the journeys, the rituals and the losses. He also came to realize that the horse was his totem animal. In 1996, both Linda and Gary decided that they wanted to learn more about incorporating horses into their therapy practices so they attended a training retreat for drug and alcohol abuse counselors at The Ranch in Nashville. In retrospect Gary considers this the most spiritual experience he has had as an adult and still feels a stream of emotion just recalling the events of the week.

In particular was his interaction with a Lakota woman named Toomi who was one of about 30-40 therapists there for training. She and her colleague were from the Pine Ridge reservation in South Dakota. During an evening dinner when they first arrived, Toomi had sat with Linda and Gary and shared part of a dream she had about the experience, two weeks before. She had seen a white horse and that she would be on that horse at some point during training. The next day when the two vans full of therapists made their way to the pasture, everyone now well aware of Toomi's dream, they all saw that among all the different horses, there was in fact one white horse waiting for her to arrive. She became excited upon spotting her intended partner and called out to everyone within earshot, "Did you see my horse?" The first exercise had four therapists at a time entering the pasture and picking out a horse. They then returned and spoke to the instructor about why they chose a particular horse, often being surprised to learn that the experience fit closely with what was going on with them in their own personal or professional life.

On another day, the therapists were again grouped in fours; this time Gary found himself in one with three other women, including Toomi. The exercise for the day involved being blindfolded and laid on their stomach across the back of their chosen horse while two people they had chosen helped them stay balanced. During this exercise, there was always an equine specialist monitoring the horse to ensure everyone's safety. For her helpers, Toomi chose her Lakota colleague and Gary. The difficulty of this exercise depended on the horse, the helpers chosen and the range of physical ability of the subject. In Toomi's case, she was short and stout and not very flexible, so she was extremely apprehensive in attempting this feat. The instructor coaxed her by asking, "What are you feeling? What do you need help with? Has this happened before, this sense of not being able to see?" She replied, "Yes, I am not able to see the final outcome in my work. I don't know if I am doing any good." Toomi proceeded to lay across the horse. The horse could sense her anxiety and began to tense up and started moving nervously.

Gary was on the side where her head was. He told her to breathe, that he would hold onto her arm. And then without any warning, Toomi began to sob, just wailing. The horse on the other hand, began to relax and didn't move at all. The instructor encouraged Toomi to share with the group what she was feeling. She shook her head no. He then asked what she was afraid of happening if she should share her feelings. "Nobody in the group will understand," she replied. The instructor dug further, "Who won't understand?" Toomi shot back, "Gary won't understand." Gary felt flustered and embarrassed as all eyes focused on him wondering how he could be the type of person that Toomi would be afraid to say what she was feeling because he wouldn't understand.

Coaxed further, Toomi relented and shared, "My people, your people. Why did you kill my people? Why did you have to exterminate us?" His head swimming in the emotion, Gary sensed the focus on him was about him being this tall white dude, the only one present in a cowboy hat, representing all that had gone before him in the time of frontier expansion. He was flooded with a profound sense of loss and guilt, all prejudges of the past came forward. Sadly, Gary had to admit that there existed the possibility that if he were there in that time and space, feeling the cultural pressures of the day, he could not say beyond a shadow of a doubt that he would not be guilty of the crime now being accused.

Toomi took off her blindfold and realized how calm the horse had become as she had become emotionally distraught. The question remained for Toomi, "How much is this about the work you are doing now and how much relates to your people dying?" The answer was that they seemed inseparable. Further complicating the experience was that when someone died in the tribe, it was always a white horse that brought the warrior for burial, the body laid on its stomach across the back of the horse.

She was there for them, those that were dying. She was there to participate in their spiritual journey, but could not control the outcome. Toomi sat upright on the horse and Gary took the lead, together making a slow progression around the arena while everyone else followed behind, a tribe of helpers and healers.

Shortly after this experience, Gary and Linda enrolled in training out of Salt Lake City to become certified by the Equine Assisted Growth and Learning Association (EAGLA).

My Fascination

As we wandered down to the pasture from the barn, I was still feeling pretty confident that I was up to whatever challenge Gary wanted to throw my way for the day's session. In hindsight, this seems rather irrational when I stop and consider that all my previous attempts at riding a horse had been somewhat disastrous, or at the very least pretty comical. It would be quickly apparent to any horse that I was clueless as to what I was suppose to do when it came to riding or even working with a horse, yet somehow I felt prepared for whatever was to come.

Gary gave me a ten to fifteen minute safety lesson and my confidence started to waiver just a tad. He reminded me that his horses were spirited and quite unlike the horses that are in a disassociative state that you are apt to find available for trail rides. He instructed me how to protect my personal space and stand my ground if a horse should come up and start head-butting me to see what I was made of. At first I didn't think getting nudged by a horse's head sounded all that threatening until Gary reminded me that their heads are extremely powerful and can pack a heavy punch with all that bone mass.

He also showed me the proper way to shake hands with a horse and no, you don't reach down and grab a hoof like you would a dog's paw, rather you extend your hand and let the horse sniff the back of it. Horses, like many herd animals, have monovision which means they can only see you with one eye at a time. They can't see you if you are directly in front of them or behind them. For that reason, among others, you always want to approach a horse from the side and if you are behind them, you want to keep close contact with a hand on the rear of the horse so they know you are behind them.

All these important instructions started swirling in my head and while I could understand the logic of it all, the question was whether I would recall the desired course of action in the heat of an actual situation. Gary went on to explain what my assignment was going to be as he handed me a halter. I was to go into the pasture where he had sectioned off two of his big geldings, and I was to go make a connection with one, put a halter on him and lead him out of the pasture and into the arena. Well, now, this was starting to sound a little dicey. Gary quickly added that he would be going in there with me and keeping a watchful eye to ensure I didn't get into a dangerous situation. With that, Gary asked me what my strategy was going to be. I was quick to reply that I wanted to see if a horse would pick me instead of me forcing myself on one of them. Without a judgment or confirmation of whether that was right or wrong, Gary suggested we give it a try.

With some trepidation, I marched into the pasture with halter in hand, determined not to break a sweat. Dan, the alpha horse of the herd, approached us first. I extend my hand to give him a good whiff of my scent. Within a minute his head was butting me and invading my space. I remembered what Gary had said and made a fist and formed a right angle with my right arm, holding it to the right of my body indicating my perimeter. Dan's nudging continued, but seemed fairly restrained, almost as if he needed to do it only out of a sense of tradition rather than an intent of making a statement. It took all my balance and strength to try and keep him from moving me and he still managed to move me a bit. During the course of this engagement, I somehow lost my focus and Dan started connecting with Gary. Before I knew it, he became disinterested in the whole process and walked off.

Hmmph, I thought. Guess that means Dan is out of the picture. I hoped I would have better luck with the other gelding, named CJ. I approached CJ and extended my hand. CJ took one whiff, and then ran from me like greased lightening. It was kind of a shocker at first and then Gary asked me what I thought about the situation. I shared that so far it seemed to mimic real life. People with strong personalities are often drawn to me and will test me out to see if they can control me. Yet others are intimidated by me and will shy away from me. In the latter case, I usually don't pursue further communication because I am not interested in being around someone who is afraid of me. In typical psychologist fashion, Gary asked me why that was. I said the first thing that came to mind which was that I didn't like to be around low-energy people or ones that would find me intimidating. It just wasn't interesting for me. Now as I consider it further, I suspect it is also because it makes me uncomfortable to be around people who are feeling uncomfortable, especially if I detect that I am the cause of that discomfort.

At this point the two horses had congregated over by the pasture fence and were huddled with the other two horses in the adjacent pasture. I was feeling a bit apprehensive. Neither horse seemed that keen on making a connection with me. I was also uncertain how I was going to make my way over to that bundle of horse legs, slip a halter on one of them, all while managing not to be kicked. The horse nearest to me this time was CJ, so I decided I would try him first instead of making my way closer to the fence to try Dan.

Magically, CJ did not run this time. He appeared calm and open to communication. I talked to him and rubbed his face and asked him if he was going to let me put the halter on him. It seemed like he really knew what I wanted to do because he made it easy for me to slip the halter on him and stayed still and calm as I hooked the metal clip to secure it on his head. I don't know who was more surprised, me or Gary! Then I started walking and just as easily, CJ followed behind me.

When we got inside the arena, Gary informed me that we were going to groom CJ. I asked if I should tie him to the fence post and Gary replied that it was up to me. I thought about what Gary had told me, that you should treat a horse like how you would want to be treated and that it needs to feel safe and secure. Putting myself in CJ's shoes, I knew I wouldn't want to be tied up and feeling vulnerable so I left his lead rope hanging loose. I figured the worst that could happen would be that I would try to bring him back to this area of the arena and he would have decided not to let me near him again. But, if he was feeling that way, I wouldn't want to force him anyway.

I did some of the grooming, but Gary helped me because the dust from the caked-in mud was a bit of a challenge for my lungs. When we finished this exercise, Gary handed me a tool to clean the hoofs and asked me if I thought I could do it. I figured this was part of the experience and I wanted the maximum experience so let's do it. Of course I got no instructions on how to go about it, so I had to use the old brain logic. I figured I would just keep talking to CJ and telling him what I wanted to do and ask him if he was going to help me out and let me do it. I reached down for his front left hoof and he lifted it up and let me clean it. Then I went to the back left hoof and he didn't lift this one up for me, so I was a bit puzzled. I tried lifting it up, but it was barely leaving the ground. My instincts were telling me that there must be some trick I was not aware of with the hind legs so I slipped over to the right front hoof and completed that task before attempting the hind legs again. Studying the situation out, I realized that that the horse was putting more weight on the hind legs and so maybe it was a balance issue. So I re-approached this part of the assignment with a new expectation and managed to get the two hind hoofs cleaned when CJ just barely lifted his hoof up. The whole time I kept a running conversation going with CJ and remembered to keep thanking him for his cooperation. Gary later told me that CJ doesn't normally like to have his hoofs cleaned, so that was a pretty amazing demonstration of cooperation from the get-go.

Next came the climax of the whole challenge in that I had to talk CJ through a course made up of construction cones and logs to be stepped around and over without touching the horse or using any kind of lead. Just to get the idea set on what the expectation was, I was able to lead CJ through the course once with a halter on. Then I had to remove the halter and with a metal rod in my hand (that was never to come in contact with the horse) I was to lead CJ through the course. When I was about to start, he got spooked by something and took off towards the fence of the arena. I gave him a few minutes, and then talking to him and approaching him with my arms open, ready for an embrace, I walked back up to him. He decided to trust me again and came back over and let me lead him through the course. I was bursting with pride at this accomplishment and was waiting for Gary to tell me how spectacularly I had done. Gary paused and then said I did well, but I had broken the rules. Huh? I thought, what did he mean I broke the rules?

I never touched CJ with the metal rod. Gary explained I wasn't supposed to touch the horse at all, and I had been patting him and rubbing him with my right hand the whole way. Oh, I had missed that part about not touching the horse at all! So I asked if I could try again. And he said sure, if I wanted to. So we lined up again and this time we walked the course up and back with no touching, just a friendly conversation and my mind remaining focused on what I wanted CJ to do. With the challenge complete, I was completely full of pride and feeling the same kind of elation I have felt when I had maneuvered through a foreign country by myself. Success was mine and an adrenaline rush over the satisfaction of knowing I did it was flowing through my body!

Gary shared in my joy and told me that I really demonstrated strong leadership skills, but just as importantly was the way I had worked those skills, with great compassion and concern for CJ. He also told me that he found it quite amazing that CJ had been so timid in the beginning and yet bonded with me later so quickly, to the point of complete trust. As we stood there talking, I kept rubbing CJ's face and patting his side and let my fingers play with his lips and mouth like I use to with my dog Zachery.

I told Gary that I knew I had strong leadership skills based on my past career performance as well as results from executive training exercises, so that was not such a big surprise to me. I also admitted that while I loved to be the compassionate, gentle leader, that part may become somewhat suppressed if I find myself having to drive a team to success under a tight deadline. It is my preference to let everyone work at their own comfortable pace, but a corporate environment doesn't always afford such a luxury.

When asked what lesson I learned for the day, I said it had to be not to be so judgmental when people or horses shy away from me at first. To give them a chance to warm up to me and I just might have a rich experience like I did with CJ today. Gary quickly added that he thought that was my lesson for the day too. And with that, as if he knew exactly what we had just said, CJ nodded his head up and down to validate our conclusion.

My Belief

I believe horses do mimic human interactions. I had to witness it myself to really understand what that meant. But having experienced metaphor after metaphor that day as I worked to establish a connection with the two geldings, I could easily relate the scenes to many of my past experiences. What an amazing, mystical day!

I believe I have fallen in love with CJ and only wish it were possible that he could come live in the house with me. I would like to have him in my office while I am working on the computer or in the TV room watching a good movie with me. I liked the way I felt in his company and the return of warm, loving thoughts and appreciation I received from him.

I believe the whole experience has been filled with synchronicity. Many of my intuitive friends have raised my awareness to look for it to validate whether you are on the right path or not, and clearly I was: the fact that I had two occasions to meet Gary earlier this year and learn of his passion for horses; that he was able to find time in his busy schedule for me on short notice; and that a show horse in North Carolina that I had been attracted to have an experience with was unavailable to me, so that instead I spent the time getting to know CJ.

Finally, just two short days after spending time with Gary reviewing how he had come to know horses in such an intimate way; I find myself touring the fabulous new American Indian Museum in the Smithsonian complex in Washington D.C. There among the exhibits is a spot dedicated to the Lakota people of the Pine Ridge reservation in South Dakota. A quote from a drug and alcohol counselor, Cecelia Fire Thunder, reads, "We want to let others know that we are still alive as a nation; that we have not been killed off. Regardless of the hard times we have gone through, we still have our ways, our knowledge, our wisdoms and our elders." Another quote from Robert Two Crow that seems apropos to the experience went on to say, "The Lakota Universe can be described as Mitakuye Oyasin. That means everything is connected, interrelated and dependent in order to exist. The Universe includes all things that grow, things that fly-everything you see in the world or the place that you walk on. These are all included in what the Lakota see as the Universe. All of this is related."

The Value

Self examination through a mirror held up by these magnificent horses was very telling and enlightening. It brought an adrenaline rush through accomplishment, made possible only through connection with someone to whom I gave a second chance. For someone who is so passionate about encouraging others to not judge so quickly, I learned I still have some work to do in that area myself.

{15}

Psychics, Dowsers, Intuitives, Channelers
Incredible Journeys, Enlightened Souls

Psychics, Dowsers, Intuitives, Channelers….what do these terms mean? I have checked in with psychics since my early twenties from time to time, often amazed at what they could tell me about myself and what was around the corner for me. Some were consistently, astoundingly accurate on a myriad of topics. Others were hit and miss and most were not accurate at predicting the timing of events. But all in all, I've always found my visits helpful in that they provided me with insight about myself and urged me to view life and its possibilities from a fresh perspective.

Events that were previewed for me included being married within a year even though I didn't have a boyfriend. Becoming immersed in an international project that would take over my life which became the summer I was involved with a Russian Circus. Spending extended time at the beach which turned into a six week stay in Ponte Vedra, Florida and extended work and travel in Europe which manifested in a 3 month project in Frankfurt, Germany that included weekend excursions all over the continent. I was also advised that, in conjunction with this European travel, Paris, France would be of significance. This was the same trip where my wallet was lifted and I spent the whole day with the Paris Police to get a theft report filed and ultimately had my wallet returned to me once I was back in the States.

In the last couple years, I have come to know several new sources of alternative information through the good fortune of meeting some wondrously interesting and gifted people. Along with these new friends came new terms that seemed to be used interchangeably and were causing me great confusion. I began to wonder if the terms psychics, dowsers, intuitives and channelers were actually different names for the same gift, or were they really in fact different gifts? There didn't seem to be a widely accepted means of delineating between these terms. In fact, everyone I talked to always prefaced our discussion by saying that they could only speak from their own point of reference. This appears to infer that there really isn't a generally known or accepted resource that defines the field of alternative sources of information for the average person.

Below is my attempt at providing some clarification based on discussions with several people in the field.

The toughest delineation was between psychic and intuitive. Delineations that emerge from time to time are not standard and seem to be based more on social preferences and desired market stratifications versus true delineations based on distinguishing standardized attributes. One definition I like is that intuition is something everyone has to some degree and is considered less threatening in society than psychic powers. Intuitive information comes more from a direct knowing without the aid of an intermediary. A psychic and/or channeler on the other hand has developed their abilities to access entities from other dimensions and this ability is developed in fewer people. Dowsing is a combination of both psychic and intuitive powers.

Psychics or Intuitives

These terms appear to be used interchangeably.

Tools:

Cards, Crystals, Stones, Numerology, Astrology

Source:

Information may be received as a clairvoyant (clear seeing), clairaudient (clear hearing) or clairsentient (clear feeling) or some combination of the three.

Information is mainly received through the crown chakra (7th chakra) and third eye (6th chakra). Information may come in the way of symbols that must be interpreted; through visual scenes that may include motion like a mini clip, a slide show or a direct download of information through hearing or knowing. Sometimes the information is received through the aid of other higher beings.

Preparation:

Needs to be well rested and in alignment, treat the body like a temple.

Must release their own personal emotional baggage and not be judgmental.

Must be relaxed, yet in an alert state of mind, in an "alpha-wave" state. Intent must be for the highest and best good.

Specific Challenges:

To learn to correctly interpret the symbolism they receive and to validate the source as being in the highest and best good.

Dowsers

Tools:

Pendulum, L Rods, Y Rod, Bobber

Source:

A connection between an individual's sensing system and their conscious mind. Information is received in the form of a yes, no or maybe response to a skillfully formed question.

Preparation:

Needs to be well rested and in alignment; treat the body like a temple.

Must release their own personal emotional baggage and not be judgmental.

Intent must be for the highest and best good.

Specific Challenges:

Learning to patiently attune their tools before they use them, to ask properly formed questions that are not open-ended or subject to interpretation, and to validate the source as being in the highest and best good.

Channelers

Tools:

Body

Source:

A higher being or spirit guide enters the body through the crown chakra and temporarily takes over part (becomes the information generator through a person's mouth or via automatic writing) or all of the mind and body.

Preparation:

Needs to be well rested and in alignment, treat the body like a temple. In addition, a channeler's mind may or may not go to sleep in a semi-trans state, and in a full-trans state both the mind and body go to sleep. When the person enters a state of sleep, they may be watching the event outside of their body, but it is like they are in a sound booth and are not privy to any of the information.

Must release their own personal emotional baggage and not be judgmental.

Intent must be for the highest and best good.

Specific Challenges:

Learning the channeling process and how to let go. This is a more limited method of sourcing information for many individuals because it is very hard on the body.

I am fascinated by the different paths people have traveled to arrive at the point in life where they can use their gifts to help others maneuver through the storms of life. Some have known their gifts since early childhood; others discovered them through a series of events, often starting with a personal crisis. Below I have endeavored to sketch individual awakenings of gifts and provide an understanding of how they apply them.

Deborah Hill
Atlanta-based Intuitive Coach and Clairvoyant
Author of *The Writings of the Masters:*
Enlightening Lessons for Everyday Life

Deborah grew up among Midwest sensibilities in a family basically unaware of psychic phenomenon. As a result, when little Deborah started demonstrating her adult insight in a two-year old's body, her revelations were not welcomed. Even more alarming, her truth was not filtered by society's decorum of what was appropriate to state and what was not. She would often get in trouble for saying what was obvious to her and doing what came natural.

Confused by the negative reactions she received from others, she started to withdraw and relate more often to a whole host of energy friends, invisible to others, who would amuse and play with her. This tendency was considered acceptable for a while, but eventually was considered problematic by her parents when it continued beyond the normal age for children to have "imaginary friends." Deborah's saving grace was that she was wise beyond her years and soon concluded it was best to keep much of her existence hidden from others in order to "fit in" to the acceptable realm of behavior. Though she could not stop herself from hearing and knowing things, she began to discredit her intuitive messages and sight, as many children do when faced with societal pressures to rely on the information and insights of the logical mind.

At times throughout her life Deborah existed out of body. She describes this as managing her life like someone driving a remote control toy car. When she was not fully present, the energy from other beings was able to inhabit her without realizing it. She explains that we all live out of body at some point such as when we find ourselves zoning out in a conversation, we feel we are walking around like a zombie or we have found ourselves driving without being consciously aware of how we got from point A to point B. She refers to our spirit as an energetic, vibratory being and to our conscious point of spirit as our center of awareness. Out of body is when our center of awareness has left our physical presence.

Deborah lost touch with the understanding of her abilities and began a quest to learn more about herself and God. For thirty years she looked for God and explored her path as a spirit. About seven years ago, Deborah began to enter mid-life and felt an urge to explore her intuitive abilities. She found a book on how to develop your psychic abilities and was surprised to find out that she had all of the abilities mentioned in the book. She immediately asked for a teacher and soon found a few who had been teachers and leaders at the Berkley Psychic Institute. Over a 6 year period she traveled around the country to take workshops from these teachers and also took courses from instructors who set up a curriculum in Atlanta. This proved to be a period of great unveiling to her about her life to date. She learned that she was psychic and developed her abilities. She was positively astounded as she identified behaviors and skills that she had that others did not, that the life she was experiencing was much different then that experienced by most other people. She also realized that she had been allowing other beings to inhabit her body energetically and she shut that access down.

Deborah also learned that we all tend to get "polluted" by the energy of others. Occasionally other beings try to attack us energetically from other planes, just as they do on Earth. A great deal of what she studied and now teaches is how to protect yourself from the energy of others and clear it from your body and energetic field. She doesn't go looking for energies that have a negative intent, but avoids them. She says it's the same as not allowing yourself to wander into a dangerous neighborhood or place where you feel threatening energy. It's the same when she accesses other dimensions. She doesn't go where she senses there is a negative threat.

Deborah has been doing private intuitive coaching sessions for clients since the year 2000. She receives her information verbally and visually – like seeing a movie in her head. She can talk to what she sees and she can also hear beings respond. She shares that people can center themselves in their 6th chakra (also referred to as the third eye) to see clairvoyantly. Centering or being aware from the 7th chakra (also referred to as the crown chakra) leads to knowing things and centering in the 2nd chakra (a couple inches below the belly button) enhances the feeling of things.

She describes her experience like always having radar on and receiving information but not always consciously tuning in. She participates in her earthly conversations while monitoring other conversations on other planes. Deborah does not actually attune to the steady stream of information that could fully absorb her attention. Rather, she accesses these other conversations when specific voices or signals compel her to do so, or when she needs a specific answer or information. It's similar to being in a restaurant having a conversation with someone. You might be aware of the noise of diners at other tables and of music and food being served, but you don't focus on it. She will consciously turn her attention to the information if she senses a need to do so, or if someone in that dimension starts speaking to her loudly to get her attention.

Deborah has a number of guides that assist her. Archangel Gabriel is always with her as a guardian and guide. At the end of her sessions, she always includes time for healing and is guided by two healing masters, Jahna and Sam. Both of them appear to her in human form and look like regular men you might meet on the street. They have lived many lives on earth as healers in the past. She may also be guided by many of the Masters and angels, and often works with Jesus, Buddha, Archangel Raphael, Archangel Metatron, Archangel Michael, and Elijah the prophet. Each is especially adept in relating to specific aspects of life, such as Michael, who understands and functions as a protector from negative energies and beings.

Before she begins a session, Deborah puts up a protective barrier and works under the premise that it is not her job to carry around anybody else's energy, including his or her pain. She tries not to carry her clients' stories and issues and makes a deliberate effort to clear out after a session using a number of techniques, including visualization. At times she'll also use other forms of clearing including tuning forks, aromatherapy and bath salts. When a client returns for another session, she finds that she easily picks up where she left off because the information is again visible to her.

Deborah notes that there is a difference between a belief and an experience. A belief is an idea you have taken on without any real proof, while an experience is when you take that mental concept further and own it through understanding it in spirit. One of the biggest lessons she tries to pass along to her clients, and teaches in her lectures and workshops, is that we are all intuitive beings and have the ability to communicate with our higher selves and guides. She guides people to be fully present, with the center of awareness focused from within the body. We are all powerful spirits in bodies with a great capacity to create joy, abundance and understanding, and to enlighten the world around us.

Carolyn Cummings
Atlanta-based Intuitive Psychic Medium
Author of *Beneath the Mask: An Empowerment Card Deck*

Carolyn was born with a developed sense of psychic abilities and can remember seeing things and knowing things, thinking everyone was having the same experience. She was around five years old when she discovered differently and became concerned that something was really wrong with her. Her intuition told her to be careful of what she said and to whom, don't broadcast it. People would say things like "Carolyn is sure perceptive" or "She has great intuition".

Fortunately her mother was always open to extraordinary events and new things, taking Carolyn for her first psychic reading while she was in her teens. In hindsight, she realizes that her mom was psychic and so was her grandmother; they just didn't talk about it. Her mother would tell her that she had eyes in the back of her head and could see what Carolyn was doing all the time, and she seemed to really have them there too. Her grandmother always encouraged her to follow her heart and do what you believe, advice which would eventually lead her to the place she is today.

Her father, on the other hand, was an analytical army colonel and he only wanted to hear about things that were factually based. After earning a degree in nursing, Carolyn married another military man, Fred, who was a Westpoint graduate. He shared the same objection Carolyn's father had to anything psychic and often commented that only uninformed people believed in this bunk. If she tried to share that she had been visited by her great grandmother, Fred would chastise her for losing it. Again Carolyn found herself in a restraining situation that prevented her from exploring the world from a psychic perspective to the degree she desired. This time her confidant into the realm of the extraordinary became her son Kevin who is also very intuitive and psychic.

Eventually Carolyn and her husband divorced which gave her the freedom to start pursuing classes that focused on the paranormal. She found that as she raised her awareness, she started becoming more receptive to what she was supposed to do. While walking along the water one day in Virginia Beach, a friend told her out of the blue that she should read Shirley MacLaine's first book, *Don't Fall Off The Mountain*. She took the advice and found the book really spoke to her. When she called her friend to thank her and discuss what she had read, the friend informed her that she had no idea why she told her to read the book, having never read it herself. She continued to explore different tools, consulting a Ouija board which told her to move to Atlanta and started doing automatic writing. Carolyn became preoccupied with a desire to learn whatever it was she had come here to learn about. She became adamant about surrounding herself with close friends that shared the same philosophies and beliefs, being careful not to include any nay sayers in her inner circle.

The draw to Atlanta became stronger and even though she had no particular plans, she gave in to the compulsion when Kevin ended up going to the University of Georgia. She continued her career as a nurse, reading for friends and her friends' friends as a hobby. While she was standing in line at a grocery checkout one day, she heard that little voice telling her that it was time to become a psychic full time. Practical Carolyn argued with the voice, saying that she couldn't quit her job to do readings, I can't wear the hat of a psychic full time. But the urging continued and wouldn't let up. Carolyn challenged the Universe to send her a sign right then and now if that was what she was suppose to do. At that moment, and well out of sight of any fruit counters or any approaching grocery baskets, a single apple came rolling down the floor, stopping right in front of her feet.

Since Carolyn was a home health care nurse, she had the type of flexibility that allowed her to comfortably transition into making readings a part of her livelihood. At first she felt guilty having to charge for spiritually advising people, but she also knew that if she was going to devote a major portion of her time to this task, that she had to make a living doing it. She never advertised, yet she quickly developed a client base that ended up becoming a full time job. Carolyn also continued with her nursing duties full time, so in effect she was doing two full time jobs for years. She kept feeling the pressure to drop nursing and focus solely on her psychic consulting. She slowly transitioned to part time, then just one weekend a month. That weekend became a bear and she dreaded it for the whole week before it arrived knowing she would get the hardest cases that required the most effort for the least pay. Finally, six years ago, she gave it up entirely without regret and followed her heart to devote all her time to psychic readings.

Carolyn receives her information in an even mix of seeing, hearing and sensing. When she sees something, she will see it in scenes like a movie clip. Each day before she starts her work, she thanks God, breathes in the energy of God and her teacher, and asks that nobody take anything from her, or her from them, energetically.

Carolyn believes our sole purpose for being born is to address our fears. To assist us during this journey, we each are assigned a single teacher that is with us our entire experience, a teacher who is part of God and in charge of our lesson plan. The teacher's role is like a movie director, setting up the scenes so we can learn our lessons to help align with our higher selves, or souls that are all knowing. We also have guides that come in and out of our life for a particular purpose. They are always there during that time if you call them, but our relationships with them are temporary.

We have to live many lifetimes to learn these lessons and come back in all different forms so that we can have the experience of being male, female, rich, poor, black, white, thieves, charitable, etc., to feel what everyone feels in every walk of life. How we treat others in these roles will impact how we ourselves must experience the role. In this cycle of karma and reincarnation, the old adage applies, pay now or pay later. If you think you've escaped from your mistreatment of others, you are wrong. If you stole something two lifetimes ago, what you stole will be taken from you in another lifetime. God loves everyone equally and this whole cycle of reincarnation is to move you in the direction of God-like love, unconditional love. We can't get it in one lifetime and sometimes we spend several lifetimes on the same lesson. It behooves us to learn.

Carolyn also believes everything is based on intent. In her heart she asks to be used as a conduit for information and guidance that will help her clients become empowered and healed. Everyone is dealing with their inner fears, what she likes to call the screwed up kids, of not being smart enough, not pretty enough, not worthy enough, etc. as well as our egos. In her sessions, she always wants to make sure to remove both the client's and her own kids so that they won't interfere with the message.

Before she starts a session with a client, she always asks that only God and her teacher, the client's teacher, Carolyn's higher self and the client's higher self be present. That both her and her client's inner kids are not allowed to interfere with the reading and that they only receive information for the highest and best interest of the client. She then asks permission to do the reading.

At first she started asking permission because she thought it was the polite thing to do. Then one day she actually got a "no". In the past they had always been in sync so she wondered what could possibly be going on. She asked them again, three more times, always getting "no".

Puzzled by this turn of events, she decided to continue anyway, but nothing came. She drew a complete blank. She asked them, "What's the deal here?" They responded that they, "always wanted her to know who was in charge, they were. That this was considered serious business and this man was not serious about what they were about to tell him." This has only happened to her four times since she has been doing readings.

Carolyn is very serious about the role of the teacher and will not reveal their name to her clients unless she is directed to do so. She believes finding that information out is part of your journey. The same is true of your power animal----an animal designated to be your spirit guide and protect you. Carolyn will share with you what has been given to her spontaneously, but she will not ask for you.

One of her cherished abilities is that of mediumship, the ability to connect with people that have passed over. Someone will often show up during a reading and give her clues as to who they are. One of her favorite stories is about a man who would check in with her fairly often on business matters. On one such visit she was approached by a spirit who said his name was George. She told her client that there was a male gentlemen here named George who would like to speak to you. Her client shook his head and said he didn't know anyone named George that had passed. "Are you sure you don't know anyone named George? He is showing me short legs." Again she got a no. She then asked if he knew of someone with just the letter "G". Still a no. So she told George, "I think it's over George, he doesn't recognize you." Just at that moment, her client had a light bulb go on and said, "Wait, George is my father!" Astonished, Carolyn was thinking, what do you mean your father, wouldn't you know your father's name? Her client went on to explain that George was a nickname that he had made up for his father as a kid. The short legs reference was an appeal to Carolyn's nursing background. George had suffered from poor circulation in his legs all his life and thought short legs would be a helpful clue.

Bill Phillips
Atlanta-based Dowser
Mechanical Engineer

Bill developed an interest in alternative sources of information while he was in high school. He was fascinated by a book a friend told him about called, *Psychic Discoveries Behind The Iron Curtain*. The book was written in the 1970's after two women, Shelia Ostrander and Lynn Schroeder, relayed their accounts of traveling through Eastern Europe and meeting various Soviet scientists studying the paranormal. Bill found himself excited about their accounts of encounters with superlearning (accelerated learning through the use of very specific, relaxing Baroque music), hypnosis, psychotronics (interactions of matter, energy and consciousness), psychokinesis (power to move physical objects by thinking about it) and subtle energy (non-physical energy).

This book stimulated his mind and made him want to explore further. But available information on these subjects were slim and most of his friends didn't share the same enthusiasm he had for the possibilities they presented. In college, he found another book that piqued his interest called, *The Secret Life of Plants,* by Peter Tompkins & Christopher Bird which discusses the ability of plant life to communicate with man, to serve as a lie detector, an ecological sentential, adapt to human wishes, respond to music and demonstrate curative powers. It was also at this time that a friend introduced him to dowsing and one of the dowsing tools called L Rods.

Dowsing is the art of communicating with the Universe through one's subconscious mind and inner body knowing, typically in conjunction with a specific dowsing tool, to receive answers to carefully formed questions. Dowsing may be used to locate mineral veins, electromagnetic fields, noxious rays, geopathic zones, lost objects and information within a book. It can help identify spiritual, past life and health issues and even the source of your car problems or other electronic issues. Dowsing may also be used to identify probable outcomes to specific actions under consideration. L Rods are angular rods that are held at waist height, like pointed pistols, and swing outward or cross inwards to indicate the presence of water or a mineral vein being sought. They also can be used to indicate yes, no or maybe answers to questions posed to them.

Bill was intrigued by the fact that the L Rods would move and give him results. However, his friends were unfamiliar with the structured methods involved in dowsing at the time, so it was viewed more as a curiosity than a reliable source of information and Bill put dowsing on the back burner. He continued his studies and completed his degree in mechanical engineering which served as a basis for his career in instrumentation and control systems.

In 1990, he was introduced to people from the local Atlanta chapter of the American Society of Dowsers. There he learned how to properly use the L Rods and the results moved from random to reliable when he focused on keeping them straight, had a mental concept of what he was seeking and learned to ask specific questions that were not subject to interpretation.

He further learned that dowsing is the most efficient and cost effective way today to locate a water well. People can spend thousands of dollars on a hydrologists with expensive sonar reading equipment and perform test drills only to come up empty handed, while a water dowser can locate an underground source quickly and cheaply. The same can often be said for locating an electrical line. You can use a magnetic detector, but it can be thrown off by interference. An experienced dowser can actually find the line easily and accurately.

Dowsing Tool	Description	Use
Pendulum	1/2 to 4 ounce weight suspended from a 3 to 8 inch string or chain.	Chain is held between the thumb and forefinger and a movement pattern indicating yes or no is established, or a variable (such as 0 to 100%) from the direction of the swing.
L Rods	Angular rods that are made of metal and 1/8 to 3/16 inch in diameter and from 18 to 24 inches long. The two rods should be bent at a point approximately 6 inches from the ends to form a right angle "grip.	Held at waist height, like pointed pistols, the rods will swivel, either crossing inward or diverging outward, as you pass over the target. They also can be used to indicate yes, no or a variable (0 to 100%) answers to questions posed to them.
Y Rod	Wooden, metal or plastic stick in the shape of a fork.	Held upward and swings downward to point to the target.
Bobber	2 to 4 foot wire wand with a flexible spring section and weighted end.	Operates like a horizontal pendulum. Can give quicker answers than a pendulum because it swings much faster than a pendant.

When a person first decides to try dowsing, they need to select a tool they feel comfortable with (see chart above). They will then need to program their tool for a positive, negative or variable result if they are posing a yes, no or maybe type question. Some people prefer to have a consistent indication for yes. Others prefer to check their tool each time they start a session to ensure they understand the response they receive day by day.

Next you need to form a mental concept of what you are seeking and/or formulate a specific question that can be answered in a yes, no or maybe manner. You also need to clear your mind of conscious thoughts and beliefs, those preconceived notions that could influence the answer. The key is to open yourself up to receiving the information without exerting influence.

Bill cautions that you really need to be very specific about what you want to know. This includes what, where, when and sometimes instructional information relating to the question. Make the question a definite request for information that exists somewhere versus an opinion. Do not ask open ended questions or use terms that are subject to interpretation.

Finally you need to ask permission to proceed with the following questions:

> *Can I: Do I have a proper connection? Am I ready and able to access the proper resources for the answer? Am I calm and focused enough to get accurate results.*

> *May I: Do I have the proper permission to proceed and be involved? This typically pertains to when you are asking a question on behalf of someone else in regards to their health or other personal matter at their request.*

> *Should I: Would it be appropriate, possible and suitable to seek an answer to this question?*

After you get your answer, check the precision level by asking, "What percent accuracy was attained?" With an L Rod or a Pendulum you can get a vector reading of 12 o'clock for 100%, 3 o'clock for 25%, etc. or you can pose specific percentage of influence questions on an ascending basis for a yes, no or maybe response.

Bill's interests guided him toward geopathic dowsing which involves identifying ley lines or earth energy grids. Energy ley lines are natural flows of positive or negative energy that connects with the earth at places we called power centers. Many accomplished ancient cultures from around the world were aware of these power zones and built some of our most impressive sacred sites over these areas through the ages. In North America, the Native Americans use ley lines to position medicine wheels. The Mayans and Incas built all of their ceremonial structures on them. In Egypt and China pyramids and other sacred structures are built on them. In England, Stonehenge and many of the churches were built on former pagan worship sites that had been built on ley lines.

Often Bill will use his geopathic dowsing skills to help assess the energies in someone's home. Positive ley lines will boost your energy level and increase your metabolism, while negative energy lines will make you feel fatigued and shutdown. There is also a need to balance between these positive and negative energies. Positive energy will boost without limit which can be counterproductive. Negative energy is the balancing energy that will keep positive energy from overexerting its influence. In a healthy person, positive energy will give your system a boost, but in a person that is sick, it can actually boost the spread of disease. If an imbalance is detected, the energy may be shifted through the use of minerals. It requires only a minimal investment in the cost of materials and the time required to survey the property.

Negative subtle energy is also believed to be able to travel up through the power wiring in your homes. Bill and a colleague have conducted dowsing tests and discovered that not only can energy emit 4 feet from your television when it is turned on, but it can also radiate when it is turned off. The same is true with light bulbs which can radiate 3 feet based on their testing.

The effects of ley lines are all based on the theories around subtle energy. Bill shared that, "Theories and related technologies around subtle energy have been around for a long time from people like Wilhelm Reich (active ingredient of life called bions), Nikola Tesla (over 700 patents, including AC power distribution, radio, and high voltage technology), Thomas Henry Moray (energy conversion devices) and Thomas Bearden (theoretical foundations), but Bill believes much of the discoveries have been classified and not available to the general public. Subtle energy is basically something that is not observable, it is non-physical so that it is not electrical nor is it magnetic; yet it influences things in the physical world.

It is nothing that is "spooky". It is just a mental concept that can't be held like an object. For instance we have an environmental law where people or companies are not allowed to dump mercury based chemicals into the water. The law itself doesn't exist physically. It may be printed physically on paper, but you are not able to pick the mental concept of the law up and touch it, look at it, examine it. To go even further, a belief doesn't even have to be written down like a law. Someone may believe that harm will come to them if they venture a few miles away from their home where they were born. This belief will prevent them from traveling and will actually influence their physical action.

Although we know more about subtle energy then most people are aware of, we still do not have accurate processes and instruments to detect and/or sense them with the exception of our subconscious biological senses. You can't measure it autonomously because you won't get any result, there is no physical component, no magnetic field or pressure. But it still produces influence. In fact, it is the greatest influence that exists on our biological systems for both plant and animal life as discovered through the work of Wilhelm Reich with bions. His work in the 1920's isolated a gray gel-like substance that could not be inactivated and is thought to be what animates life at the cellular level. It is theorized to be the active ingredient that takes the chemistry, electricity, molecules and DNA of the cells in our bodies and makes it come alive.

It always has puzzled Bill why people can become so polarized over new ideas and often are quick to put negative labels on people who want to explore these theories. He finds amusement that these same people are apt to be the ones that would have applied these same labels to someone trying to tell them that we would someday soon have a box in our house that sat on our desktops and would allow you to see thousands of miles away or that prior to the invention of the telephone, would have laughed hysterically over the idea that we would be able to talk to people around the world over wire.

Bill, and others like him, remain on the polar opposite side of the innovation scale and welcome new thoughts and ideas that they can explore further.

Lori Lothian
Vancouver-based Clairvoyant

Lori takes exception to the overuse of the word "gifts" when it comes to accessing a greater knowing. She believes we are all born with the ability, some with a greater range than others, yet all having a choice on whether we want to acknowledge it, hone it and use it. "It's more like a life tool than a gift," explains Lori, who likens it to deciding to sing. Of course there will always be a few who would find singing extremely challenging, but most can manage to carry some sort of tune. "For example we can enjoy the music of Madonna or Whitney Houston, the former being a highly trained singer and the latter a highly gifted singer." So we might come by our psychic tools naturally, or we might have to work hard at honing them, nevertheless they are there for us to choose to use as we journey through life.

Lori really wouldn't describe herself as psychic as a child, more like being from a family that was psychically inclined and growing up in a place that was home to paranormal phenomenon. She attributes her awakened abilities to not being inhibited by a belief system that was telling her she couldn't do things. Her mom was psychic and used it in ways to help her daughters understand who to trust and who not, and what to expect from people and various situations. She also encouraged her three girls to have fun with it and play simple games like guess which Hollywood square was the secret square on the popular 70's TV show or which cup had a penny hidden in it. One of Lori and her sisters' favorite games growing up in Canada was going to the store and waving their hands over the potato chip bags or soda bottles to determine which one had the winning package or bottle cap. What really tickled the girls was that they usually picked the winner.

Lori's major awakening of her spiritual self came shortly after graduating from university with her journalism degree. She was excited about taking off for Europe for an extended backpacking trip and shortly before she was to leave, she found that her beloved Grandmother had been diagnosed with cancer. They had always had a very special connection, but being young, it really didn't register with her that Grandma might not be there when she returned. Caught up in her excitement, she said her goodbyes and left with promises to call and write postcards, neither of which she did.

She can still recall today the exact time she entered a strange dream state on Oct 23rd, about a month into her trip. She was in Seville, Spain at dawn and not really asleep, nor was she awake. Somehow she found herself in between and Grandmother was there with her in this nothingness that consisted of white noise static. She was surprised at her appearance, now very, very thin, and weak with a yellow jaundiced look to her. Lori started to speak to her about her condition, but her grandmother wanted nothing of that, only to hear of Lori's exciting escapades. Lori obliged with all the riveting tales she could think to share, including spending time with a man in Rome who she knew she would marry (and indeed married two years later). As the discussion ended, her grandmother morphed from her 77 year old deteriorated body into a vibrant and beautiful 25 year old young woman. They hugged, said their goodbyes and then it was over. The next morning, Lori made an entry in her travel log/dream journal and then made her way towards her next European adventure.

When Lori returned to Canada, she was met at the bus station by her mom who began to try and find the words to tell her that her grandmother had died. She began sharing that she had some bad news, but before she finished, Lori told her that she knew that Grandmother had died on October 23rd. The even more remarkable news came when the two of them discovered that Lori's visit from her grandmother occurred exactly during a three to four minute period when she had stopped breathing in the hospital that day. All her daughters were at her bedside and thrown into a panic at that moment. They shook their mother, begging her to return. She did return, resumed breathing and went on to live three to four more hours before she passed.

Even in her death, Grandmother had made a point to treat her connection with Lori as a special bond and made sure she did not leave her granddaughter with a lifetime of guilt. This final parting also served as a pivotal moment that became the catalyst for Lori to embark on the big metaphysical inquiry into "What was real and what was not?" At the same time, Lori put her journalism degree to work, becoming a "Pen for Hire". For ten years she covered entertainment and general interest stories for newspapers and magazines including work at a technology trade magazine out of Manhattan.

In 1996, Lori shifted from mainstream journalism to being a full time psychic. This metamorphosis was a huge undertaking at this point in her life because she really hadn't been consciously applying her developed talents on behalf of others seeking advice. She had experienced premonitions and/or forewarnings of deaths of those close to her like her father or her close friend Alexander who died of AIDS in New York, but taking on the duties of peering into the future full time was a huge leap of faith. As she prepared for this undertaking, she began digging deeper into her spiritual self, which unveiled such truths to her as: "Material reality is just a veneer. Our spirit lives on and transcends time and space, backwards and forwards." "Life is like a kaleidoscope, constantly in motion, like a story constantly under production. Our plot line is always being decided on in the present moment." "Fears and pain of our past experiences too often influence our future. It is like using a map of where you have been to get to a new place of where you want to go."

Lori describes her work as acting as a satellite dish and tuning in to her client's own trajectory or planned course. She serves her purpose by preparing them for a death of those close to them, helping diagnose a health problem so that they can seek proper medical attention, and giving them material to deal more easily and/or effectively with a life crisis. For instance, she told a woman that her daughter would need her on October 31st but that everything would work out to be okay. The woman's daughter was hit by a car that day, and as she was by her side in the hospital, she had strength in believing that everything would turn out for the good. She later contacted Lori to thank her for the gift of comfort and faith in a positive future outcome during this dark moment.

Lori receives her information through her crown chakra and processes through her third eye. She has a few symbols that come to her like an Ace of Pentacles tarot card may appear to symbolize a job offer or a rainbow will signify a successful outcome, she may even see a tombstone with a name and a date. But mostly she receives her information as an inner knowing/sensing or in the form of picture stills like a slide show or a short movie clip like an Internet download. From the visuals, she will be able to get a mood or tone of the conversation through body language. She describes her information mix as knowing (60%), seeing (30%) and hearing (10%). The hearing, or command to tell her client something, typically comes into play when she is avoiding addressing something she is getting through a knowing or seeing a scene.

Two very important preparations Lori employs in her readings are to set her intent for the client's highest and best good at the start of a session and also to keep her own heart chakra open. By setting the intent, only nuggets the size of serving the highest and best good will come through for her client. By keeping her heart chakra open, she makes sure she shares information with compassion and keeps a keen awareness of each client's divinity and beauty. She shares that we are all radiant beings of light but sometimes we allow our light to be shrouded by lifetimes of accumulated shame, fear, doubt and all other emotional pain that distances each of us from the true nature of our core self. It's when we awaken our everyday self, to our big self, meaning our connection with our own divinity, we form a spiritual marriage of sorts and truly began to shine. Her hope is that she can help her clients strengthen and enhance that connection through their session.

To protect herself from taking on her clients issues, she always works to stay grounded. Lori explained that people who have a developed sixth sense, tend to not be in touch with their bodies. This might be evidenced as being fantasy prone, extensive day dreaming, and not particularly coordinated when it comes to sports, following the rhythm of music or dancing. This can lead one to binge on food and go overboard on alcohol consumption just to feel connected with the earth again. When she first started doing readings professionally in 1996-97, she would get headaches and feel fatigue, especially when she worked with clients who were depressed, or on a very negative vibration level. To counteract this situation, she began practicing Kundalini yoga which helps her stay connected to the earth and prevents her work from negatively impacting her health. She also doesn't hold on to her clients' information. She can remember what she told them five minutes later, but it is gone by the next day.

Lori takes pride in knowing that she can perform her work under pressure and has been successfully tested while being observed through the scrutinizing eye of TV cameras.

Shannon Sambells
Calgary-based Channeler and Intuitive
Advisor to Individuals and Corporations
Author of *To Touch The Hand of God*

Shannon's counsel is often sought by other intuitives and channelers because her high frequency allows her to access information from high energy frequency bands for those who operate at elevated frequencies. She has been on a fascinating spiritual journey and shared the following experiences on how she came to awaken and apply her gifts.

Her natural state is to be a channeler and access information from the Universal Mind. Her clearest desire is to access the mind of God so she tries to get as close as possible to the Divine so that she can obtain pure information that is not subject to interpretation. When she channels, she enters a semi-trans channel state where she remains fully conscious of the information being said, it just happens to be coming from another spiritual being that uses the brain wave functions of her body. When she opens her mouth, another energy uses her brain waves and she doesn't know what will come through until it has been said. She is allowed to remain conscious so that she may learn from the information as it is shared and always sees the information in the form of scenes on her third eye movie screen. The voice that emerges continues to be Shannon's but with a different cadence.

She explained that Edgar Cayce was a full-trans channel and his spirit guide would take over both his mind and his body when he channeled. In these cases, the person's mind is pushed to the side and is able to watch the channeling event , but it is as if they are in a glassed-in sound booth and are not privy to any of the information being said.

Shannon did not start out with a developed sixth sense. In fact she can only recall one incident, as a very small child, when she saw a cloud-of-light rise from her father when he died. His early death was followed by a highly traumatic event where, although raised as a Protestant in the United Church of Canada (similar to the Methodist Church in the US), Shannon and her elder sister were temporarily placed in a Catholic Convent while her mother went back to school. The sisters suffered from the loss of contact with both parents simultaneously and, to make matters worse, Shannon was molested while in the church's care. Eventually she and her sister were returned to live with their mother and youngest sibling, and grew up into adulthood.

Her intuitive gifts continued to remain dormant until she was 33 years old. Then in November of 1982, as a young mom with two small children, Christ appeared to her. He stood in front of her with one hand extended and later turned and bent down to pray. Although she felt her soul and all its inequities was known completely, she felt no shame, embarrassment or judgment, upon her, only unconditional love in the purest form and the mostly indescribable feeling of ecstasy. Shannon recalls that in her mind she pleaded with him to take her with him, she didn't want the feeling to go away. But as the vision disappeared, she felt her body shifting and the energy around the visitation still present. Time had literally stood still during His visit and she is still unable to fathom whether it lasted 30 seconds or 2 minutes.

Shannon's interpretation at the time was that He must be telling her she was going to die or that she wasn't praying enough. Soon she began to feel unwell and her condition rapidly declined. She couldn't feel her left arm, lost her vision, and her legs and ankles became numb. In short, her entire system was shutting down. By the beginning of December she was unable to interact with people all together. Shannon's GP ran a number of traditional medical tests to determine if she was failing from pituitary cancer, multiple sclerosis, diabetes, etc., but the tests results always turned up negative. In a meeting with her doctor on New Year's Eve Day, he told her that he thought her soul was talking to her. At the time she didn't understand what he was talking about, but later came to realize that she was being called to do God's work.

Well into January, there was still no traditionally identifiable reason for her decline and she had yet to discover alternative modalities. She was given antidepressants, sought counseling and continued to look for answers. During her search, she stumbled upon the writings of Ruth Montgomery, a former war correspondent and past president of the National Press Club, who had discovered she had the gift of automatic writing. At the same time she began reading Ruth's books, January to March of 1983, Shannon started hearing her name being called. She decided to try her hand at automatic writing to see if she could identify who was calling her. Automatic writing is writing done in an altered state of consciousness that is attributed to spirits from other dimensions. In some cases, the spirits literally manipulate the writing utensil in the hands of the channeler and at other times the spirits may also communicate by forming messages in the mind of the channeler, which is reproduced on the page.

It was through this medium that she was introduced to Mimikula, a doctor from Atlantis, whose name means Great Healer or Mountain of Help. He first appeared to Shannon in human form. He was tall and slim with a thin face, beautiful dark eyes and longish shoulder length dark brown-black hair. He wore an Atlantean head piece – a band around his head, and long robes, mostly blue. He would appear in her mind's eye and as their two year tutorial progressed, he eventually became known to her in his balls-of-light energy form. They became so close, that he was as real to her as any human being. During their time together she learned much about the Atlantean culture that thrived over 14000 years ago. The Atlanteans were very Imperialistic, much like England, and had different classes and structures of races and many traditions. They had many colonies throughout the world including Italy, Greece, Egypt, Phoenicia and the Yucatan. When the great flood came and destroyed Atlantis, the survivors took the records to India and to Egypt. Many of the souls that were on Atlantis have reincarnated during the time of Christ and again now. They, along with the Atlantean predecessors called the Lemurians, are referred to as the Souls or Children of Light.

Eventually it was determined that she was becoming too attached to him and she had to work with another spirit guide. She was terribly upset with this turn of events and strongly rebelled, refusing to channel, quit praying and in all was really quite uncooperative. But her tactics didn't change the situation and eventually she accepted her new guide, Clement of Alexandria, a Father of the Roman Catholic Church. Later the Oracles of Light, a group of angels from the Angelic Realm, introduced themselves to her. With each new guide, she ascended to a higher frequency, which gave her stronger information, but also created a bigger drain on her body. Finally she met Haliel, a Throne Angel which is close to the Divine. We often hear of Arch Angels overlooking our universe, but Throne Angels are beyond our own universe. Haliel supports Shannon in her readings and most people, when actually physically present for a reading, find themselves surprisingly emotionally overwhelmed by the energy and release in the form of tearing.

The first ten years of working with her gifts, she spent channeling for people in absentia. But channeling takes a greater toll and she has gradually blended this form with intuition. With this blend of methods, Shannon receives about 80% of her information directly and 20% through symbolism. When she was instructed to choose her instrument to use with her intuition, a friend presented her with Egyptian Cartouche Cards which she has used ever since. As an intuitive, she uses all four forms of receiving information: channeling, clairvoyant, clairaudient and clairsentient. She still considers channeling to be the purest form to give her specific and clear information. Most of her readings are now done in a mild channeling state along with her Egyptian cards. Once she turns on her recording machine, it signals the start of this channeling and she doesn't remember what's she has said after a few minutes.

Shannon always makes a point to be well rested and ensure her body is in alignment before she does readings. She cautions that everyone is different and their bodies become sensitized to a particular routine. For her, she needs to refrain from any alcohol and includes occasional red meat in her diet. She strongly believes that mind altering drugs are not suppose to be in the preparation for anyone intending on receiving reliable information.

Sandra Cheek
San Antonio-based Psychic

Sandra has had clairvoyant experiences and sensed insights about people for over fifty years in some form or fashion. She was raised in both England and the US in a very intellectual family, but not one that was particularly spiritual or religious. As a child, Sandra felt Godly love and would feel messages from angels. She also found herself drawn to churches and synagogues and would wander inside out of curiosity as she came upon them. At 13, she was chosen as a soprano to sing in the adult choir of an Episcopal Church and she always felt a strong energy going on when they sang. Sandra wasn't too big on the church doctrine, but she was into the feeling of love that the church offered. One day while the choir was performing, she felt this great huge tall, energy in front of her and she knew it was an angel, perhaps Archangel Michael. She invited him to sing with her and she remembers feeling this great rush of wind and great strength. Visits like these would only happen spontaneously however, nothing that she could call upon at will.

As a teenager, she became more telepathic and first utilized her psychic abilities in games with other teenagers when she attended high school in England. One of the favorite games was where a group of classmates would put objects on the ground and choose a telepathic subject. They would ask the subject to leave and then as a group, decide which of the objects they were going to focus on. The subject would return and pass their hands over the objects to try and determine which one the group was focusing on. Sandra was very good at this game but she found psychometry, reading objects versus living energy, always gave her a headache.

She continued to follow her compulsion to explore religion, especially Eastern dogma. Her mother could be rather flippant about this fascination and she recalls a time when her mother asked what she was doing. Sandra was studying Buddhism and responded, "I am trying to reach Nirvana." Her mother replied, "Try to be back in time for dinner." But it was this lack of seriousness on her mother's part that allowed Sandra the freedom to explore without limitations. She was further encouraged to reach into the unknown through the good fortune of being immersed in a land known for its historical spirits and ghosts. England was a place where past, present and future seemed to be happening all at once and Sandra fondly recalls picnicking on such mystical spots as Stonehenge.

When she turned thirty, she saw a real acceleration of her gifts. She was a middle and high school art and English teacher with a focus on comparative literature. A normal and natural progression from Sandra's profession led her to embark on an intellectual journey into the worlds of psychology, Jung and the collective consciousness. It was the 1960's and she was raising two little girls by herself at the time, not consciously trying to become a full time psychic or clairvoyant. But she kept feeling and seeing unusual things and felt the presence of a great love energy.

Sandra shared that, "people, no matter what religion or even no religion, still have a common link in what we feel about being here as a human in this particular time in history. Do we like it or are we ashamed of being human? Do we feel connected with everything in the Universe or isolated? Every atom is connected. Does a person feel on fire all the time, that there is a reason for their existence? They don't have to be hugely philosophical or religious to feel this passion.

"A person's greatest clairvoyant growth often evolves out of pain and difficulty. People turn to prayer and mediation more and get a sense that although things are not perfect, everything will be alright in the future. We receive greater then what we ask for, but not always in the form we ask for it to arrive. Your gifts are often not activated until they are needed by the Universe."

Sandra started to do readings part time, growing her business only through client referrals. In 1982, her youngest daughter was preparing to start college. It was at that time that Sandra had found herself faced with another divorce and everything seemed to be pushing her to make a dramatic change. She decided to leave the teaching profession, stepping out in faith to start doing readings full time. This horrified her daughter who didn't see how she would be able to complete college without her mother's financial support from a dependable job.

Much later, when her daughter found herself stricken with Lou Gehrig's disease, she told Sandra that she would not have done what she needed to do if Sandra had not made the decision to take on readings as a full time occupation. Sandra's daughter was referring to the need for her to pursue a 3 year work study program which led to a number of job opportunities.

As she followed her calling full time, Sandra was also invited to lecture teachers and counselors at a local university on right brain and intuitive abilities. She kept it rather intellectual and did not dive too deeply into the spiritual aspect. Sandra did share with her audience that she always had felt that a connection with the creator should remain a very personal experience. She didn't do it as a matter to convince anyone of anything, but afterwards she remembers a military man coming up to her with tears in his eyes thanking her for her insights.

It is not uncommon for Sandra to be able to see 12 years out. Since her location and educational credentials made speaking in front of an air force or army audience a fairly common practice for her, she hadn't expected her lecture at Webster University to be such an impactful event. The room was full of doctors, nurses and pilots all preparing to depart for the Gulf War in 2 days. Someone in the audience requested that she do a reading for him, more or less looking for a confirmation, "We are going to take care of this in hurry, aren't we?" Sandra doesn't do readings for someone in front of other people, but that day she felt obliged to fulfill his request. As she focused in on the energy of the audience, she saw the military people looking out with great compassion for the people they were engaged in battle with and what we have gone through over in Iraq and not too long ago Afghanistan. She saw that some in the crowd wouldn't make it back. It was an example of knowing the answer to what was not asked, but what you should know.

Shortly after that, she quit lecturing and focused on personal readings. Sandra always feels one has to be respectful and careful of what is being shared, yet find a way to tell the truth. Two years before her daughter died from the disease she had contracted, Sandra had been gently forewarned of the need to walk through fire, while given reassurance that she would come through spiritually unscathed. Often people say you can't read yourself, but Sandra believes one can if they are able to lift the veil of influence and have the courage to do so. Sometimes you must witness the difficult and awful, but there are also the joys and the miracles to celebrate. Some people don't like their gifts. But Sandra finds the greatest comfort in them; the forgiveness, to seize the moment and rejoice, and the humor of the angels.

Sandra does not do readings for entertainment. Rather she considers it an honor to go along for the spiritual ride and is always amazed at how different people can be; the wonderfully unique balls of light that are the essence of their being. She has never advertised and doesn't even own a business card to this day. Sandra always makes sure she allows plenty of time for her reading, 1 to 2 hours, because she never wants people to feel pressured or rushed. One of the things she finds extremely odd is when people try to compare readings as if a spiritual gift could be reduced to a commodity product. She views calling upon these gifts as creating a painting or singing a song, it is not something that lends itself to comparison. Sandra is quick to point out that nobody has an exclusive library card to universal knowledge.

Angels are often present and her client's guide is present, but other than that Sandra does not work with a particular guide. She can sense the presence of beings that have crossed over and return as angels of light, often feeling her own daughter's energy present as well. "The guides and angels appear, not to make choices for us, rather to appear as a holy cheering section, giggling and shouting with joy." One time she was in the middle of a very heavy reading for a man in her downtown office when all of a sudden a parade with a big brass band went marching by blasting "Play that funky music," and totally broke the somber mood. There was no way to resist the lightness of the tone which was an obvious signal for the reading to shift into a more balanced mode.

Sometimes angels will appear without Sandra focusing or meditating. She was vacuuming her living room one day with the music on after her youngest daughter had passed. Her children's father was now very ill in the hospital with the oldest daughter, a nurse, by his side. Sandra and he had not remained close and she hadn't seen him in a very long time. She remembers distinctly hearing her youngest daughter's voice, "Mom, Mom, stop vacuuming. Listen to the song that is playing." The song was singing, 'I remember only good things.'

She was feeling a great weakness. Sandra explained that when someone you are connected to spiritually is about to pass, it can be like experiencing a birth that drains you. Again she beckoned her mother, "Listen to the song". It continued, 'On my way home. I remember only good things.' Almost thirty years had passed and it was time to remember only the good moments together so Sandra began sending out good thoughts to her former husband, sending out light, thanking him for their children, all the positive things from their relationship that she could think of. By taking the time for spiritual forgiveness, to release all unresolved issues, remembering only the good, it freed them both. As soon as that happened, she received a call from her eldest daughter, informing her that he had passed.

Before a reading, Sandra will meditate and focus on being grateful. The quietness allows her to tap her right brain energy which triggers an endorphin shift into the higher consciousness. Her crown chakra becomes lighter and she elevates into nonjudgmental energy. During a reading, she will see images first in the form of a painting, slideshow or movie with her clairvoyant abilities. Then the details start filling in which could be something she hears, clairaudient, or knows, clairsentient. Sandra likens it to sharpening a pencil, the points become finer as you sharpen deeper and deeper. She doesn't try to translate anything; she just conveys the information exactly as it comes to her.

When she gets a view of a past life for a person, she finds it always pertains to something going on in their life now. She is also able to view her client's spiritual geneticism, not their aura, rather their higher consciousness or authentic self which is why they are here and what they have to do. She's always found it fascinating that as human beings cross over to the other side, they become Beings with a capital "B" meaning they retain their personality and memories, but they are much greater than that, all knowing and aware of all of their spiritual essence.

Sometimes Sandra remembers what she tells her clients, but she doesn't make a conscious effort to do so. A few people will not want to record their session and they will opt to take notes instead. The trouble is that the information comes faster than you can write it down. Then it may not be accurate because it was paraphrased or incomplete. Sandra can feel the energetic pull of her clients even when they are not having a reading. She explains that, "each individual has an energetic fingerprint. The spirit itself feels tall, light, peaceful and has a nobleness about it."

My Fascination

While tapping into this realm of advanced understanding, I've always been puzzled by a number of questions that float through my mind. Through my interviews with the people over the last year, I have come to have a greater understanding of their abilities and what they do to access the best information possible for their clients. The responses listed below to my questions are from those individuals I've profiled above as well as an incredibly fascinating mystic which I like to refer to as OB1.

Q: How do you know you are receiving guidance from a helpful and knowledgeable source?

Shannon: When you are validating your source, you need to ask questions like, "Who are you? Are you of the divine consciousness? What is your purpose?" If the source does not reply that it is to serve others, then it should be told to go away.

Lori: I receive the information in the same manner I receive any other form of internal guidance. It is in my voice, with expressions that are commonly used and known to me.

I can speak to dead spirits, but it is not a comfortable experience for me. My ears start ringing and the hair stands up on my arms. I will only engage these spirits when it is paramount to my clients' journey.

Deborah: I don't accept any information from anyone, whether on earth or out of body, without validating the source. I ask such questions as, "Who are you?" "How do you know this?" "Where are you from?" Fortunately, out of body beings can be evil, but they cannot lie or be deceitful. Lying is part of the human experience. I also pay attention to the vibration level of the being's energy. I look for the same type of qualities I look for in a human: High vibration, loving, compassionate, light, funny and respectful.

OB1: My information doesn't flow from the astral level of spirit guides and/or higher beings. But when information is received from these sources, a good way to validate the source is to look at what type of information is being provided. Is it articulate and intelligent? Is it giving guidance that inspires greater understanding and enhances the ability to make the best choices for the person's highest and best good, or is it telling them exactly what to do? I am always suspect of information that is directing specific actions. I also think it is extremely important that people do not reinterpret the information given to them for their clients, adding their own layer of fears and judgment.

Carolyn: First of all, you need to have done the work to heal your own inner kids--fears, judgments, etc.—before you apply your abilities to help others so that you can make sure of the clarity of the information and you are not putting your ego or other issues into the mix through reinterpretation.

I always ask that only God and my teacher, the client's teacher, my higher self and the client's higher self be present. That our screwed up inner kids have left and that we get only information for the highest and best interest of my client.

I also ask that I am not sent people that are not serious about the session, what has been referred to as the want to get "laid or paid" crowd. When you set the tone for a spiritual experience, then you get more clear and accurate information.

Sandra: I assess the type of energy I am working with. It needs to be loving, pure, positive, non-judgmental--nothing but kindness. There is also the energy behind the energy to consider as everything can have a positive outer appearance, but at the core be negative and manipulative. I also find it to be a red flag if the energy does not appear to be wise.

Fortunately I receive a lot of guidance about when to be part of something or not and I have learned to fly above the storm of negative or lesser energy. When you can access the information at this level, you have learned to be more objective and can view the situation from a higher level of the lesson versus the act itself.

As an illustration of this concept, I was approached by two psychiatrists to help a woman who was very sensitive to energy and was caught up in the trauma of another young girl's disappearance. In this particular case, the young girl's father was suspected of foul play but a body could not be located and the police were unclear as to whether in fact she had been killed or not. I don't involve myself with many police cases but felt compelled to help this woman learn to get above the storm so she wouldn't continually be feeling this young girl's death and be haunted by the imagery. What we learned beyond the act that caused heartbreak, anguish and trauma was how this was suppose to turn out, ie the father was suppose to confess to the crime and he eventually did. By elevating beyond the emotion of the situation and operating on a higher plane of understanding, the woman was able to be unaffected by the negative energy surrounding the situation.

Bill: For dowsing, one of the major sources of inaccurate answers arises out of lack of control over the body to keep your tool focused consciously so that only the subconscious is allowed to move it. When people are first learning to dowse, they need to practice walking without moving their L Rods, Y Rod or Bobber tool. They also need to learn to keep their arm still when using the pendulum. The other potential problem is if people have not cleared their mind of pre-conceived notions about the answer to their question or if they are too emotionally attached to the outcome.

Q: Do you ever feel like your information is somehow off base?

Shannon: Something is off if it doesn't feel right in my tummy. When I get a feeling that this is the case, I back up and go at from a different angle and use another instrument to come at it from a different perspective.

Lori: I become wary of my information when it feels like a struggle. I am straining to find the information and find by the end of the session that I am completely drained. I am most accurate when there is a sense of playfulness and fun to the reading.

Deborah: When something is true for me, I feel empowered and strong. When I receive information that makes me feel uneasy, I check it out further. Sometimes I have a resistance to it, though it is true. In those cases, I attempt to broaden my perspective and clear the resistance within. At other times the information just doesn't work for me. I wouldn't say that the information is incorrect, but rather an incomplete perspective or perhaps, one-sided. It may also be coming from someone who doesn't have a broad awareness of life, or is of low vibration. At these times, when the energy doesn't feel right, I dismiss it.

OB1: Yes, and I just say, whoops, time out. Typically this happens if the information has not arrived spontaneously. So if I am not getting anything, I just share that I really don't have a clue on this particular issue or turn down clients because I feel I can't give them the information they are seeking.

Carolyn: Can't really say that happens. If I get up tired or don't feel physically well, I will ask God to please take it away so it doesn't interfere with my work.

Some people can drain you energetically if they don't own their own problems and don't take responsibility, which can impact the completeness of the information. There can be no healing without ownership. The blame card is always disempowering.

We keep pulling the same things to us if we don't own the lessons and become responsible for our role.

Sandra: I get a different feeling and share with my client that this feels a little wobbly or it's iffy. It is apt to depend on people's actions and decisions.

Bill: Experienced dowsers are typically 80-90% accurate in the information they receive. One way to validate the information is to have 7-8 dowsers all pose the same question and then correlate the results.

Q: How do you determine accurate timelines for events?

Shannon: Figuring out timelines is not always easy. I may be seeing several scenes and will need to determine which ones are for the past, present and future. There may be obvious clues in the appearance of my client in these visions, but if not, I might have to ask questions to determine which time period goes with which scene I am seeing. For instance, if I see two different scenarios where one takes place in a bungalow and another in a condo, I might ask my client whether they are currently living in a condo to determine the appropriate point of time reference.

Lori: My clients consider me a timeline specialist. I actually see calendars with exact month, day and year dates. Whenever information comes to me spontaneously, typically the date I've been given will be highly accurate. As the timing given gets less specific, the variation becomes greater. So if I get a specific month, day and year that is generally highly accurate. If I get a month, than that has a tendency to fluctuate either side by a month. If it's only a year, well, then be prepared for a hiccup in timing.

I also find it interesting that when a client asks me for information, my timing is apt to be a little more off. It is almost like the spontaneously provided information has been offered up by the Universe for their highest and best good and it has been delivered in a way that will prove most helpful. When a person is asking for information, they are now trying to pull information out that has not been freely offered and it shifts into a different dynamic.

I've also noticed that the Heisenberg Uncertainty Principle from quantum mechanics seems to come into play which basically says you can't accurately measure both the position and the momentum of a sub-atomic particle at once. So when I go in search of information in response to a particular question, I will either get accurate specifics on the event or specifics on the timing, but almost never specifics on both the timing and the event. Either the "what" or the "when" will end up being very general, while the other is likely to be specific if the information is meant to be delivered to the individual.

Deborah: I receive information in several ways. However, I understand that time and events can change and I tell my clients this. My client can change the timing of the event, as can those around them. I believe that we create our future in the present, working with the universal creative force. Sometimes our actions are preempted by the larger power. Most times, we create our reality moment by moment. If we change, we can change the future, and even the past.

That said, I receive information in the following ways: A

voice will tell me the exact time and date, the person in spir-it or their guide will tell me, I project a timeline and see where the event falls on the line, or the information may just flash across a screen and I see it.

OB1: I don't. This is the most common area of mistakes. We are on a linear timeline. The other dimensions are not oper-ating with this same point of reference. You can give an accu-rate course of events, but not the when. For instance, when I am asked to give stock market assessments, I can give gen-eral trends and even graph those trends to illustrate a pat-tern. The question I can't answer is how long it will take for that pattern to play out. Alternatively, if I am looking at a single day, I can pick which stock is going to be the most volatile within that day.

Carolyn: Timelines are terrible and I always explain that to new clients when I first meet with them. Accurate timetables are often elusive, so is the gender of energy for a fetus.

I try to come at it by asking other questions rather then ask-ing for a specific date. I may ask, "How old will she be then, which gives me a range of time to work with. Sometimes it can be dead on, but that is usually if it has come to me spon-taneously, and then it is still questionable. If I get a date that is like Sept 10 at 2pm, I don't believe it. If I get September 2004, I am more apt to believe that it is within a month or two. But I try to focus my clients on the bigger picture of what is unfolding versus the when.

Sandra: When I receive timelines spontaneously, they tend to be accurate and represent a high point in a person's life in terms of number of days or months. It can also be shown to me on a calendar or in a timeline and I do get instances where I get all three: day, month and year. I find in these situations I am often right about the month, but may be wrong about the year.

When someone asks me for the timing on something they are impatient about, it is more likely to be something that will be dependent on some action of the person I am reading or someone else that can influence the situation. This is particularly true when people are anxious about meeting a mate. Often they need to work on cleansing themselves of some issues before this person is going to show up for them.

The good intention is always there. The Universe brings us what we need but when everything is ready. People cannot prevent what is for their greater good to come to them, but at times they can just not be appreciative of it because it might not be in the form they had envisioned. Often with the passage of time, they can understand the greater meaning of the situation.

Many people who have developed their psychic abilities could sense a horrific event was looming over us prior to Sept 11th. We could also sense that, along with the horror and tragedy, there would be a flood of worldwide compassion, that there would be more cooperation among one another. As awful as it was, for some reason it was supposed to happen.

Bill: Dowsing for past dates is possible with artifacts and other objects where you are trying to assess their age.

Predicting future dates is indeterminate and you can only assess what and when something is probable to occur at that very moment in time. There are too many intervening variables at play to pinpoint anything with absolute certainty. You also run the risk of accessing information relating to a parallel reality.

Q: Sometimes you can find that someone that has given you good information in the past may be totally off base during your session. What can cause this to happen?

Shannon: This can happen for a variety of reasons including the person may not be well rested or emotionally calm with their own issues causing interference. They need to be centered in order to receive accurate information. They also need to be neutral or nonjudgmental, setting aside their own prejudices.

There may also be interference caused in the ethers level causing them to have difficulties in energetically relaying information to the recipient. Earth is an experimental and experiential world and with our current activities, we have been drawing more and more spirit beings and angels to us, some to help, others only to observe. When angels witness humans being inhumane to another, the angels actually wail at the loss of compassion within humanity. The dearth of spirits can cause energy interference.

Lori: I find personally that this can be the case if I am too tired or not feeling well. Sometimes it may be attributable to the client too if they really don't want a reading. Energetically they may be shutdown and resisting the information.

I also believe that if a person visits their psychic counselor too often, the reader has too much conscious knowledge about the person and their information is influenced by the familiarity. The shorter the intervals in-between the sessions, the more likely there is to be an opportunity for there to be this kind of interference and for the information to become deteriorated. In order to avoid this problem, I will not see clients more than once within a six month timeframe.

Deborah: My information comes from me seeing it or a guide/angel/master telling me something. There are several reasons why it can be inaccurate at the time. If I'm biased and wanting a specific outcome or information I will inadvertently influence the incoming data. It's clear to me when this occurs and I clear my own energy so that it doesn't influence the truth. At times the information is true for the person saying it, but it is not true for my client or myself. We all have different perspectives and understandings. What's true for one person is not necessarily true for another. There may also be interference with the incoming information. When this occurs I have to stop and clear the field around me from this disruptive energy.

OB1: When someone is giving a reading for someone, they are sharing with him how the events are likely to unfold for them based on the highest probability at that point in time, where they are that moment. But life doesn't stand still and all sorts of factors can alter the plan momentarily. It could also be as simple as the person doing the reading is just having an off day. Then again it could be that a dependency has evolved over time and the spirit feels compelled to let go and cease to work in a client relationship. It's as if the person providing information has just hit a brick wall.

Carolyn: It may result because they missed a lesson with their inner kid and they need to address it or the scenario has changed through the person or those around them exerting free will.

Sandra: It could be good information as to a life theme and it just hasn't unfolded in the timeframe or manner they are anticipating. If the information doesn't ever ring true, then it could be attributed to the person's health who is giving the reading in terms of how much they are feeling drained. Or it may just be that you are not supposed to get any information on this particular situation, a deeper level of your own soul may be calling for a greater growth.

Bill: Most likely it is a bad day that is adversely affecting their health. Those that are very proficient can focus and eliminate interference during the time required for dowsing. It could also occur because the person has lost the tuning connection with the person they are dowsing for, especially in a health related dowsing. You may also have an outside energy influencing the information.

Q: If you have an especially troubling matter and seek the counsel of more than one person, each of whom has been reliable in the past, sometimes you find that they provide conflicting answers. How does this occur?

Shannon: This can happen for a number of reasons. First of all, the timing of events is very hard to read and people may be accessing different time periods...one could be viewing tomorrow, another eight years from now. Another influencing factor could be your own consciousness. If you go to the first person and they tell you what you don't want to hear, your conscious focus to change events may have already started in play to change the course of action. There is also free will involved of those around you that could also be changing the course of action.

Lori: When a client has such a burning question that they feel compelled to seek the counsel of several individuals, the issue then becomes very potent and highly charged energetically. It is often a time where they are facing a big fork in the road and their decision will cause a major life shift. This is apt to be a time when a decision is part of their life journey and needs to be a conscious choice made through personal reflection and not on the advice of another. Their higher self is not going to let them get off the hook by being told what to do. The soul needs to make the decision and be responsible for owning up to their karma or life story. In these cases, the role of a psychic counselor becomes one of presenting the infinite possibilities before their client so that free will emerges and choice comes to the forefront.

Deborah: There can be several reasons for this. Something may have shifted and what was once true is no longer so. Also, every person has a different perspective. When I attended a psychic institute, we would have classes where a small group of us would sit in a line and read one person. During one of the sessions we each saw something different. One of us saw a lake, another a barn, another grass and someone saw a little girl. The place was the person's grand-mother's farm. We all saw the truth, but we each saw a dif-ferent aspect of it. The situation might best be illustrated by the old story about the six blind men describing an elephant. One feels an ear, and describes it. Another feels the tail, and another the trunk. They each sense the elephant differently. It's important that the individuals gather all of the informa-tion and then decide what is true for them.

OB1: Well this could really mess with a few minds, but there are different levels of reality, the same thing happen-ing in different frequency levels with different outcomes. The concept is often referred to as parallel lives which may be taking place in the past, present or future. Some are identical, some slightly different. For instance, we might not be having this conversation in another parallel life or we might be having a different conversation. You could be engaged in one lifetime to a person and marry someone else in another lifetime. These parallel lives have common denominators, same people, different relationships and/or experiences, but all working on the same problems. So as different people perform the readings, they may be reading different frequency levels and accessing different parallel lives. What's important is to be present in the here and now. Deal with the issues in your life and use your talents and abilities to serve humankind.

Carolyn: The conflicting answers come up because the per-son is not taking care of the issue himself. We are here to learn by exercising free will. The person needs to decide for himself.

Sandra: The information is provided as spiritual advice, not a spiritual instruction book and should not be used as a basis to make specific monumental decisions. The person always needs to gravitate towards what resonates with them personally and use that as a guidepost.

People should also keep in mind that different clairvoyants focus on different levels of information and that information is sometimes incomplete. For instance, for one of my clients I saw many people wearing funny looking hats and a Viking ship. A reinterpretation of this vision might make one think this referred to a past life. But by explaining exactly what I saw without adding my own spin, the information remained pure and in hindsight was discovered to represent a trip to the Lillehammer Olympic Games where the skating arena was designed to look like an upside down Viking Ship.

Bill: It could be that the dowsers were getting good information but from parallel realities. You may try rephrasing the question to be specific to "what this person is going to experience in this lifetime."

Q: How do you advise others to use the information you give them?

Shannon: Whatever information you receive you always need to check against your own body. What do you feel in your heart and in your gut. You should never live your life by what someone has told you. Rather you should listen to your tape once or twice, then put it away and live your life with that extra bit of insight that just might help you see a situation in a different light.

Lori: Don't hand your personal power over to another and let them create the outcome. Always understand that you have the power to invoke free will and can create your own reality that may align or be different than which has been foreseen for you at this particular point in time. It is as if someone is saying to you, if everything is later as it is now, this is what is likely to happen. However the world is dynamic and we are part of that dynamic, so use your influence if you don't like the direction you are heading.

Deborah: I like people to understand what I am seeing so that they can process it and make up their own minds about what to do themselves. I strive to provide information that they can apply to their areas of concern versus giving them specific instructions on how to proceed. The information is to be used as a tool to help them to respond to the world in a more effective manner. I usually give information that helps people to have a better perspective on themselves. Often the knowledge allows them to transform during the reading – to grow and change with the understanding of what I'm telling them.

I also advise people to never give up their own power to me or anyone else, no matter if they are in or out of body. We have to know and follow our own truth.

OB1: Always evaluate the information along with other known information. For instance, in my corporate work, the information I provide is used in conjunction with feasibility studies focusing on the market or scientific innovations, internal reviews and other sources of information. The piece I provide can involve future trends and market shifts. This creates the opportunity to look at a situation from a multi-dimensional perspective, a holographic view that allows the executives to turn it around and look at it from various angles.

The same is true for an individual. They should take the information provided to them and evaluate it in light of other information they have and most importantly, with how it resonates with them on an intuitive level, does it feel right.

Carolyn: Their life is in their own hands. My information may facilitate making a decision that would be best for them. First and foremost trust themselves.

Sandra: Throw your tape in the drawer and forget about it for awhile. The information should be viewed as guideposts or sideposts. Don't expect things to happen and don't cause events to change by concentrating on them too much. It is really always up to the individual to exercise free choice and free will.

Bill: It is always up to the individual to make their own conscious decision. People should never feel forced into believing something.

Q: What is the biggest risk in using these gifts for others?

Shannon: The worst misuse of such gifts are when people give bad readings. Bad in a sense that it can be incorrect information, but more in the sense that they can let their own ego be involved and deliver information in a cruel manner.

People have come with an open soul to hear something different, to receive help. And the delivery of that information can be devastating. It is not to say that you can't deliver difficult and challenging information when it is truth, but you must choose how you put it in front of others in a kind and compassionate manner. You need to honor that person as you would want to be honored. For instance if you foresee that a plane ride could be dangerous, you would not want to deliver a warning that could cause the client to be afraid to fly the rest of their life. Instead the information may be delivered by telling them, "If you are traveling on a plane in the near future, and if you feel it is not correct to do so, than listen to your instincts and make other plans." It is important to maintain control of the delivery, to raise awareness, but not issue dire warnings.

Lori: Having your clients fall into a trap where they believe that their psychic counselor knows best and forming a co-depend relationship. In those cases clients take their freedom to choose and hand over to another person, in essence giving up their power to create their own wonderful life.

Deborah: There are a few risks involved. One is with clients who are looking for someone to tell them what to do, instead of taking responsibility for their own lives. These people want to call often, and they don't change much. I discourage clients from becoming dependent on me. I try to get them to transform so that they see the truth for themselves. The ones who use the information wisely call rarely. They learn from the information and transform.

It's also important to not predict events as if they're set in

296

stone. When this is done the client comes away feeling doomed, as if he has no free will. The client is programmed, in a sense, to create a life to achieve this aim.

It's also important to honor the client's need to hear or not hear certain information. When I see a traumatic event in a person's past, such as a child rape, I ask the spirit if it's time to learn about this. I then gently steer the conversation to help the client to uncover the event on her own, so there's no damage to the psyche or emotional integrity of the person.

OB1: The more I do work for others, the more my own challenges come up. My own reality changes as more information comes through.

As your spiritual perspective changes, it helps you broaden your understanding and not judge people. If you don't want to grow and change, than that could be a problem for some people.

It is also a problem if you have an emotional stake in the outcome. There are a lot of humble, balanced people that offer these services. There are also a lot of people with big egos.

Carolyn: The biggest risk is that people listen to me. I must be accurate so it is important for me to learn my own lessons and heal my own kids. I see it as a major responsibility and it is not a laughing matter with me. I believe in my information, otherwise I wouldn't do what I do.

Sandra: It takes a lot of your energy to do this type of work. It also takes a lot of understanding in a personal relation-

ship, you need to be surrounded by people who understand it. People can also be disrespectful. But all in all it is a great adventure.

Bill: The biggest risk is getting messed up in someone's karma by showing him the wrong way or you have too much sympathy or empathy with a situation. Or in the case of medical intuitives, you can take on the sickness from people. You really need to block another person's energy from coming into your space.

My Belief

I do believe there are people who can and do tap into a higher knowing than our human experience and consciousness affords us. The best information and therefore guidance will come from someone with this well-developed connection who has also learned to take their ego out of the communication, is not judgmental and can check their emotional baggage at the door.

I think this information can often give us the gift of insight into past events and their relationship to the current dynamics of our life; our journey and purpose on an individual and global basis; our personal gift package and how we might best use them; and upcoming challenges and opportunities—what they are and potential outcomes.

As a person seeking this information, we are challenged to find someone we can trust as we bare our soul looking for hope and guidance in the area troubling us. We must then take this information under our own advisement and decide if it rings true with our own intention and belief system. It should be received as potentially helpful counsel, and never as an absolute pronouncement of unyielding truth.

I also believe that our thoughts wield tremendous power over our reality. I recently went to the movie playing in art houses called "What the Bleep?" It focuses on quantum physics and quantum mechanics and explores the possibilities behind our reality through the minds of a number of people who spend a lot of time pondering these thoughts. The overriding message that we can influence and co-create reality is one that resonates with me, but I think they forgot to specifically add, but we cannot fully control it. And that to me is an important part that needs to complete that thought. People want to believe that by the power of their mind they can manifest anything. I think you can manifest some things and only influence others, especially those that are not autonomous acts.

A demonstration at a meeting of the Atlanta chapter of the American Society of Dowsers illustrated the power of our thoughts over others by using a volunteer from the audience and a pair of L Rods. An expert dowser, Red Morris, asked the volunteer to stand in front of the room. She then proceeded to walk up to the woman and as she approached, the rods swung open to indicate the presence of the volunteer's energy field about six feet from the person's physical body. Red then asked three people in the front row to send the person negative thoughts. After a couple minutes, another measurement was taken and the volunteer's energy field had shrunk to within about a foot of her body. Then Red asked the whole audience to send the volunteer positive thoughts and took a final measurement. This time the L Rods indicated the presence of the volunteer's energy field to be nearly doubled from the original size or approximately twelve feet.

The Value

I have often had very revealing information given to me through these sources that has helped me anticipate and leverage highly specific career opportunities and how best to handle potential pitfalls. I have been gently prepared for upcoming illnesses and ultimate recovery of family members and the passing of my beloved pets. I have had remarkable previews of relationship changes and been able to anticipate spectacular travel opportunities.

I've also had an enormous mirror held up to me as an individual to objectively look at my actions, inactions and reactions to situations and the people involved. A very valuable learning opportunity indeed.

{16}

The Traveling Soul
Robyn Reynolds

D uring my journey through alternative sources of information, I have also had the opportunity to meet Robyn Reynolds, a traveling soul who has shown me how to open myself up to communicating with spirits from another dimension by preparing me mentally, emotionally and spiritually. Of course I realize this is a place that most people can't fathom as possible until they have actually traveled there themselves and until recently, I would have had to include myself on that list. Fortunately for me, I've moved off that list and onto the one where it has become part of my life experience. It has brought me so much joy and a sense of wonderment for my spirit; I thought it was one worth sharing with you.

I was introduced to Robyn through an email when Brent Atwater sent me pictures of spirit orbs that Robyn had photographed. I thought the photos were kind of interesting, but I figured it was probably just someone with extra time on their hands messing with a graphics program. Brent suggested that the two of us should meet and that perhaps this was material for my book. While I was a bit puzzled how this was suppose to fit into my healing journey, my curiosity was still piqued and I emailed back with a copy to Robyn saying I'd like to get together. A couple of months went by and nothing ever came of it. I was occupied with other writing projects and didn't think too much about it, figuring it was just one of those passing thoughts that wasn't going to materialize into anything more. Then I went to listen to Brent speak at a meeting of the Atlanta chapter of the American Society of Dowsers and who should end up sitting right next to me but Robyn. We both got a chuckle out of this and decided we were getting a message that shouldn't be ignored.

I chatted with Robyn by phone and she invited me to come visit her and her partner Connie at their home, which is situated on a historic property in north metro Atlanta. The plan was to get to know one another over dinner and find out about the personal book projects we both felt driven to deliver, mine of course being about exploring alternative sources of information and healing, and Robyn's being the message that there is a spirit world that we can all communicate with if we so choose. She was also prepared to share insight into the catalytic event that started her on her deep spiritual path that has lead her to now regularly commune with the other side. Over the last year she has shot close to 10,000 pictures and about 2,500 of those photos have captured visiting spirit orbs, some on their property, some while at the homes of friends and still others while traveling to other cities. Robyn further engaged my curiosity by offering to do a photo shoot that night and hopefully introduce me to the phenomenon of contact with the other side. This sounded like the type of evening that Cathy Horvath would also enjoy so I finagled an invitation for her as well.

My Fascination

It seemed like the drive took us forever, but finally we arrived and were simply enchanted by the vision before us. The two women had managed to design and lovingly build a very mystical-looking place. Although part of a subdivision, the properties were spread out amongst a heavily wooded area so each home had a good measure of privacy. In their backyard setting, there is a half moon shaped pool, a large plant-filled pond brimming with koi and the sound of water running over rocks, a 15 foot curved stone meditation bench supported by a stone wall and little charming surprises of angels, fairy nymphs, deer, frog couples, squirrels, rabbits and more poised tastefully about the property. It all added up to a sight that delighted the senses on many levels.

As we settled in on the back patio for the evening, we began learning about the nightmare that interrupted their idyllic life in June 2003. Late one evening, they had suddenly lost their twenty-year old son Kyle in a tragic car accident. He had always been the center of their family life, in fact everything was always planned around how it best served his future including the house they designed and built. The hollowing event became the catalyst for a deep spiritual journey for them both, ultimately filling them with hope for the future when they reconnected with Kyle through his appearance as an energy orb in photographs and through meditation.

He has confirmed to them that we are all spiritual beings living a human experience and that through accepting and giving love, we can commune with our loved ones and spirit guides. As a result, Robyn founded a practice to teach others how to connect with those that live in another place and provide evidence of these encounters through spiritual photography.

By that time it was dusk, the perfect time to start taking pictures in hopes of catching spirit friends in a photo. Robyn prepared us with a quick mediation and then off we strode around the property, our four digital cameras flashing away. Cathy was able to capture a pretty spectacular orb and I got a small one, but the pictures Robyn took were phenomenal and got us all very excited. We could not view the orbs with our naked eyes, only sometimes through the viewfinder of the camera and sometimes not until we actually had the picture in full screen on the computer. Mostly they are white lights of energy balls, but sometimes they are blue, purple or a multi-colored green, red and gold. Most do not have a great deal of detail, but some are truly spectacular with faint faces of humans or animals that can be detected.

The evening got me so jazzed that I returned the following Friday with a new friend in tow who was an engineer with a strong passion for innovative sound equipment. He was also highly intuitive and quickly felt the energy of the property once we arrived. Through a meditation he saw signs of a civil war battle and was also able to tell us that some of the spirits were actually souls that hadn't moved on. This was before Robyn had researched her property to discover that indeed, there had been a bloody battle where 2,000 lives were taken on the very spot they now lived. He felt certain that all the spirits were friendly and that we needn't fear any of them. We smiled and thought that was good as that was a confirmation of the feeling we already had. We spent another evening running about the property taking the most intriguing photos and this time I actually was able to capture quite a few on my camera. Robyn's favorite picture of me is where I am intently focusing off into the dark trying to use my intuition to determine where I should point my camera lens while all the time there is a big sphere hovering right behind me and a little one on my pant leg. It really is quite the humorous scene.

My Belief

While this introduction into another dimension, which proved to me to be undeniable proof of its existence, was a lifetime find of great magnitude, there was still more exciting unveiling to take place. Weeks later I was sitting in my office one night and decided I should take my camera around the house and see if I could locate anything. A couple of people who seem to be sensitive to energy had told me tales in the past of hearing things or even seeing things, but I hadn't paid it much mind because I hadn't seen or heard anything and I have an extremely sensitive ear. How could anything possibly be happening in the house and I not be able to detect it?

I kept my camera adventure to the upper level of our house and found nothing in the master bedroom or bath, nothing in the guest room, other bath, hall or TV room. But then I started scouting around my office and to my amazement, just five feet from where I sit day after day writing at my computer, my beautiful friend Georgee said hello! Okay, he didn't really say hello, but he appeared on film the 27th of August and has been there every night in September I have chosen to grab my camera and look for him. He is a gorgeous red sphere with two red balls of light inside and blue emanating from the balls within the sphere almost like the iris of an eye. He is totally mesmerizing and I find myself being infatuated by the sight of him for hours. The best pictures appear when he is in the window, but I also have pictures of him on the wall, woodwork and paper tray.

He mostly likes to hang out in this corner of my office. But he also has obliged and ventured to other areas after Robyn had suggested to me earlier one day that I should see if I could get pictures of Georgee in some other room. Late that night without consciously asking him to follow me, I grabbed my camera and headed out into the hall. I saw a big ball of red energy flash by my camera lens, but I was not quick enough to snap the picture. After that, he continued to play games with me for about an hour, appearing as a tiny red blinking light, darting across the viewfinder, sneaking up and peeking just above the lens than popping away again, then sometimes stopping long enough to pose so I could in fact get some pics of him on the hall walls, the wine colored hall carpet and the white carpet back in the TV room. Another night when I was trying to take pictures to see if my sister had any spirit guides around her, Georgee followed us back into the TV room to her office area, too. There I got a really interesting picture of him on the door knob.

I was going to name him, but when I started focusing on that exercise I kept getting the name Georgee in my head. I would have gone for something more exotic, but the idea was insistent, so I went with Georgee. Later I discovered that the blue rectangles that often appeared in the window, and which I was dismissing as a camera reflection, might also be another being, this one's name being Ann. She has also been photographed on the curtains and woodwork and does not appear as consistently as Georgee.

The Value

I've been told by intuitives that Georgee is here to be an amusing Leprechaun type diversion to me while I write my book, to validate that these wild mysteries that I seem to be discovering for myself are in fact reality and to also help guide me in finishing my project. They also have said that their visitation might just be temporary which I find to be a bit sad, I will certainly miss their playful spirits if they move on after my book is finished!

{Epilogue}

I embarked on this journey over a concern for my physical health and
have come to the conclusion it was more about a journey for my
soul. Especially as I have been guided to meet and talk to those I've
profiled in the last chapter.

While discussing my odyssey with OB1, I told him how I felt certain that a cure for my lung problem would be found if I just opened the
right door. And then we laughed about my surprise in learning that I
seem destined to continue through a hall of doors that grows longer
each time I opened a new one. We also discussed the effect that my lung
painting, one of Brent Atwater's Paintings That Heal, seemed to be having on me over the last several weeks. I have the painting resting on a
drawer of my armoire directly in front of the foot of my bed and have
tested the energy emanating from it with L Rods, some homemade ones
that Ray Horvath presented me with after dinner at their home one
night. What I found interesting was that when I tried using the L Rods
directly in front of the painting, nothing happened. But if I walked up

to the painting from the side, the L Rods swung wide open as I encountered the energy field. I do that some nights before I go to bed as a way to reassure myself that I am not crazy, I really am getting energy from the painting. It has been having an effect on me too.

I had heard that when you are going into a core healing mode, the ailment you are battling can often get worse, before it gets better. That is exactly what seemed to be happening. I had nothing else to attribute it to except for a recent compulsion to forgo my restraint from wheat and dairy, but I didn't think that was enough to warrant the type of change I was experiencing. And so the journey continued and I felt a bit like Dorothy after a visit to the land of OZ, knowing that the power to heal myself was inside me all the time.

In sharing my journey with you, it has not been my intent to convince you of anything, only to open doors for you to peek through. Ultimately you will need to decide if these avenues are something that might benefit you and something you feel compelled to explore further.

Some people have asked me what type of healing modality I have found the most effective and I would have to say that is like asking who your favorite child is. Each one has something wonderful to offer and it does not lend itself to ranking them on some sort of arbitrary effectiveness scale. People will resonate with different modalities and different healers more than others. My best advice is to not be discouraged if you don't find the answer you are looking for on your first venture into the alternative healing world. More than likely you are not trying something by total accident; there is a plan and some sort of need for the experience. Be brave, be curious and don't let the judgments of others prevent you from taking a valuable journey that inspires the spirit and evolves the soul.

{Pictures}

The Sandbox

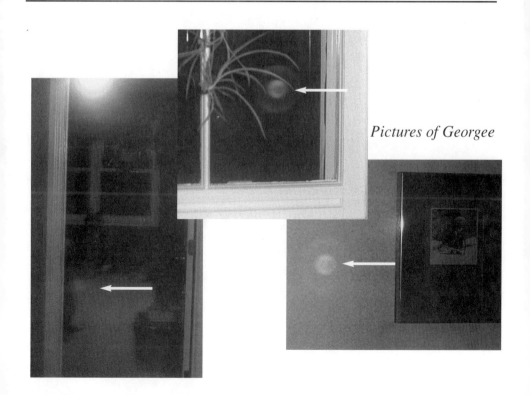

Pictures of Georgee

{Glossary}

Acupoints   Acupoints are specific anatomical locations on the body that are believed to be therapeutically useful for acupuncture, acupressure, sonopuncture, or laser treatment. There are nearly 400 basic acupoints on the meridians. Many of these basic points are rarely used. Some points are considered more therapeutically valuable than others, and are used very frequently for a wide array of health conditions.

Acupuncture   Acupuncture is the practice of puncturing various acupoints on the human body using specific needles for proper manipulation to relieve pain, treat specific diseases and problems.

Akashic Records

Some people believe that everything that has ever happened - every event, every thought, every action, every feeling since the beginning of time - has been accurately "recorded" in "Akasha," an astral light which exists beyond the range of our natural senses.

Asthma   A condition often of allergic origin that is marked by continuous or spastic labored breathing accompanied by wheezing, by a sense of constriction in the chest, and often by attacks of coughing or gasping.

Astrology   Astrology is a lifeprint that can give you a lot of information about your journey and how best to navigate it. To identify and explore

311

your individual lifeprint, you need to provide an astrologist your specific date, time and location of birth so they can determine the exact planetary configuration, or your natal chart, when you entered this world.

Atlantis　A legendary ancient culture and island, whose existence and location have never been confirmed. It was originally mentioned by the classical Greek philosopher Plato, who said that it was destroyed by a natural disaster (possibly an earthquake or tsunami) about 9,000 years before his own time. Recent esoteric writers such as Helena Blavatsky, Edgar Cayce, and Jane Roberts/Seth proposed that Atlantis was an ancient, now-submerged, highly-evolved civilization. The metaphysical significance being that it was a land from which many of us continue to reincarnate, with Cayce adding that the Atlanteans also had ships and aircraft powered by a mysterious form of energy crystal.

Aura　The electromagnetic field around our bodies that express the true intention of your spirit, invisible to all but gifted/trained individuals and through processes such as aura scans and Kirlian photography.

Automatic Writing

An individual receives a free-flowing message from an entity in the form of the written word. The writing comes quickly and without judgment, with the person putting down whatever comes to mind on paper or in a computer via a keyboard. Automatic writing allows the person access to the entity for guidance and can also serve to retrieve information from the individual's unconscious.

Azna　A name referenced by Sylvia Browne for the Female Divinity, Mother God, who gives you your emotions which causes movement in Creation. The other half of the divinity is The Father God called Om. He gives you your intellect and is the one who conceived of Creation and keeps it stable. Together they are One.

Bell's Palsy　Bell's Palsy is a condition that causes the facial muscles to weaken or become paralyzed. It's caused by trauma to the 7th cranial nerve, and is not permanent. Most people either wake up to find they have Bells Palsy, or have symptoms such as a dry eye or tingling around their lips that progress to classic Bell's Palsy during that same day. A warning sign may be neck pain, or pain in or behind the ear prior to palsy.

Bifidophilus Flora

Used to repopulate the intestinal track with good bacteria that is needed for effective digestion. Imbalances often occur when there is an extensive use of antibiotics.

Biofeedback
A system evaluating the biological signals produced by the body, specifically biological functions (i.e. heart rate, breathing rate, skin temperature, etc.). These functions are monitored by surface electrodes (sensors) and electronically amplified to provide "feedback" to the patient.

Bions
Discovered by Wilhelm Reich when he isolated a gray gel-like substance that could not be inactivated and is thought to be what animates life at the cell level. It is theorized to be the active ingredient that takes the chemistry, electricity, molecules and DNA of the cells in our bodies and makes it come alive.

Black Energy
When a Healer channels black energy, it brings a state of grace, silence and peace with God.

Blue Energy
Blue strengthens the immune defense system as it calms the body and calms irritations and inflammations. Many healers claim that blue is the most beneficial color of all for those with pain. When used by a Healer, blue energy represents energy cooling, calming and shielding from pain.

Blue-Purple Energy

When a Healer channels blue-purple energy, it provides pain relief for deep tissue and bone cell work.

Bobber
2 to 4 foot wire wand with a flexible spring section and weighted end. In dowsing, operates like a horizontal pendulum. Can give quicker answers than a pendulum because it swings much faster than a pendant.

Chakras
There are seven main Chakras or energy points located in a line starting at the base of your spine and going up through your head. Each of these chakras relate to a specific area of your body and specific emotions. The chakras process subtle energy and convert it into chemical, hormonal and cellular changes in the body. When they are in balance, your life force flows freely. When they are out of balance, it can manifest in physical illness until you address the situa-

tion causing the imbalance. People who have learned to shut down their analytical filters can see the charka points.

Channeling   The phenomenon whereby an individual allows their mind to sleep and a higher level of consciousness to flow through them, often verbally, as in trance channeling, but also through automatic writing; or channeling the higher self or 'other being' consciously.

Chi   Life force or living energy that sustains life of organs, cells, tissue, and blood. As a spiritual entity the life force is considered our connective flow to the creator. Chinese refer to the life force as "chi" or "qi". Hindus call it "prana". Greeks know it as "pneuma". Japanese refer to it as "ki".

Chronic Fatigue Syndrome
A disorder of uncertain cause that is characterized by persistent profound fatigue usually accompanied by impairment in short-term memory or concentration, sore throat, tender lymph nodes, muscle or joint pain, and headache unrelated to any preexisting medical condition.

Clairaudient   Literally it means someone with the ability to hear clearly (clair is French for clear). Clairaudients have acute intuitive insight or perceptiveness and are able to hear voices or sounds outside the normal range of human perception. Some people hear in the form of voices of someone they have known, some hear in a voice they don't recognize and still others don't recognize their psychic ability initially as the messages just sound like them thinking to themselves.

Clairsentient   Literally means "clear feeling" or "clear sensing." Experiences of clairsentience can be physical or emotional. They can vary from smells to tastes, to pains or cramping, to emotional feelings such as happiness or fear.

Clairvoyant   Literally, it means someone with the ability to see clearly (clair from French). Clairvoyants have acute intuitive insight or perceptiveness and are able to see images or pictures outside the normal range of human perception. It is different from telepathic – displaying the art of reading someone's mind. Clairvoyants perceive events directly, rather than through the mind of someone else. It is the ability to look beyond the everyday world and see far away people or events, or can include seeing into the future, known as precognition.

Colon Therapy   The process of cleansing and flushing out the colon, or large intestine. Also called colonic irrigation or colonic hydrotherapy, the treatment is similar to an enema but more extensive.

Colonics   See Colon Therapy.

Color Therapy   Each color vibrates at a specific, individual frequency, as do the glands and organs of the body. When we are ill, the body is not functioning at its proper frequency and becomes out of balance. Colors are the result of the eye perceiving light vibrating at different frequencies. The eyes convert light (color) into a kind of energy which travels through our nervous system and affects various body functions. Studies have shown that exposure to color can cause cellular and hormonal changes that bring the cells into synchronization or balance. Color therapy is used to treat both physical and emotional problems and may involve exposure to colored lights, massages using color-saturated oils, contemplating and visualizing colors, even wearing colored clothing and eating colored foods.

Crown Chakra   The seventh chakra located on the top of the head. It is used as a tool to communicate with our spiritual nature and to learn to live in the NOW. It is through this vortex that the life force is dispersed from the Universe into the lower 6 chakras. It is associated with wisdom, understanding and transcendent consciousness. It connects one to divine purpose, universal consciousness, enlightenment and unity with the Supreme Being.

Crystal Therapy

Use of crystals or gemstones and their related vibrational qualities to facilitate balance and healing.

Cupping   Cupping is a natural therapy that is usually used in conjunction with acupuncture. Air is heated inside the cup and is put on certain meridians and acupoints to treat and prevent health problems. The cup usually is made of bamboo, pottery, glass or plastic. Cupping does not break the skin or cause pain, only a feeling of suction and causes clients to have red or purple bruises the size of the cups.

Distance Healing

Distance healing encompasses spiritual healing, prayer, and various derivatives and has been defined as "a conscious, dedicated act of attempting to benefit another person's physical or emotional well being at a distance". It includes strategies that seek to heal through some exchange or channeling of divine energy.

Divination

The word divination is based on a Latin word that means "the faculty of foreseeing." The word comes from the Latin word for "divine power," "of the gods" or "to make divine." The art of divination reveals itself as a spiritual science that seeks to discover the divine meaning behind "chance" events.

Doctor of Naturopathy

Doctor of Naturopathy (ND). Naturopathic physicians undergo a four-year training program that includes training in homeopathy, clinical nutrition, manipulation, herbal medicine and hydrotherapy.

Dowsing

An intuitive skill used for finding hidden or lost objects and mineral resources, and for diagnostic use and healing illness and disease. Often a tool such as a pendulum or L Rod is used and the manner in which a question is asked is critical for the accuracy of the type of answer sought.

Dr. Hayashi

Dr. Hayashi was a Reiki student of Dr. Usi and he developed standards for hand positions, the system of three degrees and the attunement process.

Dr. Usi

Dr. Usi's discoveries formed the initial basis for Reiki treatment; he seems to have focused on further developing the spiritual aspect of Reiki.

Drumming

Referring to the use of rhythmic drumming to assist in conscious dreaming and journeying to the lower, middle and upper worlds.

DVAP

The DVAP (Dean Voice Analysis Program) is a software application, developed by Vickie Dean, which helps pinpoint low frequency and/or weaken areas of her body so that specific sound and color therapy can be created to repair and restore a client's health and wellbeing.

Earth Goddess Worshippers of the Female Divinity, Mother God, who gives you your emotions which causes movement in Creation. Often associated with fertility and vegetation.

Electrolytes Electrolytes are the minerals in the body (mainly sodium and potassium salts) that maintain the proper electrical charge and pH balance (acid and alkaline balance) in the various organs and tissues of the body. Each one of these tissues, organs and body cavities has a certain proportion and balance of minerals to maintain the necessary pH balance. For example, the stomach should maintain an acid pH and the duodenum (first part of the small intestine) should be alkaline in order for proper digestion to occur. If this balance is disrupted, then digestion will be impaired.

Enema Liquid put into the rectum to clear out the bowel or to administer medications.

Energy Work Focused attention on an individual's energy field, chakras, internal frequencies and energetic bodies to ascertain imbalances and commence rebalancing for optimum health and wellbeing.

Equine Assisted Psychotherapy

Equine Assisted Psychotherapy (EAP) is an emerging field in which horses are used as a tool for emotional growth and learning. EAP is experiential in nature and is a collaborative effort between a licensed clinical therapist and a horse professional. Participants learn about themselves and others by participating in activities with the horses, and then processing (or discussing) feelings, behaviors, and patterns.

Feng Shui Also known as Chinese "geomancy". The art of positioning physical objects in environmental locations that stimulate wellness, wealth, and happiness.

Five Elements All things in nature can be classified in five types: metal, wood, earth, water and fire. In Traditional Chinese Medicine, these five elements are also metaphors and symbols for describing how things interact and relate to each other. The five elements are further defined as both a production cycle and a control cycle acting upon the elements. In the production cycle, wood produces fire; fire produces earth; earth produces metal; metal produces water; water produces wood. In the control cycle, wood controls earth; earth controls water; water controls fire; fire controls metal; metal controls wood. The interaction of five elements becomes a tool that helps sort observations and data in order to draw high level conclusions or predictions based on the element types. In Chinese medicine, each organ of the human body is associated with an element and refers to phases, system, and energies in the bodies.

Food Allergy　　A food allergy develops when the body's immune system becomes misdirected and attacks harmless food proteins. An allergic reaction is an immune system response to a substance perceived by the body as a harmful allergen. The immune system attacks the allergen, releasing substances (such as histamine) that cause inflammatory reactions affecting different areas of the body. Symptoms involve the digestive, skin, and/or respiratory systems.

Food Intolerance

Food intolerance is the term used to describe a pharmacological reaction to a food component and does not involve the body's immune system. A pharmacological reaction refers to the drug-like side effects caused by a range of chemicals which may be present in food as natural or added components in food processing and preservation of foods. Food intolerance is much more common than food allergy. The range of symptoms which can be induced by food intolerance is very similar to those caused by food allergy. However, food intolerance may also lead to more diffuse symptoms such as drowsiness, fatigue, irritability, headache and muscular aches and pains.

Gelding　　An animal that has been castrated. Often referring to a male horse.

Gemstone Therapy

Use of crystals or gemstones and their related vibrational qualities to facilitate balance and healing.

Gold Energy　　When used by a Healer, gold energy is charging and restores the energy field.

Green Energy　　Green is a cool neutral color. It helps balance and restores clarity of focus. Green is useful for conditions which surface from stress and tension, such as migraine headaches. When used by a healer, green energy brings general healing and balance.

Guided Imagery

Guided imagery focuses and directs the imagination towards a specific action of healing. It involves all the senses and calls upon you to not only visualize an act, but to also sense how it would feel. When you have a healing guide that you resonate with to lead you to the place of power in your mind and body, imagery has the capacity to deliver multiple layers of complex, encoded messages that will call your body into action. It is a right-brained activity and engaging in it will often be accompanied by other right-brain functions such as sensitivity to music, openness to spirituality, intuition, abstract thinking and empathy.

Hawayo Takata

Hawayo Takata was a second generation Japanese immigrant who experienced the dramatic healing powers of Reiki when she was visiting her parents in Japan. She convinced Dr. Hayashi to teach her Reiki and eventually return with her to Hawaii to establish Reiki in the West.

Healer

A Healer uses gifts to help transform the energy from a place of disease, disorder, or dysfunction to enhanced health and wellbeing.

Healing Energy

Healing Energy is energy that has been transmuted from a higher power, focused by intent and directed to repair damage that has occurred in a person's energy levels or to places that have manifested into physical problems. The study of energy medicine and the part Energy Healing plays in health recovery continues to gain ground in the West. It has been an accepted part of Eastern Medicine practices for over 6,000 years. Healing Energy modalities that seem to have gained the most acceptance by health professionals and in traditional hospital settings include Healing Touch, Reiki and Acupuncture. These modalities, along with other Energy-based Healers who channel energy, continue to be the focus of complementary alternative/ integrated medical research. This acceptance and use of Healing Energy in perplexing cases to diagnose and aid in the recovery process, is considered to be on the cutting edge of integrated medical research.

Healing Touch

Healing Touch is an umbrella term for a number of energy based healing treatments. It is a hand-mediated technique which requires certification through a standardized curriculum. Practitioners either use their hands close to the patient's body in their energy field or use light touch to influence and harmonize the energy system. These methods can restore any previously detected imbalances to the desired state and allow individuals to access their full healing power. The therapies support a person's immune system and self-healing process, thereby enhancing the effect of other therapies. Healing Touch methods have been credited with reducing pain and anxiety, decreasing stress and tension, accelerating the healing process, preventing illness and activating mental clarity.

Heart Chakra The fourth chakra is located in the chest. Repairing the wounds in this center of our human energy system is often the focus in bringing about a healing. Hurtful situations that can affect our emotional being include divorce or separation, death of a loved one, emotional abuse, abandonment and adultery. Physical illnesses brought about by heartbreak require that an emotional healing occur along with the physical healing. Healing the heart chakra involves forgiveness, unconditional love, letting go, trust and compassion.

Hemorrhoid A mass of dilated veins in swollen tissue at the margin of the anus or nearby within the rectum.

Hippotherapy Hippotherapy is a treatment that uses the multidimensional movement of the horse; from the Greek word "hippos" which means horse. Specially trained physical, occupational and speech therapists use this medical treatment for clients who have movement dysfunction. Specific riding skills are not taught (as in therapeutic riding), but rather a foundation is established to improve neurological function and sensory processing.

Horoscope Generalized "Sun Sign" horoscopes that do not take into account the year (or hour and minute) you were born or the town and country you were born in. Since your "Time and Space" are not really known, these entertainment based "horoscopes" are only based on an estimate of where the Sun was located on your date of birth, and thus are far less detailed and accurate as a Personal Horoscope Reading based on your full birth data - which will include the positions of the Moon and ALL the Planets, and what that means about you as a unique individual.

Hypnotherapy Psychotherapy that facilitates suggestion, reeducation, or analysis by means of hypnosis.

Ignatz von Peczely

Pioneering physician that studied the changes in the eye as a result of disease, injury and/or surgery. He created the first chart of the iris based on his findings and is considered the founder of the science of iridology.

Indigo Energy   Indigo is the soothing color that plays upon the mental and emotional bodies. Indigo restores free-flow and movement making it particularly helpful for cysts and tinnitus.

Intuition   Quick and ready insight seemingly independent of previous knowledge gained from experiences. The ability to perceive or know things without conscious reasoning.

Iridology   Iridology is the science and practice of analyzing the markings in the iris of the eye to identify the presence of inflammation in the body, where it is located and in what stage it is manifesting.

Irritable Bowel Syndrome

A chronic functional disorder of the colon that is of unknown cause but is commonly considered to be of psychosomatic origin and that is characterized by the secretion and passage of large amounts of mucus, by constipation alternating with diarrhea, and by cramping abdominal pain.

Kinesiology   Kinesiology or Muscle Testing is a means of testing the body's knowledge about a certain topic. A yes or no type question is posed to the body and then pressure is applied by the person asking the question to see if the body's muscle supports a positive answer and therefore resists the pressure or folds to the pressure indicating a negative answer. Often the test is performed with the person being queried extending an arm out to the side while the person asking the question tries to push the arm down. The body's ability to respond is based on the electrical network it has within it and surrounding it. If anything impacts this electrical system that does not maintain or enhance your health, your muscles are unable to hold their strength when physical pressure is applied by an outside source.

L Rods   Angular rods that are made of metal and 1/8 to 3/16 inch in diameter and from 18 to 24 inches long. The two rods are bent at a point approximately 6 inches from the ends to form a right angle "grip. In dowsing, they are held at waist height, like pointed pistols, the rods will swivel, either crossing inward or diverging outward, as you pass over the target. They also can be used to indicate yes, no or a variable (0 to 100%) answers to questions posed to them.

Law of Correspondence

The law of correspondence states that we are all connected in some shape or form since we have all been originally created from the same source.

Law of Similarity

The law of similarity states that a photograph or even a memory of a person can be used for psychic purposes to direct healing at that person.

Ley Lines   Natural flows of positive or negative energy that connects with the earth at places called power centers. Many accomplished ancient cultures built some of our most impressive sacred sites around the world over these areas through the ages.

Lifeprint   A blueprint for the soul based on planetary alignment at the time and location of birth.

Lillith   Queen of the Fairies and is known to protect animals and children.

Lost Continent of Atlantis

See Atlantis.

Lower World   One of three interconnected spirit worlds. The Lower World resembles a beautiful landscape and is where power animals reside. The advice you receive in this spirit world is very earthy, practical and specific.

Lung Biopsy   Lung biopsy is a medical procedure performed to obtain a small piece of lung tissue for examination under a microscope. The procedure may involve an incision followed by a use of a biopsy needle or it may involve removal of tissue while the patient is under general anesthesia. Needle biopsy is a less risky procedure but there is still a risk that the lung may collapse because of air that leaks in through the hole made by the biopsy needle. If the lung collapses, a tube will have to be inserted into the chest to remove the air.

Possible complications of an open biopsy include infection or lung collapse. Death occurs in about 1 in 3000 cases. If the patient has very severe breathing problems before the biopsy, breathing may be slightly impaired following the operation.

Medical Intuitive

A medical intuitive is someone that uses their intuitive gifts to help identify conditions present in their clients which have manifested as physical health problems. They may or may not have had formal medical training, but have been infused with diagnostic knowledge and the ability to see the source of health problems that may have eluded discovery by traditional medicine.

Meridians

Meridians, as it relates to the practice of acupuncture, are represented by fourteen major channels and/or pathways in which energy flows throughout the body. When this flow along one or several of the meridians is obstructed, the result may be disease or injury.

Middle World

One of three interconnected spirit worlds. The Middle World is similar to our conscious world and you can visit places and times that are important to you. This is the place where you can visit with the spirit of another person or a part of nature. It is also a place where illness resides as well as wandering spirits.

Moon Lodge

The moon lodge was created in indigenous cultures to house women during their moon or menstrual flow. This is considered a time of power for the woman and she is believed to be more open and receptive to spirit. It is a time to go within and listen. In earlier times when roads were poor and traveling difficult, Secret societies have also created Moon Lodges. They would meet on the date of the Full Moon or, in some instances, a certain number of days before or after the Full Moon so that those going to and from Lodge Meetings would have the light of the moon to make the journey safer and easier.

Mother Earth

See Earth Goddess.

Multiple Sclerosis

A disease marked by patches of hardened tissue in the brain or the spinal cord and associated especially with partial or complete paralysis and jerking muscle tremor.

Muscle Testing   See Kinesiology.

Natal Chart   It is a chart of where the Sun and Moon and Planets were located in Space, in relation to each other, and to a particular place on Earth, at a particular instant in Time marking your birth.

Neuro-Linguistics Programming

Neuro (neurothogy) represents the brain/mind through which we process our experiences. Linguistic refers to language or communications (both verbal and non-verbal). Programming refers to the ability to process our mental experiences and choosing to model our responses in ways that will bring our goals forward.

Orange Energy   Orange is the symbol of the feminine aspect containing the energy of creation. Orange is believed to combat depression and transmute negative into positive. It is also believed that the color orange can affect mental, emotional and physical properties. When used by a healer, orange energy works on your immune system.

QXCI   A device developed by Professor Bill Nelson that resonates with thousands of tissues, organs, nutrients, toxins and allergens for one hundredth of a second each and records how the body reacts. During this testing, it is looking for viruses, deficiencies, weaknesses, allergies, abnormalities and food sensitivities to determine the energetic state of your body. Once it measures the frequency of all intended variables, it then compares it against an established norm and identifies areas at risk. Depending upon the assessment, it may send electronic impulses that raise or lower the frequency to effectively move towards a healthier energy balance.

Paintings That Heal

Paintings That Heal are a unique therapeutic modality consisting of rare interactive art with a Healing Energy component. To date, there are only a handful of distance healers around the world that have discovered an ability to channel, capture, and infuse Healing Energy on canvas.

Past Life Therapy

Tapping into your mind through hypnotherapy, guided meditation, or visualization techniques to learn patterning from past lives.

Pendulum   1/2 to 4 ounce weight suspended from a 3 to 8 inches string or chain. In dowsing, chain is held between the thumb and forefinger and a movement pattern indicating yes or no is established, or a variable (such as 0 to 100%) from the direction of the swing.

Power Animals Protective Spirits that helps us in our daily life and in our spiritual search for harmony with the Universe. Everyone has a power animal that is their personal medicine. This animal often reflects a person's innermost self and can change over your lifetime as your needs change. You can find your power animal through dreams, meditation, intuition, synchronistic sightings or through a shaman.

Psychic   Ability to use Extrasensory Perception (ESP) to perceive objects, places, thoughts, or events without the mediation of any of the known sensory channels.

Psychokinesis The power to move physical objects by thinking about it.

Psychometry Receiving information about a person or object by touching an object.

Psychotronics Interactions of matter, energy and consciousness.

Purple Energy When used by a Healer, purple energy is healing a spiritual connection.

Qi   Life Force.

Quantum Mechanics
          The branch of quantum physics that accounts for matter at the atomic level.

Quantum Physics
          Physics based on quantum theories that suggest an unstable world, that the observer's mind is the only reality, or that there may be parallel universes.

Raheim   Raheim is a Master Healer. He can be called upon for any type of healing, just like the other Master Healers.

Rayid Eye Pattern

If a person's left eye has more characteristics or a higher concentration of color, that person has a dominant right brain and uses the left side of the body more. Left-eye dominant people are generally flowing and agreeable, prefer to sleep with the left cheek down, and usually have a closer relationship with their mother. Right-eye dominant people are generally structured, organized and ask more questions, prefer to sleep with the right cheek down, and usually have a closer relationship with the father. Left-eye dominants are attracted to right-eye dominants in mate relationships.

People with a predominance of dot-like pigments in the iris (Jewels), tend to be thinkers and precise verbal communicators. People with a predominance of curved openings in the iris (Flowers) tend to be emotional, feeling-oriented and spontaneously expressive. People with a uniform fiber structure in the iris (Streams) integrate life through sensory experience, communicating through touch and movement. Those with both jewels and flowers in the iris (Shakers) tend to be dynamic, progressive, and even extremist in nature. For more information see www.rayid.com.

Rayid Iris Identification

The practice of identifying behavioral, communication and relationship patterns based on the structural constitution of the iris of the eye.

Red Energy   Red is thought to destroy bacteria and raise body temperature. Red is also thought to create warmth, hence aiding circulation and raising body temperature. When used by a Healer, red energy burns out cancer and warms cold areas as its restores the life force.

Regressed   The act of reasoning backward from an effect to a cause.

Reiki   Reiki is designed to be used for healing, connecting people to their spiritual path or for personal empowerment. For healing it invokes deep relaxation, strengthens the body to heal itself and speeds up recovery. From a spiritual perspective, it is about learning to detach from the outcome and being present in the moment. It is not about a particular religion or belief system, rather it focuses on the basic values of unconditional love, caring, peace, and compassion for all. It is also about honoring each other's individual path. Reiki can also be used to enhance your natural abilities. Working with the Reiki energy will help you connect with your path, your skills, and develop your senses. With practice, it can enhance your creative, intuitive and business abilities. Reiki doesn't do harm and will not work if harm is intended. It cannot be used to control people or situations. It works to bring the best result or highest outcome for all.

Reiki Master A person who has received all of the necessary initiations and attunements for the three levels of Reiki including the 4 Reiki symbols and knowledge of their use. The first degree covers the history and philosophy of Reiki and gives the hand positions for working on oneself and for working on others. Second degree imparts the power symbols and gives instruction in their usage. Third degree gives further instruction in symbol usage and teaches the student how to perform the 'attunement' procedure. In each degree, the teacher performs a series of attunements upon the student to open and clear the subtle energy channels within the student and connect him/her with the healing energy.

Reverend Nils Liljequest

Discovered the relationship between the use of drugs and the specific discoloration in the eyes as a result of his experiences with illness in youth. This discovery was instrumental in the development of Iridology.

Ring of Harmony

Ring of Harmony is a Rayid Eye Pattern that indicates an individual which has high ideals about social and environmental issues. They dislike disorder and have a deep desire to experience the world as one big happy family. They often have a loving disposition, but are quick to point out negativity.

Ring of Purpose Ring of Purpose is a Rayid Eye Pattern that indicates an individual who feels they have a strong sense of special purpose. Constantly searching for their mission in life, many times unclear about how to achieve their objectives, they find that through diligence and commitment they are capable of anything.

Shaman A priest/medicine man or woman, secular and sacred leader of a tribal circle, a "technician of the sacred".

Shamanism   For 40,000 years, shamanic healers all over the world have had one foot in ordinary reality and one in non-ordinary reality, bridging the gap between humans and the spirit world. Whether the need was for physical, emotional, mental or spiritual healing, the shaman journeys to seek help from guides for healing for their clients. Techniques of journeying differ among indigenous people, but most use the sound of percussive instruments like drums and rattles to enter into the altered state through which spirit contact is available. From the shamanic perspective, all life such as plants, rocks, animals, stars and the earth are filled with spirit and have power. The shamanic seer has a vision of this wholeness and uses it for healing.

Solar Plexus   The location of the third chakra varies depending on the source. Some put it below the navel, some above the navel and some right on the navel. It is associated with personal power, control, decision making and ego. Its lesson is about mental understanding of the emotional self and self-love. It also houses our gut instincts.

Soul Retrieval   A shamanic practitioner seeks to retrieve actual, multi-dimensional parts of a person's soul which exist outside of our normal concept of time and place. Soul parts can splinter off out of pain for many reasons including childhood abuse; death of a spouse, parent, sibling or friend; the end of codependent relationships or as a result of divorce; or at the time of an operation, car accident or other physical trauma. The soul parts either leave on their own, taking refuge in non-ordinary reality, or are stolen by others. If stolen, the shaman must work to "steal" them back.

Sound Chair   A chair outfitted with transducers that turns sound into a vibration so you can feel it through your skin and deep down into the bones. The sound actually penetrates you in the different chakras and fills you with deep relaxation that allows you to be mentally quiet.

Sound Therapy The body resonates at a specific frequency for each gland, organ, system and subtle body. Each must resonate at that certain frequency for optimum health. Sound therapy utilizes frequencies and wave forms to balance and re-harmonize areas of the body that have become weak or diseased to initiate healing.

Subtle Energy   Non-physical energy.

Superlearning   Accelerated learning through the use of very specific, relaxing Baroque music.

Ten Planets   The planets are represented by the position of Earth's eight sister planets (Mercury, Venus, Mars, Jupiter, Saturn, Uranus, Neptune and Pluto) as well as the Sun and the Moon. Astrologers, interested in the relationships between the positions of all ten objects call them the Ten Planets. Their cyclical movements act like a giant cosmic clock that marks off past, present and future time and events.

The Houses   In astrology The Houses indicate when a planet's energy is most likely to affect your everyday life.

The Planets   In astrology, The Planets represent the energy affecting you.

The Signs   In astrology, The Signs indicate the type of energy given to each planet.

The V.I.B.E.   The V.I.B.E. (Vibration Integration Bio-photonic Energizer) is a relatively new patented energy device developed by Gene Koonce with the objective in mind to create the optimal model of healthy resonance, much like a tuning fork, so that when used, the device allows your cells and organs to remember how to operate at optimal frequency. Once an individual is exposed to this tuning fork, their body recognizes the optimal performance level and begins resonating and shifting in an effort to emulate this desired frequency state. The change can trigger the release of toxins and signals the body to start healing damaged tissue.

Third Eye   The sixth chakra is located in the center of the forehead and is often referred to as the "third eye" or the "mind center". It is where visual images are received and our avenue to wisdom where we learn from our experiences and put them in perspective. It is also our place where we develop intuitive reasoning.

Throat Chakra   The fifth chakra is located in the throat and neck region. This chakra is our will center and its purpose is learning to take responsibility for one's own needs. The healthfulness of the fifth chakra is in relation to how honestly one expresses himself/herself. Lying violates the body and spirit. A challenge of the throat chakra is to express ourselves in the most truthful manner and to receive and assimilate truthful information.

Traditional Chinese Medicine

Traditional Chinese Medicine (TCM) is the official name used in China for a degreed branch of medical science that covers the practice and use of traditional Chinese medical theories, therapies, acupunctology and natural herbal material. The fundamental difference in TCM and western medication can be simply described as:

Western medication cures disease by using external forces. TCM attempts to reinforce and stimulate body's internal strength to cure disease.

Western medication is based on the theory that disease is caused by bacterial and other external means. TCM believes that disease is basically caused by the "weakening state" of a body as a whole.

Western medication often cures diseases more effectively and quickly, but it may also cause temporary or permanent damage to the internal system of a patient. TCM may take longer time to cure a disease but it strengthens the overall health of a patient. Western medical practitioners have started to use TCM to offset the side effects that can occur with medication or when they are unable to cure certain conditions.

Trauma Release Trauma Release Therapy can take on a number of forms and was developed by Karl Nishimura, D.D.S., M.S. It is based on the assumption that a trauma to the body (either physical, emotional, mental or spiritual in origin) needs to be released from the cellular memory in order for the person to heal from the trauma. If traumas are not released, over time, the mind and body adjust and compensate to allow continued function up to a saturation point. An overload of the suppressed traumas can eventually manifest in the form of pain and deterioration of the body.

Universal Law The universal law states that a person attuned to the universal energy can call upon the energy forces around them to help send healing to a certain individual.

Upper World One of three interconnected spirit worlds. The Upper World is a place where you meet spirit teachers that offer philosophical and general advice.

Violet Energy   Violet is the color of spiritual energy. Notice the color of vestments worn by Priests during high holy days. Violet strengthens spiritual awareness and heightens insight.

Voice Analysis   Analysis of individual voice prints, similar to uniqueness of finger prints. When the body becomes weak and diseased, the frequency of the previously healthy area of the body will disappear from the person's voice print.

White Energy   When used by a Healer, white energy brings peace and comfort as it takes away pain.

Y Rod   Wooden, metal or plastic stick in the shape of a fork. In dowsing, it is held upward and swings downward to point to the target.

Yang   Yang represents the active energy aspect of the complimentary opposites in Chinese philosophy. It reflects assertiveness, movement, speech, the sun or light and positive aspects. Everything is believed to contain the opposite forces of yin and yang which are mutually exclusive, yet interdependent, e.g. female (yin) vs. male (yang), front of the body (yin) vs. back of the body (yang), fat (yin) vs. muscle and bone (yang).

Yellow Energy   Yellow repairs and heals, particularly beneficial for skin problems. Yellow is believed to improve judgment and stimulates mental processing abilities. When used by a healer, yellow energy clears a foggy head.

Yin   Yin represents the receptive energy aspect of the complimentary opposites in Chinese philosophy. It reflects more passive, still, reflective, moon or dark and negative aspects. Everything is believed to contain the opposite forces of yin and yang which are mutually exclusive, yet interdependent, e.g. female (yin) vs. male (yang), front of the body (yin) vs. back of the body (yang), fat (yin) vs. muscle and bone (yang).

{Index}

{Resources}

Advanced Tachyon Technologies (*)
www.tachyon-energy.com

Brent Atwater
Medical Intuitive, Healer and Artist
Energy Works, Inc.
PO Box 475
Southern Pines, NC 28388
Office: 910-692-5206
Email: Brent@brentatwater.com
www.brentatwater.com,
www.paintingsthatheal.com

David Bina, CEO (**)
Aura Video Systems
4051 Glencoe, Suite 10
Venice, CA 90292
Office: 1-888-692-8722
Email: david@aura.net
www.aura.net

Z. Budapest
www.zbudapest.com
Author, *Goddess in the Office*

Bhimi Cayce
Owner Vitality Unlimited
V.I.B.E Machine
172 Spalding Trail
Atlanta, GA 30328
Office: 404-303-0965
Email: bhimiuip@earthlink.net
www.conscious-coaching.com

Sandra Cheek
Psychic
San Antonio, Texas
Office: 210-212-4019
Email: saseer2003@yahoo.com

Geraldine (Jerry) P. Connor
Licensed Professional Counselor
5390 Peachtree Industrial Boulevard,
Suite 21-D
Norcross, GA 30071
Office: 770-441-3878
Email: jerconnor@mindspring.com

Mary Cote
Certified Colon Hydrotherapist
The Star Wellness Center
275 Carpenter Drive, Suite 202
Atlanta, GA 30328
Office: 404-497-9268
Email: info@starwellnesscenter.com
www.starwellenesscenter.com

Carolyn Cummings R.N.
Intuitive Psychic Medium
Author of Beneath the Mask:
An Empowerment Card Deck
Universal Insight
Office: 678-495-1480
Email: flyeagle@bellsouth.net

Carol Dallas, M. M.
The Dallas Center, P.C.
Physical Movement for the Brain
Neuromovement * Neurodevelopment
Private Counseling *
Workshops & Classes
Certified Brain Gym Instructor
4651 Roswell Rd., NE Suite 604G
Atlanta, GA 30342
Office: 404-781-0284
Email: cmdallas@comcast.net

Vickie Dean
Vocal Imaging
Dean Voice Analysis Program
Office: 770-429-8707
Author, *Sound Creations;
Sona Soma, Changing Your
Environment*

Mariette Edwards
Star Maker Enterprises Inc.
Business and career strategies
for executives and creative professionals
Email:
mariette@starmakercoaching.com
www.starmakercoaching.com

Florestas Organic Botanicals (*)
Skincare Products from the Amazon
PO Box 1060
L.I.C., NY 11101
www.florestas.com

Barbara Gray (**)
Gas Discharge Visualization (GDV)
camera imaging and interpretation
Starlight Productions
Office: 770-971-0179
Email barbaragray399@Comcast.net
Author, *Secrets of Energy, Energy
Management, How To Increase Your
Positive Energy Levels*

Deborah Hill, MSN
Intuitive Coach, Author, Speaker,
Teacher
Energetic Healing
Office: 877, 462-5292, or 404-459-0590
Email:
debhill@writingsofthemasters.com
www.writingsofthemasters.com
Author: *The Writings of the Masters,
Enlightening Lessons for Everyday Life.*

Rochele Hirsch
Life Consultant
Division of CommExpress Int'l, Inc.
Office: 404-521-0362
Email: info@rochelehirsch.com
www.rochelehirsch.com

Ines Hoster, MS, CHTP/I
Certified Healing Touch Practitioner and
Instructor
Trauma Release/Guided Imagery
Healing Quest
Office: 404-257-1843
Email: ihenergy@mindspring.com

Li Hua L. Ac.
Licensed Acupuncturist
Certified by NCCAOM
Traditional Chinese Medicine Doctor
Sandy Springs Professional Building
275 Carpenter Drive, Suite 200
Atlanta, GA. 30328
Office: 404-250-9903
Email: lihua@aac2000.com
www.aac2000.com

Jeanne Johnson
Usui and Karuna Reiki Master/Teacher,
Shaman
Certified Brain Gym Instructor
Atlanta, GA
Office: 770-313-3622
Email: jeannecmj@bellsouth.net

Gary Kimbrough, M.DIV. and EAGLA
Certified
Equine Assisted Psychotherapy and
Corporate Training
Deer Ridge Farm
Dallas, Georgia
Office: 678-363-3561
Email: Cgkimbrough@aol.com

Lori Lothian
Psychic
Vancouver, Canada
Office: 604-898-3397
Email: Tarology@aol.com
www.accessnewage.com/tarology

Justine E. Owens, Ph.D. (**)
Energy field imaging with the
Gas Discharge Visualization (GDV)
camera
Energy Imaging Associates
Office: 434-823-5963
Email: owens@virginia.edu

Bill Phillips
Geopathic Dowsing and Subtle Energy
Research
Email: billphillips@speedfactory.net

Linda Potter
Certified Master Hypnotist
Specializing in Past Life Regression
Spirit Guides, LLC
1852 W. 11th St. #404
Tracy, CA 95376
Office: 209-835-1146
Email: Linda@spiritguides.info
www.spiritguides.info
Co-Author, *The Healing Room*

Mother Earth Pillows (*)
Karen Kowal, RN, LMT, NCTMB
CEO, President
Office: 314-316-7075
Email: Karen@MotherEarthPillows.com
www.MotherEarthPillows.com

Robyn Reynolds
Spirit Photography
Office: 770-855-4365
Email:robyn@sphericallyspeaking.com
www.sphericallyspeaking.com

Stephanie Maxine Ross, M.H., H.T.,
C.N.C.(*)
Medical Botanist
Specialist in Women's Natural Health
Holistic Practitioner to CEO's and
Celebrities
Omni Botanicals
Office: 215-441-9353
Email: smaxinross@aol.com

Shannon Sambells
Channeler and Intuitive Advisor to
Individuals and Corporations
Author of To Touch The Hand of God
Office: 403-238-5217
Email: oraclesoflight@aol.com
www.shannonsambells.com

Lisa Seelandt
Editor Health and Healing
PlanetLightworker.com
Email: lisa@planetlightworker.com

Sis Sewell, N.D
Doctor of Naturopathy
Specializing in Holistic Care For
People and Companion Animals
Certified Iridologist (by B. Jensen,
D.C., N.D)
c/o The Herb Garden, Inc.
1465 Daholnega Hwy, Suite 1
Cumming, GA 30040
Office: 770-887-0875

Sylvia Browne Corporation
Society of Novus Spiritus
35 Dillon Avenue
Campbell, CA 95008
Office: 408-379-7070
www.sylvia.org

Ko Tan
Nationally Certified Reflexologist
Board Member International Council of
Reflexologists
Radiant Lotus Thai-Yoga Body Therapy
Teacher
Academy of Radiant Health
P.O. Box 2322
Roswell, GA 30077
Office: 770-843-2993
Email:
KoTan@academyofRadiantHealth.com
www.academyofradianthealth.com

Toni Thomas
Astrologer
Astrology Source
Atlanta, GA
Office: 678-474-9498
Email: javamist@aol.com
www.astrology-source.com

(*) Although I do not specifically mention my recent work with
Stephanie Maxine Ross in any of the
chapters, I am so impressed
by her abilities, and the products and
services she has introduced
me to, that I wanted to share them with
you through a listing in
this resource section.

(**) Aura Imaging resources I've utilized.